ROUTLEDGE LIBRARY EDITIONS: GERMAN POLITICS

Volume 7

I0025218

EUROPE FROM BELOW

EUROPE FROM BELOW

an assessment of Franco-German
popular contacts

JOHN E. FARQUHARSON AND STEPHEN C. HOLT

Routledge
Taylor & Francis Group

LONDON AND NEW YORK

First published in 1975

This edition first published in 2015
by Routledge
2 Park Square, Milton Park, Abingdon, Oxon, OX14 4RN

and by Routledge
711 Third Avenue, New York, NY 10017

Routledge is an imprint of the Taylor & Francis Group, an informa business

© 1975 George Allen & Unwin Ltd

British Library Cataloguing in Publication Data
A catalogue record for this book is available from the British Library

ISBN: 978-1-138-83837-6 (Set)
ISBN: 978-1-138-84750-7 (Volume 7)
Pb ISBN: 978-1-138-84753-8 (Volume 7)

Publisher's Note
The publisher has gone to great lengths to ensure the quality of this reprint but points out that some imperfections in the original copies may be apparent.

Disclaimer
The publisher has made every effort to trace copyright holders and would welcome correspondence from those they have been unable to trace.

Europe
from Below

an assessment of
Franco-German popular contacts

JOHN E. FARQUHARSON

STEPHEN C. HOLT

London   George Allen & Unwin Ltd
Ruskin House   Museum Street

First published in 1975

© George Allen & Unwin Ltd 1975

ISBN 0 04 940046 0

Printed in Great Britain
in 10/11 point Times Roman type
by The Devonshire Press Limited, Torquay

Preface

In the West European societies of the present day the average man possesses opportunities for travel available in previous eras only to the fortunate few. Even if he denies himself the chance, the mass media will provide him with at least some information about foreign lands. It is the consequence of this for international relations that concerns us in this book. We wish to say immediately that how different nations regard one another still largely depends upon the relationships existing between their respective national governments. Nevertheless, the balance in the field of international relations has tilted some way towards making popular sentiment a more influential medium in understanding, as a result of the factors described in our opening sentence. The thesis of this book will accordingly be that whilst governmental policies and attitudes still take precedence, popular contacts now have a part to play in their own right, in that they may be utilised to reinforce such policies as European integration adopted at higher levels.

An illustration of this is the treaty of collaboration in 1963 between France and West Germany. It is hard to imagine how this could have been brought to fruition without a political background comprising joint adhesion to such organisations as the ECSC and the EEC. The Cold War, and perhaps the personal relationships between Adenauer and de Gaulle, were also of great importance. All these implied a degree of reconciliation already, but we shall say, nonetheless, that once the treaty had been signed the exchanges at popular level which have followed have in themselves reinforced the *rapprochement*. For this reason we feel that Franco-German contacts are worthy of study; additionally, they need to be evaluated as a potential model for the kind of multilateral organisational framework which the European Community needs if integration is to become a reality rather than a mere phrase.

We shall return to this theme in our last chapter, but throughout the whole work an analysis of the Franco-German experience as a possible European model will be implicit in what we say.

Moreover, many of those who work for reconciliation, especially in the realm of private initiative, do so with a European end in view. Franco-German friendship is seen very much as an essential prerequisite to a wider unity. This is implicit in many twin towning links and associated activities such as school partnerships and family exchanges. It finds official recognition in the treaty of 1963 itself, where bilateral youth contacts are described as a stage on the path to those at multilateral level.

There is another way in which the bilateral co-operation which we shall describe is informative from a wider, European standpoint. For even between two neighbouring peoples such activities are fraught with hazards, as the social and administrative institutions of one country only rarely coincide in practice with those of another, irrespective of any theoretical equality. We hope to show that in the realm of cultural collaboration goodwill is necessary, but not in itself sufficient. Hard work and careful preparation are essential to secure the success of international contacts at popular level. If this applies to bilateral relations, then clearly it will also hold good for the multilateral links implied in the objectives of European integration.

Connected with this whole matter is the problem of a common language; the lack of one in Franco-German exchanges has frequently led to difficulties. Again, at the level of multilateral contacts this will equally be the case. The implications of the language question for Europe are considered in our final chapter.

In our description of popular relations between the French and West Germans in recent years we shall inevitably have to make some criticisms where we feel that they are justified. Our picture cannot always be a rosy one, in view of the events of Franco-German history between 1870 and 1945. But we wish to make it quite clear that our own attitude is one of qualified optimism; relations are really now surprisingly good between the two neighbours, perhaps much better than anyone could reasonably have foreseen at the end of the last war. There is, we believe, a considerable fund of goodwill on both sides, and certainly a psychological readiness towards mutual comprehension. If, therefore, we criticise such things as their youth exchanges in this book it is not in order to undermine them, but rather because we genuinely wish to see them improved. We also feel that there are helpful lessons to be learned for other European countries. As third parties in the matter, we are anxious to see Franco-German relations as close as possible, in view of their significance for the EEC as a whole.

Clearly the most important aspect of mass contacts between different peoples is the problem as to whether or not they can help to dispel a false picture of the neighbour (or of oneself). How such stereotypes arise is a complicated question but in a work of this nature obviously we have to draw attention to it, even if space precludes an exhaustive description of the whole phenomenon. There are many different ways, as we know, in which prejudice can arise between peoples, quite apart from the effects either of history or of current political events, the influence of both these being obvious enough. It may be as well for us just to list some of the contributory factors here, in order to remind ourselves of just exactly what can give rise to a distorted image of oneself (the autostereotype) or of one's neighbour (the heterostereotype). Our book is devoted in the main to describing what efforts are now being made in France and Germany towards mutual comprehension; but when we read this account we have to bear in mind that in the background there may well be still some other aspects of our society which are working against understanding at international level.

For example, there is education itself, strangely enough. The most influential sector here in image-building is history, as written in national textbooks. We shall investigate this question more fully in Chapter 3, but here we just have to remind ourselves that school books produced in different countries frequently carry quite different interpretations of the same event. Of course, seen from a purely national standpoint, there is no reason why they should not do so. But if the concept of Europe is to become meaningful in any really concrete way, and mutual understanding between peoples is required for this to happen, then we cannot really afford to ignore that in some educational areas a 'national standpoint' has been overtaken by changed circumstances. Even geography books can contribute to false impressions. An undue concentration on the home country, for example, can easily help children to exaggerate its importance in the world. Language manuals can, even unconsciously, present a distorted picture of the life and customs of another people in the way in which the text is presented. In the case of history or language learning, these considerations would apply equally to books written for adults as well as to school textbooks.

Further to education in general there is today the obvious influence of the mass media in creating prejudice. Here we have to be careful, because how people obtain their information on current events differs widely, not just between countries, but between individuals themselves. Whether we rely more on TV than on the press or radio is in itself a question of personal inclination. Political beliefs and social class are frequently determining factors in the choice which we make. Because of this, generalisations may be dangerous. As far as the press goes, journalists on both sides of the Rhine are in any case conscious of the role they have to play in Franco-German relations, and how they can help understanding. Joint seminars have been held on this theme since the war, which is surely a hopeful sign in itself.

One fairly obvious way in which the mass media and historical events may coincide as factors in giving a partial view of an entire people is in accounts of the last war. The Germans here are obviously rather more the victims of the recent past than are the French. German correspondents in Paris have told us that meetings arranged between the political leaders of both countries are almost invariably preceded by ORTF programmes on French television dealing with the Resistance, or with the SS and concentration camps. In May 1973 the then director of ORTF virtually admitted in a speech in Düsseldorf that French TV gave a one-sided picture: he pointed out that the French people naturally wished to pay homage to their heroes, but conceded that the risk here lay in the possibility of giving a partial view of contemporary Germany.

Films are yet another area where the same situation applies. A great number of war films have been produced in France since 1945, and no one would seriously deny that in many Germans are depicted either as uniformly brutal or stupid or both. There have been exceptions, of course, and no doubt as time goes on the events of 1939–45 will lose their fascination for film-makers. But until now no one could pretend that the image of Germans in post-war motion pictures has been anything less than unsatisfactory.

Literature has also played some part in presenting one people to another. The fluctuating image of the Germans in France and of the French in Germany have now become the objects of specialist study in both countries, and a considerable body of literature now exists on the theme of Franco-German relations as such. Here we can only draw attention to the influence of fiction or non-fiction as being yet another factor in image-building. It is true that books now play a less important part than in previous centuries because of the mass media, but their effect on public opinion still cannot be completely overlooked. In fact, between 1945 and 1953 over seven hundred works on Germany appeared in France, either by Frenchmen (or others) on the country or as German books translated into French. This is still an opinion-moulding factor of some considerable scale, in other words. Even children's books are not exempt from this point. *Astérix et les Goths* for example, dealt with this famous fictional hero of French children repelling a Gothic invasion of Gaul by warriors who wore spiked helmets and marched together in the goosestep. It is rather difficult to estimate the exact effect of this, it may even be quite harmless, but in terms of image-forming we feel it is a point to be considered, at least.

The same applies to two other relatively minor points, advertising and linguistic expressions. It has been pointed out that even the way in which French goods are promoted in Germany, or German in France, is often linked to preconceived national images. The point here is not so much whether the image of another people brought before the public is accurate or not, but whether it is true that any product is typically German or French. The way in which brands of German beer are sometimes sold in France seems to rely on the idea that there is some kind of perpetual 'Germanness' which this particular product incorporates. This obviously implies a fixed national character for the Germans; we want to ask whether or not this is the real question. Surely any preconceived concepts of national character are doubtful, even if they are favourable.

Our own language is another area in which prejudice may be expressed, albeit unconsciously. By way of illustration we can offer 'to take French leave', which in French becomes *filer à l'anglaise* and in German *sich französisch empfehlen*. Leaving without permission seems to be regarded as a French custom in Britain and Germany, and as an English one in France. Equally we have *travailler pour le roi de Prusse* in French, which means working hard for little reward. The effect of these expressions is a little hard to quantify, however, as it is rather doubtful if anyone now using them really thinks about their origin or their implications, when he does so. Again, however, it is a point to bear in mind when we discuss how prejudice arises.

There are in sum several different factors involved in the construction psychologically of false auto- or heterostereotypes. When we come in the main body of the book to discuss the efforts being made at mutual comprehension in the context of Franco-German understanding we are conscious that there may simultaneously be some forces which are actually counter-productive. We ask the reader to bear this in mind, as clearly these factors cannot just be ignored.

This work is the first of its kind, in that its theme is that of popular contacts between peoples rather than those at the level of high politics. Because of this we have felt a description in breadth to cover as many aspects of collaboration as possible would be the right approach. It would have been possible to have written a book on the subject-matter of virtually every single chapter here, but then a coverage of the whole field of post-war popular exchanges would have been impossible. This work must be seen as an introduction to the whole area, rather than as an exhaustive analysis of each part of it.

First, however, we must express our grateful thanks to all those who helped with it. Many people in Europe, too numerous to mention by name, offered information in interviews or in writing. Colleagues at Bradford University who gave constructive criticism on various sections of the manuscript included Dr K. Whitton, A. Williams, R. Smith, J. Jochum, and J. Henderson. M. Gérard Baloup, Head of the Local Authorities Division for the Council of Europe, kindly assisted us in a similar fashion, as did Mr Hugh Beesley, also of the Council, and Dr Hallett of the University of Swansea. Professor Grosser of the Fondation Nationale des Sciences Politiques at Paris was kind enough to provide us with a copy of B. Boyer's work *L'étude scientifique des préjugés nationaux dans les rapports franco-allemands*, on which the points made here in respect of national stereotypes are largely based. We should also like to express our gratitude to the University of Bradford for the financial help of which this book is a result. For all the views expressed in it, we **are**, of course, solely responsible. Finally we have to thank Mrs Paula Greenwood for the cheerful efficiency with which she coped with our handwriting in typing the manuscript.

Contents

Chapter 1

National Cultural Policies:
Their Aims and
Execution

Official policies devised by any government in order to make the culture of its people known abroad are not new. The French were carrying out such activities even in the nineteenth century. An office known as *Bureau des Ecoles et des Oeuvres Françaises à l'Etranger* was set up in 1900 and upgraded in status to a *Service* twenty years later. 1910 saw the formation of the *Office National des Universités et Ecoles Françaises* and agreements over the exchange of assistants in schools were concluded with various individual regions of Germany prior to the First World War. Immediately before the second the French were devoting 70 million francs annually to disseminating their way of life abroad; nineteen cultural accords had been signed with thirteen foreign powers.

A roughly similar course was followed in Germany, with a section for art and science in the Foreign Ministry established in 1896. This was followed by a schools section twenty years later. After the first war a full-blown directorate for spreading German culture abroad was set up; the twenties saw the birth of the DAAD and of the forerunner of the PAD (mentioned in Chapter 3). Finally, in 1932 the Goethe Institutes were founded. The French already had an official institute at Berlin prior to 1939, where Jean-Paul Sartre among others came into contact with German thought, especially that of Husserl and Heidegger.[1] Thus both countries had established a full-scale programme of cultural activities abroad, which obviously came to an end with the outbreak of hostilities.

After the war the occupying authorities in the French zone quickly took up the task of spreading their way of life to the West Germans.[2] Pre-war intellectual contact between the two peoples was re-established in this way, even if at first on a rather modest scale. In 1948 some four thousand persons took part in cultural exchanges at a bilateral level under the aegis of the French occupation.[3] Six years later relations in general had become so improved that the newly independent West Germans could sign an accord with their neighbours across the Rhine, the object of which was to further cultural links. Despite good intentions, the agreement made little headway prior to 1958. Then an important step forward was taken with the foundation of a joint Franco-German Rectors' conference, so that educational co-operation became, as it were, institutionalised. By 1962 cultural exchanges were in full swing. The French had now built up a number of institutes in the Federal Republic as bridgeheads for their way of life, paralleled by the Goethe Institutes set up by the Germans in France in 1952. There was a lively traffic in books and periodicals between the two peoples. West Germany was the world's tenth largest purchaser of those exported from France in 1962.[4]

Before we proceed to any more detailed account, we shall have to clarify what is meant by 'national cultural policy' today. In particular, it is important to be clear about the kind of role the two governments now ascribe to cultural exchanges, and the effect of the latter on international relations.

Traditionally the French had had what can fairly be called a missionary complex in respect of their way of life. Examples of this attitude are not hard to find. De Gaulle in his memoirs referred to France as having been 'from time immemorial' a 'champion of humanity', disseminating freedom of thought, a process described as 'God's work'.[5] As a further illustration, when, in 1968, the Mona Lisa was returned from exhibition in the USA, it was no longer hung in its former position of honour on the first floor of the Louvre. In July that year the Museum's director explained that its original place had been conceded to a French painting as the Louvre was a French museum and therefore the first floor, '*l'étage noble*', was reserved for French art.[6] It would probably be an exaggeration to say that to a large extent French culture represents France for most of its inhabitants, although this may have been true of earlier more elitist eras. But there is nonetheless a tendency for nationalism in France to be centred rather more on culture and language than in some other lands.

It is not altogether surprising then that the French should see a link between foreign policy on the one hand and the publicising of their way of life on the other.[7] As pointed out, this concept was already in evidence in the last century. A more modern example of its official recognition came in the cultural section of the Five Year Plan which was published in 1964. The goals were defined essentially as the dissemination of the national language, culture and ideas, attracting others to its literature, technology and knowledge, bringing about appreciation of its educational methods, raising France's influence and in sum to represent an essential element of its foreign policy. Cultural activity by the state was said to be closely linked with political and economic transactions at international level. How the promotion of French culture has been linked with foreign affairs in Germany is exemplified by the French Week run in Berlin in 1966, and organised jointly by the city's French institute and the local French military authorities. The programme included among other things an exhibition 'Paris past and present', Jean Renoir films, theatrical presentations and films on the French countryside. It was claimed that the show as a whole had helped to dissipate doubts among the Berliners about the continued French presence in the city, thus serving a political goal.[8]

Similarly, the furtherance of academic and artistic contacts is seen officially in the Federal Republic as 'an essential element in our foreign cultural policy', itself later described as 'a pillar of foreign policy'.[9] In practice, however, the situation has been very different for the Germans than for the French, as the events of the Third Reich led to considerable circumspection after the war. For some time the Germans presented a low profile to the world in respect of their way of life and West Germany became in effect a net importer of foreign culture. When a German Consul was sent to Paris as the first official representative of the nation in 1950 he received a cool reception.[10] It was decided under these circumstances to use past German intellectual achievements as a kind of pathfinder to prepare the way for normal diplomatic relations. As one German politician has said 'culture took precedence over foreign policy, and opened the road for it'.[11] Essentially the Germans were operating in a frankly unfriendly world, which did not even wish to hear German spoken. As a result the first official cultural contacts were deliberately undertaken in the world of music. Drama followed later when foreign relations were returning to normal. The Germans have accepted, in other words, that political relations between states are really decisive in determining how different peoples regard one another, but that cultural exchanges are nonetheless an important factor. So both governments see some connection between their respective foreign policies and their activities at what might be called the presentation of the national way of life. This, in effect, is what their cultural programmes are.

An additional factor in this respect is the nature of the society in which we live, based as it is on mass media and mass communications. This means that culture is no longer the domain of the privileged few. Contacts between peoples now habitually take place at a level where what might be described as traditional culture is now much less important than it once was. Hence, more and more, a national cultural policy in France and West Germany is coming to imply the presentation of the contemporary domestic scene to the neighbouring people.[12] As one official said, 'when a Frenchman talks about Schiller now he means Karl (then Economics Minister) not Friedrich'.[13] Conferences and seminars organised by the French cultural services in Germany very often deal with aspects of current life in the home country, with topics such as French agriculture or adult education. It is undoubtedly a sign of the times that whereas only 2 per cent of lectures given by French officials in Germany in 1970 had literature as their subject, 28 per cent of them dealt with economic and social themes.[14] The need to concentrate on current affairs was seen quite early after the war, not only by officials but by private persons as well. As one of the latter wrote, 'one article on the refugee problem in Germany which appears in the French press brings us nearer to our goal (understanding) than ten volumes on Goethe'.[15] In fact, the accent now seems to be falling so much on current affairs and problems that there may even be some danger that both governments are slightly neglecting the cultural heritage of their peoples, of which the contemporary world is, after all, to a considerable degree, the product.

As far as organisation is concerned, the difference in the political structure of the two states has inevitably meant far different approaches to the problem of the actual execution of policy goals.

West Germany is a federal republic where the regional authorities have wide powers. France, on the other hand, has been traditionally a centralist state, where most authority emanates from Paris. This difference creates more trouble for the French in Germany than the Germans have in France. In fact, one French official at the embassy described to us trying to run a cultural programme for Germany from Bonn as rather like basing a similar activity in Britain on the Isle of Skye. Although this is an exaggeration one can see what he means. The German capital is by no means the artistic centre of the Federal Republic, which tends to have a large number of big cities, rather than one huge capital, as in the case of France or the UK. Organisationally the French have tackled this by building far more institutes in Germany than the Germans have in France (twenty-two as against eight), on a basis of one per city. They have also evolved a system known as *professeurs itinérants*, which means that lecturers are based at their embassy and institutes and travel around the country according to demand. One interesting difference between the countries is that whereas French officials engaged in cultural services are usually seconded academics, their German counterparts are career diplomats.

Financially, neither country seems to devote very large sums to disseminating its way of life. The French Embassy cultural services spent in round figures some 14 million francs in the Federal Republic in 1972 (approximately £1¼ million). This compares with a figure of about 8½ million DM allocated for German cultural services in France, which is now almost exactly equal to the French figures.[16] These statistics do not include any money spent on youth exchanges. It may be that the relatively high cost of this latter programme inhibits the governments from devoting more resources to other activities. Altogether West Germany devoted in round figures 182 million DM (£27 million) to the cultural section of the Foreign Office in 1970, so that its expenditure in France is by no means disproportionate to that in other countries.[17] But a true comparison between the respective financial outlays of the two countries is impossible because of administrative differences. The cultural department's budget at the Quai D'Orsay comprises scientific and technical sections as well as the purely artistic. Moreover, the need, already referred to, to build a large number of institutes in Germany would tend to make for a greater expense for the French and thus distort the figures.

Additionally, cultural work is not necessarily confined in any case to foreign ministries. In Germany a number of other government departments have a hand as well. The Ministry of the Interior is responsible for German historical and archaeological institutes abroad; similarly it is the Economics Ministry which sends out books and films on its particular theme, and the official Press and Information Service of the government naturally supplies information abroad as well. These are only a few illustrations of the non-Foreign Office cultural activities.

The institutes are the bridgeheads of French culture. In 1967 they had over 300,000 works available in their libraries for the German public, as well as being the administrative centres for other types of contact. Many of these are what might be called traditional activities, for example the presentation of French plays (128 in 1964). Films, music and artistic exhibitions naturally figure quite prominently among the events. During seven weeks in spring 1972, just to take one example, the institute at Mannheim presented a concert, two different programmes of documentary films, an evening of French medieval songs, a theatrical spectacle based on comedy in French literature and two lectures.[18] The centre at Karlsruhe holds at least one, sometimes three exhibitions yearly.[19] There are usually reading rooms attached to the institutes' libraries, with a selection of journals, etc. from France, and sometimes record collections as well. All this is admirable enough and undoubtedly helps students in the neighbourhood, but clearly is unlikely to reach a very wide audience.

Perhaps the real importance of the institutes lies in two other spheres, namely language-teaching and assistance to French trade. The two categories are clearly linked together, since many Germans learn French for commercial reasons anyway. This finds recognition in the existence of special courses at the centres in commercial French, for example at Aix-la-Chapelle.[20] In 1970 some eighteen thousand learners were enrolled for French at the various institutes in Germany combined.[21] This may not seem impressive, but as many are in business it certainly contributes to bilateral trade.

An even more direct way of furthering business relations lies in the part played by the institutes in trade exhibitions. A paradigm of such functions was the French Week at Stuttgart in mid-1962, where various aspects of French life were co-ordinated in a commercial framework. Five hundred local shops carried French goods, embassy representatives held a conference at the local Technical College, German trade unionists were given talks on French social policies. Plays and music were also brought into the programme, to which the local radio station contributed.[22] The main objects of the exercise were clearly to sell contemporary France, including its products, to the people of Stuttgart.

Another way of presenting the French way of life in its various forms is the use of the *professeurs itinérants*, previously referred to. They talk on a wide variety of topics, for example about French Protestantism, wartime resistance, or perhaps environmental pollution in France. The subjects are normally chosen by the Germans asking for the talk in the first place. Pollution was chosen by the local government officials in Bavaria, presumably so they could see how the problem was tackled in France. Sometimes the request for a talk comes from trade unions or peasant farmers. The theme, in other words, varies according to the audience. For those interested enough in the problems of contemporary France there is the offer sometimes of a subsidised visit. The whole idea of travelling lecturers is undoubtedly splendid in principle, but the scale is relatively modest. In 1970 about eighteen thousand Germans attended the 446 lectures and seminars which were arranged (three quarters of which were in German). On the other hand, the fact that much of the demand comes from organisations catering either for youth in some respect, often educationally, or from workers'/farmers' associations perhaps helps redress the balance qualitatively. According to its leader the service is at the moment hampered by lack of funds, which seems a pity.[23]

Two other aspects of French policy which deserve to be mentioned are the so-called cultural missions and the scholarships in France for German students and teachers. The first consists of what might be described as cultural teach-ins, which take place either at the institutes or at German universities. They last on average two to three weeks, and are devoted to literature, and the social and natural sciences. In 1967 there were fourteen such events all told, which are certainly more designed for students than for the more popular type of audiences who attend the lectures described above.[24]

Granting scholarships for study in France is an important part of French cultural policy abroad. These may be either of short or long duration, but the main point is to allow either students or teachers of French the chance of improving their knowledge of the language, as described in Chapter 3 (due to the fact that most scholarships go to Romanists anyway).

An examination of German policy in France shows three main differences in principle from the foregoing activities. Firstly, the scale is more modest, only eight German institutes in the whole country. Then there is an even greater emphasis on contemporary life in the Federal Republic, as opposed to the German cultural heritage in general. Thirdly, the German government has now moved to a rather different concept of cultural policy as such, with the emphasis on collaboration with other states. This is now officially coming to replace the older idea of just selling German culture to foreigners.

Although the first two of these points are logically separate they seem to be connected in practice. It is undoubtedly contemporary Germany in which the French are interested, so much so that the Germans have little need to advertise. This accounts perhaps in itself for the relatively limited scale of their activities, on the principle of 'good wine needs no bush'. German officials claim that the French are on the whole much more interested in Germany than the Germans are in France. There is independent evidence to support this thesis as French observers have noted that several publications in present-day France are devoted entirely to the Federal Republic.[25] In Germany there is no particular sign of any corresponding interest in France, at least on a similar scale. It is almost certainly the economic miracle which is responsible for French curiosity. So marked is this that the director of the Goethe Institute in Paris told us that he would turn the whole place into a market research centre for French students and businessmen if he could. The institute at Lille found in a survey that over half the people enrolled on German courses there were learning it for commercial reasons.[26] It is probably in recognition of this that emphasis in the language programmes run by the institutes tends to fall on evening classes.

Apart from their linguistic activities the Goethe Institutes do pay some heed to more traditional cultural areas, such as music and art. Over thirty choirs and orchestras performed in France in 1970 alone.[27] Plays, films and art exhibitions figure regularly in the programmes, to complement the presentation of what might be called Germany's heritage. As in the case of similarly inspired French functions in Germany it is rather doubtful whether this has much influence in producing a better image of the country abroad. The audience for these activities is relatively limited and very probably consists of people already orientated towards the neighbouring country anyway.

A much more fruitful approach to the whole question is the present German emphasis on co-operation with other countries in cultural matters. Symptomatic of this new attitude was the speech by the German Ambassador at the opening of a Goethe Institute at Bordeaux in early 1973. He described the new centre's concentration on scientific, technical and commercial German as a factor in the construction of Europe. The Germans seem now to be convinced that because of the need for European integration their bilateral relations with France have entered the third post-war phase. By this they mean that the fifties were the time for breaking the ice, whereas the next decade was devoted essentially to consolidation. According to this thesis the seventies will see sober collaboration at cultural level between the two countries.[28] The French are certainly ready to meet them halfway in this respect, and some projects have already been undertaken in common.

This kind of enterprise was foreshadowed in the 1963 treaty, and as early as July that year the respective chiefs of the information services were meeting to discuss closer collaboration. In particular radio, TV and film co-operation was debated. The stumbling-block, however, to any large scale activities in common since this meeting seems to have been once again the differing TV and radio organisational structures in the two countries. German services are decentralised to a very real extent, whereas in France ORTF is a central, national body under close governmental supervision. At the West German radio and television studio in Paris officials say that the treaty has undoubtedly been of assistance to them on the whole, especially insofar as the French ORTF is now ready to place equipment at their disposal when they need it.

In addition there has been some exchange of programme material and of co-production. A show called *Intervilles* between various towns in the two countries was projected by October 1963. In Hesse the local radio began a series of plays by French and German authors in collaboration with ORTF. After a further meeting between the respective chiefs of information services in January 1964 a joint television magazine programme for Latin

America was announced. Equally, there was a joint presentation on ORTF on the origins of the 1914–18 war.[29] Nonetheless the scale of co-production remained fairly limited, at least until 1970 when twenty-one different projects were undertaken together, with eighteen planned for the following year. In 1972 ORTF signed an agreement with Bavarian TV for fifty-two half-hour programmes, to be jointly produced. These were to be devoted to France, however, for screening in Bavaria. In other words, this is in a sense a co-production without genuine collaboration as the French public will not learn anything about Germany from the series.[30]

Exchanges of material have been similarly on a small scale: in 1969 one German channel (ZDF) took 197 minutes of material from French TV, not much for a whole year.[31] Additionally some exchanges take place at regional level, for example, between ORTF and the system in the Saar.

An interesting aspect of co-operation has been the idea of twinning radio and TV stations. The regional direction of ORTF at Strasbourg is linked in this way with the radio/TV station at Berlin, to give one instance. This produced the project for a TV film 'A Berliner in Alsace' to be followed by 'An Alsatian in Berlin'. In the general framework of a Franco-German Week in Berlin both stations devoted space to the affairs of its twin area. The whole concept appears fruitful as a way of presenting the people to the people.

Some co-operation has taken place in other spheres as well. A joint Franco-German film commission has been set up, the aim being to achieve ten films together annually, the major share of the finance (80 per cent) coming from France. Similarly, there have been some theatrical co-productions, in one case for example between Metz and Trier. The opera companies at Paris and Hamburg have also worked together.

In sum it seems fair to say that on the whole the results of joint activities have been on a disappointingly small scale up to now. But there are two important qualifications to make at once. Firstly, the very real collaboration in youth contacts and education are described elsewhere. If, in the realm of more traditional culture, co-operation has been limited, this is merely a sign of changing policies, altered to adapt to the needs of our present Western society. Not everyone would think it a bad thing that collaboration has taken place mainly at a more popular level than the one at which pre-war cultural exchanges functioned. Secondly, both parties to the 1963 treaty accept collaboration in principle, for example in the realm of mass media. This acceptance offers hope that administrative differences can be overcome, as the will to work together is obviously there. Particularly significant is the new emphasis on presenting a picture of contemporary France and Germany in the neighbouring country. It does not appear very likely that lectures on Molière or Goethe will ever be anything but caviar to the general, but learning about the current problems of the other's society and how it solves them is surely a step towards integration. Nowadays German local officials visit France perhaps to study traffic problems or communal administration. For example, French mayors from Alsace were received at Kehl to see films on Berlin and the question of the Wall. If the Grosser statement already cited on page 4 is valid, this is worth ten volumes on Goethe.

A further point which has to be raised here is the whole extent of Franco-German bilateral relations, when placed in a context of the links between them and other countries. In other words, is there now anything special about their relations as a result of the treaty of 1963? After all, the kind of exchanges which we have described take place between many European states. France and Germany themselves have a whole network of cultural agreements with other lands, especially the former. France now has an accord with twenty-six European countries, as against West Germany's seventeen.[32] Just to take one example, the latter now has a brisk exchange of, among others, young leaders and administrators with the Netherlands, in conformity with a bilateral treaty of 1966. By 1971 five thousand young people had participated from both countries, and 155 joint seminars had been arranged.[33] There is nothing unique about the Franco-German treaty, in other words, at least as far as culture is concerned. It also has to be borne in mind that the existence of an agreement does not necessarily imply any particularly large scale of activity. Switzerland manages to maintain close cultural links with her neighbours without having signed a single treaty to institutionalise them.[34]

Before we leave this preliminary sketch of Franco-German contacts it ought to be mentioned that although the German Democratic Republic has no actual agreement with France it has achieved some cultural exchanges with her. As early as 1958 an organisation called *Association française pour les échanges culturels avec l'Allemagne d'aujourd'hui* was founded in Paris.[35] The association was re-named in 1970 at a congress in Lille in such a way that the impression is given that one of its main objects was to work for recognition of the GDR in France. (This has now been officially given anyway.) It includes prominent French politicians and intellectuals among its members (until his death in 1963, Jean Cocteau, for example). Structurally the movement has local and regional committees all over France, but membership, although increasing, is still limited. Between December 1963 and March 1968 it rose from 4,000 to over 10,000. It remains to be seen what effect French recognition of East Germany will have on its influence.

Additionally, the GDR arranges visits for delegations from France. Between 1963 and 1968 there was a steady climb in the number of such events but the invasion of Czechoslovakia appeared to hamper the activities quite considerably. Another form of propaganda is a newsheet *Echo d'Allemagne* published in France as a monthly periodical. Its content can be judged from the reprint of a mayor's speech, declaring that the fight against (West) German militarism was the surest pledge of Franco-German friendship.[36] The GDR also carries out the same kind of traditional cultural activity in France as does West Germany, although on a smaller scale. Typical examples are the performance of Brecht by the Berlin People's Theatre, and the showing of East German films.

In East Germany itself an association was brought into being in February 1962 with the title *Franco-German Society in the GDR*. Its avowed aim was to set up durable links of friendship with the French people. The latter's 'revolutionary tradition' was praised by the association's president in a 1962 speech. He forecast the development of exhibitions, concerts as the basis of future cultural exchanges, and of teacher and lecturer exchange visits between the two countries.[37]

It does not seem very probable, despite French political recognition, that the GDR will supplant or even seriously threaten the firm place in France of relations with West Germany. East German leaders clearly believe that culture can be used as a kind of political spearhead, but Franco-West German membership of the EEC gives the West Germans a basis for their links to France which the GDR does not possess. But the East Germans will almost certainly increase their cultural drive. The results of the March 1973 elections in France seem to demonstrate that there is some considerable potential in the country which would constitute an audience for such activities.

In summarising the current state of official cultural exchanges between France and West Germany we would concentrate on three main points. Firstly, the two governments seem to be entering a third phase in their post-war relations, these stages having been in chronological order reconciliation, consolidation and collaboration. This movement is perhaps the most hopeful sign at present. Linked with this is our second point, the desire now to present an image of one's contemporary society to the neighbour. The French Institute at Heidelberg, to take one example, announces that the France of today is above all the theme of its programmes.[38] This seems to us a far more fruitful way of approaching culture than putting on plays by Molière or Schiller, exactly because it helps to produce understanding of one's neighbour and his problems. It is probably arguable that even today neither government really spends enough at official level on activities like seminars or information visits for civil servants or leaders on both sides of industry.[39] If integration in Europe in the full sense of the term is to be achieved, these contacts must surely be extended. The 'new Europeans' must know their neighbours as a preliminary step to understanding them.

Associated with the recent emphasis on the contemporary scene is the need to further international links at popular level. As long as culture meant Racine this was by definition impossible. Mass literacy and easier communication now present a challenge to current EEC states. For the first time in history it has become technically possible to present the people to the people, that is to make the Germans as a whole acquainted with the current French way of life under peacetime conditions. Since there is an obvious connection now between foreign policy and cultural exchanges there seems no reason why the politico-economic ties between the two peoples cannot be strengthened by a programme of mass contacts, when properly organised. In this way it should theoretically be possible to complement joint membership of the EEC in one sphere by genuine *rapprochement* at popular level in another, as the French and Germans have been attempting since 1963.

Notes

1   R. Cheval, 'Die deutsch-französischen Kulturbeziehungen' in *XV Jahrestagung des Arbeitskreis deutsch-französischer Gesellschaften*, pub. by Arbeitskreis deutsch-französischer Gesellschaften, Mainz, 1970, p. 35.

2   For accounts see F. R. Willis, *France, Germany and the new Europe*, London, OUP, 1969, and A. Grosser 'Deutsch-französischer Zusammenarbeit nach 1945', *Deutschland-Frankreich*, vol III (Stuttgart Deutsche Verlags-Anstalt, 1963), pp 17*f*.

3   *Allemagne*, no. 2, June/Aug. 1949.

4   *Correspondance franco-allemande*, no. 23, 30 Apr. 1963, p 15.

5   Charles de Gaulle, *Memoirs of Hope*, London, Weidenfeld and Nicholson, 1971, p 189.

6   K. O. Nass, *Gefährdete Freundschaft*, Bonn, Europa Union Verlag, 1971, p 75.

7   For fuller accounts of this attitude see W. Ross, 'Konzept einer auswärtigen Kulturpolitik', *Merkur*, 1965, pp 905*f*, and E. R. Curtius 'Die französische Kulturidee', *Antares*, 1955, p 13*f*.

8   *Le Monde*, 23 Apr. 1966.

9   *Guidelines for a Foreign Cultural Policy* (German Federal Foreign Office, Dec. 1970), pp 5*f*.

10 H. Kühn, 'Die deutsch-französischen Kulturbeziehungen in den letzten 25 Jahren', in *La réalité quotidienne des échanges franco-allemands*, vol II, p 15.

11 Ibid., p 15.

12 For recognition of this in West Germany see German Press and Information Service Bulletin 10/S.81 (27 Jan. 1971), giving the text of a talk to officials by the then Foreign Minister, which contained the sentence 'Culture is no longer a privilege for the few, it's on offer to everyone'.

13 Graf Raczynski, director of the Goethe Institute in Paris, in a personal interview.

14 Information from M. Haddey, director of Services Extra-Universitaires at the French Embassy in Bad Godesberg, in an interview.

15 A. Grosser, quoted in H. Kühn op cit., p 17.

16 The French statistics are from a personal interview with M. Cheval, French Cultural Attaché in Bad Godesberg.

17 *Kulturabteilung des Auswärtigen Amtes-Jahresbericht* (1970), pp 24*f*.

18 *Correspondance*, no. 202, 15 Mar. 1972, p 13.

19 *La réalité*, op cit., vol II, p 59.

20 Ibid., p 33.

21 *Correspondance*, no. 189, 15 June 1971, p D.

22 For the whole event see *Allemagne*, no. 74, May/June 1962.

23 This information from M. Haddey of the Services Extra-Universitaires.

24 For the statistics of 1967 see *Correspondance*, no. 138, 15 Nov. 1968, p 21.

25 See A. Grosser, 'Die Bundesrepublik; bieder oder nüchtern?' in F. Bondy (ed.), *So sehen Sie Deutschland*, (Stuttgart, Seewald Verlag, 1970), p 44 for this point, with a list of the periodicals.

26 F. Altmayer, 'La coopération culturelle franco-allemande', *L'Europe en Formation*, 1965, p 26. The survey took place in 1960.

27 'Kulturabteilung des Auswärtigen Amtes' *Jahresbericht*, 1970, p 92.

28 For expositions of this new approach see H. Kühn, 'Deutsch-französische Kulturpolitik im nächsten Jahrzehnt', *Dokumente*, 1969, p 369*f*, and J. Rau, *Chancen der deutsch-französischen Kulturpolitik in den siebziger Jahren*, Bonn, Institut für Internationale Begegnungen, 1971.

29 *Correspondance*, no. 31, 1 Oct. 1963, p 1; no. 34, 1 Nov. 1963, p 14, and no. 38, 20 Jan. 1964, p 14.

30 *Le Monde*, 21 Nov. 1972.

31 For information on exchanges and co-production see K. Holzamer, 'Die Rolle des Fernsehens bei den Bemühungen um die Zusammenarbeit zwischen Frankreich und der Bundesrepublik Deutschland', *XV Jahrestagung*, op. cit., p 47.

32 The lists are in G. Hindrichs, *Kulturgemeinschaft Europa*, op. cit., p 161.

33 *Federal Press and Information Service Bulletin* 77/S, 1971.

34 As pointed out by Hindrichs, op. cit., p 17.

35 S. Reime, 'Die Tatigkeit der DDR in den nichtkommunistischen Ländern' IV, *EWG Staaten* (*ohne Bundesrepublik*) (Forschungsinstitut der Deutschen Gesellschaft für Auswärtige Politik, Bonn, 1970), pp 88*f* for this section.

36 Quoted in *Mitteilungsblatt für die deutsch-französischen Gesellschaften*, no. 16, Oct. 1963, p 26.

37 Reime, op. cit., p 84.

38 *La réalité*, vol II, op. cit., p 57.

39 By 1972 the Goethe Institutes were complaining in their annual report of a shortage of funds and speaking seriously of a possible reduction in the number of such centres abroad. *Correspondance*, no. 200, 15 Feb. 1972.

Chapter 2

Franco-German Youth
Exchanges

The treaty of 1963 foresaw the inauguration of a joint organisation concerned solely with the furtherance of contacts between the youth of the two countries in order to achieve a better appreciation of the life and culture of the neighbouring people.[1] Among the activities to be encouraged were exchanges between students, young workers and children, sporting events, contacts at holiday centres, seminars, visits of an informative, i.e. educational nature to the other side of the Rhine. Also to be included were cultural contacts, the diffusion of French and German as a second language (to be dealt with in a later chapter) and even the facilitation of scientific research carried out by young people. 'Youth' in this context was to be defined as comprising persons up to thirty years of age.

To execute this ambitious programme a Council of Administration was established, composed of ten members designated by each of the respective governments;[2] of each ten, four are from the civil service and the remaining six are themselves qualified youth leaders. The Council's sittings take place alternately in France and West Germany, being presided over in the former by the Secretary of State for Youth and Sport and in the latter by the Minister for the Family and Youth. To assist the Council's administration there is a Secretary-General and a deputy, both appointed for five years by agreement between the governments. These two officials are never both of the same nationality. The administration has been divided for purposes of facility into two sections, one at Versailles and the other in the neighbourhood of Bonn, each headed by a director on a five-year appointment.

It should be emphasised that the Youth Office (henceforth OFAJ) does not usually initiate youth functions but rather serves as a medium, both administrative and financial, for private or official youth organisations wishing to arrange group or individual contacts at an international level. The OFAJ is liberally supplied with public funds, initially to the extent of fifty million francs annually, subscribed in equal proportions by the two governments. (As a result of France's financial problems in 1969 the total sum was provisionally reduced by 10 per cent.) A regular scale of subventions has been laid down for financial assistance to youth groups according to the type of contact involved. For example, in the framework of twin town exchanges, the OFAJ will pay 60 per cent of the costs of the journey for participants, plus six francs daily for youth and accompanying adults, the proportion of the latter to the former being one to ten. Priority is given in such cases to visits where accommodation with a family is envisaged. In the case of exchanges of a more educational nature, the subsidies are higher still; a worker less than thirty years old can obtain all the costs of his journey. The OFAJ will pay the entire expenses of a two-month language course as a preliminary to the exchange, and all insurance expenses. It also guarantees a minimum salary of 600 DM monthly, provided that the worker undertakes a long-term period of employment in the neighbouring country.[3]

Before we begin to describe the activities of the OFAJ we have to make it quite clear that the new body only raised youth exchanges to an official level. They were already in full swing in practice prior to 1963. Again it was the French occupation, supplemented by private initiative, which furnished the necessary organisational framework.[4] It was continued when in March 1949 Franco-German youth leaders met at Vlotho (Lower Saxony) for discussions. Religious associations were prominent in postwar contacts, for example bilateral meetings of young Catholic workers. French and Germans were among the participants at the European youth camp *Lorelei* in 1951. The initial meetings were not always without friction. One holiday centre in the Black Forest refused to take French students because of their behaviour in early 1955. Their consciousness of having been on the winning side in the war was said to have been too much in evidence.[5] Despite some trouble, however, the picture was an encouraging one on the whole, especially in the four years prior to the treaty of 1963.

By that time 200,000 French aged between twelve and thirty had visited the Federal Republic since the end of the war. Not less than 70 per cent of these had done so since 1959. [6] The creation of the OFAJ has to be seen in the context of a growing demand for travel abroad; this was especially true in Germany. In January 1964 the youth of that country, according to a poll, chose France as the place they would most like to visit above any other. [7] As far as travel motives in general are concerned, it is really rather difficult to establish them precisely. A large number of young Germans questioned in one survey as to their reasons for wishing to travel gave in many cases quite advanced grounds; nearly a half wanted to know different lands and peoples, nearly a quarter said it was primarily in order to serve international understanding. Whether these were the real motives or merely those which sounded better than those of a frankly touristic nature it is hard to say. Incidentally, international understanding tended to be given rather more by students and grammar school pupils than by those at lower educational institutions. [8]

By that month the first OFAJ projects were under way, only twelve months after the initial treaty. The first ever meeting under the aegis of the new office had previously taken place at Verdun, apparently chosen for its symbolism. The schemes now announced included sporting contacts in Berlin, a choral encounter at Nevers, financial aid for the installation of language laboratories in Bavaria and the construction of a youth centre for Germans in Paris. (This short list gives in fact a good cross-section of OFAJ activities during the first five years and the pattern did not appear to have altered very much before 1968.) For 1964 as a whole it was hoped to exchange all in all 150,000 German youth and 100,000 French. By April, however, if not earlier, it had already become clear that enthusiasm for these types of exchanges had to be tempered with a certain amount of realism. It would be useful at this point to draw attention to the inherent difficulties contained in the projected exchange projects.

To begin with, there was the whole question of what actually constituted youth exchanges. If OFAJ assistance were to be made available, should all such contacts be subjected to the discipline of an actual programme of activities, or was an exchange simply an encounter round a camp fire? Then there was the language problem and its role in assisting, or perhaps hindering, contacts. These and other organisational problems alone took three days of discussion at a Bonn meeting in April 1964. Eventually it was decided to assist properly structured and programmed projects only, based on the use of a monitor, or youth leader of some kind. As far as finance was concerned, demand was overstepping supply already, by 70 million DM against the budget of 40 million DM.

Even more pressing than points of organisation were those arising from the different psychological and historical backgrounds of the respective young people concerned. As one writer pointed out, these required that the whole OFAJ approach should be extremely cautious in both planning and execution. The French came from an atmosphere of strong national feeling which was less the case in Germany. In both World Wars it was France rather than Germany that had suffered enemy occupation. A great deal of tact would have to be shown on both sides, since this was not to be an exercise in casual tourism, but rather one where a degree of personal commitment should be involved.[9]

Just how great a task the OFAJ faced can be judged from current opinion polls. For every hundred young Germans wishing to visit France, only ten young French people felt a similar inclination in respect of the Federal Republic, so that demand was uneven.[10] This may support the previous point about the effects of history, but perhaps it was due also to a certain social difference, in that according to this poll French youth was apparently both less willing to travel anywhere, and less interested in youth organisations as such. Clearly this was likely to present a major problem to the OFAJ, quite apart from structural differences in youth organisation in the two countries.

The OFAJ was fated, in other words, to discover what almost all bodies concerned with bilateral relations find out sooner or later. This is the simple fact that no two organisations in different countries which allegedly correspond to one another ever actually do so. In the first place in France youth associations are rather more likely to be politically or denominationally based than in Germany.[11] It would also seem true that in 1963 at least they possessed a less complete administrative structure than their opposite numbers across the Rhine. The Paris office of the OFAJ therefore had a harder task in co-ordinating and planning programmes in France than the corresponding bureau in Germany (at Bad Honnef-Rhöndorf). On the other hand, it did at least have the advantage of being able to operate through a more centralised political apparatus at national and regional level.[12]

An idea of the size of the psychological obstacles in bilateral contacts may be seen in the results of public opinion polls taken simultaneously in France and Germany in late 1963, just as the OFAJ began its duties. One such sounding of opinion among young people aged between fifteen and twenty-four years of age was discouraging in its revelation of current attitudes.[13] While it was true that 61 per cent of the French had a better opinion of the Germans than had the previous generation, West Germany was placed only sixth on the list of their preferred countries, not merely behind Holland, Britain and the USA, but behind Spain and Italy as well. The Germans for their part put France in fifth position. More revealing still was the hold of old prejudices regarding certain qualities traditionally associated with some peoples. For German youth the French were 'kind, charming, happy, open and helpful'. The French saw their neighbours as 'workers, sociable, disciplined and brave' and, even more cliché-orientated, as 'aggressive, proud and reserved'.

As against this picture of generalisation carried to extremes, two points can be made. Firstly, and from the OFAJ's standpoint encouragingly, it was shown quite unmistakably that initial judgements were modified by first-hand experience, at least in some cases. It was interesting, however, that this applied rather more in the case of French visitors to West Germany than the reverse. In fact, after going to France few Germans changed their views, and in those cases where this did happen, both favourable and unfavourable opinions were strengthened. French youth who had been in the neighbouring country, however, were twice as ready as before to underline German sociability. More encouraging still, the same people were far less inclined to stress 'bellicosity' as an element in German character. Secondly, even if both sides had stereotypes of their neighbour, this seemed to accord with the opinion which they held of themselves, so that the traits ascribed by German youth to the French were usually attributed by the French to themselves, in almost equal measure. In other words, even if one nation's youth did sometimes think badly of the other, it was equally unflattering about itself.

Moreover, in tests carried out by a French psychologist at a joint holiday camp, both French and German youth appeared in some respects to be similar in outlook towards society and politics in general, in that both could be described as relatively reformist in their views. That is, both tended to be somewhat anti-authoritarian and anti-militarist; both were against Communism and capitalism, though the opposition in both camps was much stronger towards the former. It was, incidentally, observed that peasant and working-class children tended to be somewhat more prejudiced in their judgements than those from other social milieux.[14]

More evidence of the French attitude to their neighbours came from a poll carried out via a questionnaire in 1963 to over three thousand young French people, mostly males.[15] Those questioned represented a reasonable cross-section of the population; incidentally only one in six had ever been to West Germany. Nevertheless, 61 per cent felt that the 'new Europe' should include that country. (By comparison, the percentage holding the same view in respect of the UK was sixty-six.) A roughly similar proportion was ready to say 'yes' to the question 'should the past be forgotten' in terms of Franco-German relations. This poll in general seemed to confirm the picture of a youth in France relatively well-disposed towards Germany, if perhaps not always well-informed or possessed of personal experience of that country. But as in the case of the previous polls discussed, there was clearly a willingness to work with the Federal Republic. In other polls taken simultaneously in the two countries in 1963, one third of all young Germans desired particularly close relations with France, whilst over one fifth of the French youth questioned felt the same way about Germany. A still higher proportion on both sides wanted close relations, even if not particularly close.[16]

From these various soundings of opinion it would appear that several more or less definite conclusions may be drawn. Firstly, opinions could be changed by first-hand experience of the other country. This was obviously important for the OFAJ, especially as so few young French people had travelled much at all. From one poll selection it transpired that three fifths of those replying had never been outside their own frontiers. On the other hand, the same sample showed that even in the case of the German youth participating, only 18 per cent had ever been to France.[17] It appeared that in terms of the sheer quantity of exchanges required, the OFAJ had a daunting task on its hands. Secondly, even in 1963–64, old clichés about the 'charming French' or the 'aggressive, disciplined Germans' still existed, and would clearly need a good deal of effort to be removed. As against this, both sides were ready to co-operate with one another and to a certain extent, at least, ignore the past. More hopeful still was the clear impression given of a similar attitude towards life in general, i.e. of a kind of moderate reformism among young people in both countries, which might well serve in some measure as a basis for collaboration in the future. From the OFAJ standpoint this advantage was partially offset, however, by the rather one-sided impression regarding the desire to visit the neighbour's country. In one joint enquiry over one third of young Germans wanted to go to France, but their own country held a markedly lower degree of attraction for the French questioned, of whom only one in nine wished to visit the Federal Republic.

Despite this last fact, it must be pointed out that in practice the OFAJ apparently managed to maintain an even balance between the two peoples in practice. Indeed, in the first full year of its activities slightly more young French people were helped to go to Germany, than were young Germans visiting France.[18] Since relatively few young French people were interested, the only conclusion that can be drawn is that grants were more easily acquirable in France. However, before this point or any more detailed analysis of the OFAJ's relative degree of success is considered, it would be as well to give a fuller picture of activities up to 1973, together with some examples of individual, or individual group, visits, in order to give some idea of the range of contacts undertaken, what sort of people go on them and what kind of impression they give and receive.

There is no doubt at all that whatever may be said of the quality and effects of the OFAJ programme, its sheer magnitude is impressive. Whereas in 1964 the total exchanges effected comprised some 280,000 young people, included in 5,500 separate contacts, for 1968 the respective figures were 420,000 and 7,500. In fact, from 1963–68 inclusive, in the first half-decade of its existence, the OFAJ assisted 1,800,000 persons in all, included within 35,000 group or personal contacts.[19] What type of meetings were promoted can be seen from the statistics opposite.

These figures conceal a multitude of different kinds of bilateral contact. One particular group activity much favoured by the office, for example, is the short information course which takes place in one particular region of each country. Here, a group of young people of mixed nationality enjoy a form of instruction embodying both factual information about the area and visits,

Aid afforded by the OFAJ to youth exchanges 1966–68 in percentages of total budget given to different types of activity[20]

	1966	1967	1968
Group contacts: general	38·5	37·5	33·55
Exchanges between young workers	12·9	13·2	10·72
Sporting exchanges	12·4	12·8	13·39
Scholastic/student contacts	11·6	11·8	13·04
Promotion of extra-scholastic language learning	6·0	6·2	7·11
Family exchanges, holiday camps	4·5	4·4	4·29
Academic courses	5·7	5·6	9·09
Contacts in framework of twin towning	3·4	3·7	4·01

sometimes of a more touristic nature. These courses are known under the title of *Connaissance de la France* in France (in Germany *Wir entdecken Deutschland*). They have afforded a knowledge of the other people to an increasing number of participants since their inception. By 1968 this number had reached as many as 5,000 in one year.[21]

It has to be accepted that this is nonetheless still frankly rather limited quantitatively. From 1965 to 1968 inclusive, apparently only some 17,500 young people took part on both sides. However excellent in quality, therefore, this project did not appear to be reaching the youth of each country to an extent sufficient to make a real impact upon it. Moreover, it has to be borne in mind that, despite OFAJ subsidies, this type of encounter was not actually initiated by it, and would therefore be flourishing even if the office did not exist. Similar programmes to *Connaissance de la France* have been in operation since 1953 at least.[22] On the other hand OFAJ subsidies undoubtedly have augmented the scale of such activities.

Despite reservations it has to be accepted that such courses appear to be both interesting and useful to those young people taking part and who discover a region of Germany or France and its problems. Above all, they discover it together. The participants are between eighteen and twenty-five years of age and the groups range between thirty and sixty in size.[23] The district studied in common is usually, at any rate in France, about 5,000 km² in area (some 2,000 square miles, rather bigger than the average English county) e.g. the Basque country, the Rhône valley, the Bordeaux area. The economic and social life of the district is studied on a ten-day course, as well as the past, as exemplified in archaeological findings available, folklore and local art. Problems such as regional planning and urbanisation in the area are also the object of investigation. Obviously, a course of such limited duration cannot pretend to be exhaustive, but from the nature of the themes, and the fact that they are joint projects, it can be fairly deduced that they are valuable qualitatively; it seems, therefore, doubly unfortunate that they were so limited in terms of quantity. As a final point in their favour, it should be underlined that they afford young people a chance to acquaint themselves with the problems of their own regions, as well as those of another land.

One form of group contact much in favour and especially suitable for young people has been sports meetings. One example of these was an event in a mountaineering resort some 60 km from Grenoble in 1966.[24] There were in all five distinct groups brought together under one roof, three from West Germany and the others from France, in all fifty-five to sixty young people, who took a mountaineering course together. The participants were eventually split into four groups of mixed nationality, each led by an appointed monitor. A report on the whole venture struck a note of qualified commendation; the French had been willing and attentive hosts, but the organisation had been deficient in some respects. In particular, the hut where the mountaineers spent some nights had dirty beds and not enough blankets. These are relatively small points, but they serve nonetheless to highlight some of the difficulties inherent in bringing together people of any age who are the products of differing culture and backgrounds.

Other problems have also arisen regarding sporting contacts, and, in particular, the motivation of the participants. In other words, is this to be just a friendly meeting, or are we trying to win? At one camp the experiment was made of dividing the youths in each tent fifty/fifty between French and Germans, and then organising the competition on a basis of one tent against another. This meant that each team was mixed, which was a considerable risk, but in the end it was a success. It is interesting to note that in the first year of the OFAJ's life it was apparently the case that the French showed somewhat more determination to do well for France in teams selected on a national basis than did the West Germans for their country.[25]

For some group activities subsidised by the OFAJ the twin towns scheme is a useful framework. In 1968 a festival of twin towns took place at Münster, with 1,200 pupils and 300 teachers from 48 different educational establishments in both countries. It was the largest single event to receive aid that year, and the immediate sponsors were the *Echanges Internationaux entre Familles Chrétiennes* and the *Katholische Elternschaft Deutschland*.[26] The festival lasted four days and included sporting encounters, theatrical and musical presentations and dancing. This is merely one example of how youth encounters are facilitated by the twin town concept, and how OFAJ aid can be used to further contacts at the grass roots level between the peoples. The exchange of school-children in general has been a major item in meetings since the OFAJ's foundation. By 1968 over one hundred thousand had taken part from both countries together.[27]

Many youth associations as such, with a counterpart in the neighbouring land, serve as a basis for contact in the same manner. Membership of similar bodies is not necessarily equal in both countries, which presents difficulties, although these can be overcome. There are more girl guides in France than there are across the Rhine, so the French section has been obliged to resort to contacts with other feminine youth groups. This has been relatively successful so that in 1966 some 2,500 French members spent their summer camp in the Federal Republic.[28] Many camps have been run in common, in order to train future guide leaders for both countries; Arras and Limburg were apparently the first to undertake this type of joint programme. Again the short stay (ten days) at such camps is inhibiting to real understanding of someone whose reactions may be very different to one's own, as was admitted at one common camp in Isère.

The possibility which exists for a young worker to spend a year doing a similar job in the other country has already been mentioned. Unfortunately, despite generous financial assistance and the provision of a well-organised administrative framework, this scheme has been on the whole a disappointment. By the end of 1969 only 1,335 young workers had participated from both countries together.[29] (The division between nationalities was roughly equal.) Obviously, the lack of a common language is a barrier, although the OFAJ does offer a two-month preliminary linguistic course. We have been told that on the French side, at least, the differences in technical training have acted as a hindrance. Certainly as early as 1966 the OFAJ was showing concern about the lack of response. It was then alleged that accommodation was proving difficult to find for young Germans in Paris.[30] We have been told that a further factor inhibiting such exchanges was a certain resistance on the part of the employers themselves. After all, the prospect of receiving a worker with only limited ability in the language spoken in the factory is not an especially pleasing one to any manager, as it is bound to create some difficulty for him. Additionally, there seems frankly to have been little demand from young people in either country anyway, which further limited the exchanges.

A joint seminar was held that year by young workers from both sides of the Rhine who had had a stay of this nature in the neighbouring country, to draw up a balance sheet of their impressions. It was decided to set up a committee composed of former exchangees to act as a guide for newcomers to the scheme. One interesting fact to emerge from the colloquy was that many participants were from the tertiary sector of the economy, for example typists anxious to improve their language skills, but presumably not wishing to become au pairs. Thus the meagre results of the scheme were even further diminished by a rather too wide definition of the concept 'worker'. The whole problem was still unresolved in 1971, when an OFAJ representative admitted that exchanges of young workers had been inadequate.[31] It is precisely this bourgeois tinge to the whole OFAJ programmes which has led to its criticism in SPD circles in Germany, of which more later.

Apart from a stay of long duration, young workers can travel in groups to meet their counterparts. This can involve a complete change of atmosphere for them, and indeed a totally new experience. One such visit, made by young people aged between sixteen and twenty from a village in the Lower Pyrenees to North Germany in 1968, made a striking impression.[32] Everything seemed different to them on the other side of the Rhine: this included the mentality of the inhabitants and their courtesy. The economic dynamism of the Federal Republic was impressive, and the obvious newness of Hamburg made the visitors aware of how much their neighbours must have suffered in the war through aerial bombardment. It is said that the group was moved to pose interesting questions about trade union organisation etc. in the Federal Republic, and about current political problems, such as the role of the NPD.

In eastern France also many such contacts between apprentices have been effected in which a youth association in Metz called *Carrefour* has been prominent. A meeting between young workers took place at Perl, near the frontier, in 1967, at which a number of social problems outstanding in both societies were discussed in common, for example 'Woman's role in Society and at Work'.[33] Economic problems have also frequently served as a basis for youth meetings, as in Schleswig-Holstein, where fifty-five young people in a group mixed both socially and nationally, discussed such topics as youth, tourism, agriculture and industry in the framework of the local economy. Even the problem of the Danish minority in Angeln was apparently taken into consideration. Similarly, the question of the environment of Lake Constance in the Federal Republic and Lake d'Annecy in Savoy has been discussed, joint seminars being held over the extent of pollution in both areas. We feel that common activities of this nature, related to actual topical questions in both countries, can hardly be anything but informative when seriously presented, and conducive to a better understanding of the neighbour, if only because they show young people that others have similar problems to themselves.

The nature of their employment serves as a point of contact as well. Young workers are helped to pay short visits to factories across the Rhine in order to acquaint themselves with management and the system of vocational training in the other country. In one instance, a group of twenty apprentices from Krefeld (Westphalia) visited a number of enterprises in Brest during a fortnight's stay in the area. The particular factory each individual was shown depended on his own craft, so that an insight into the training and management of his direct counterparts could be afforded. This kind of project is not necessarily confined to apprentices or manual workers; in 1971 fifteen French youth leaders were sponsored on a tour of inspection in the Federal Republic in order to study municipal youth organisation in that country. Even *haute couture* in Paris has been the object of study for fashion apprentices in Munich.

Again, the actual exchange of professional people, while desirable in theory, is sometimes difficult to achieve in practice, due in some instances to language difficulties, but even more to a lack of standardisation in training and examination. This is, of course, a general problem on which both countries are working anyway, both bilaterally and within the framework of the EEC, but the possession of qualifications not recognised in the other country does not assist the OFAJ programme. The exchange of nursing sisters is only one case where this obstacle arises, and severely limits its activities.[34]

Apart from professional people and young workers, rural youth is also included in the programmes of the OFAJ, since it constitutes that socio-economic class which is normally least likely to travel abroad. The furtherance of meetings between this type of young person is therefore of some importance to the office, and strenuous efforts have been made in this direction. In France an association known as the *Centre des Voyages de la Jeunesse Rurale* has carried out more than 800 events for French rural youth in the Federal Republic, comprising some 32,000 young people in the period 1963–68.[35] The *Maison Familiale Rurale* has also been active in this field; one of their groups visiting Rindern was especially struck by the technical aspects of German agriculture.[36] Silage, grain-drying and animal husbandry were particularly singled out in this respect. Again the feeling is obtained that the inspection was more than just a courtesy call, especially when the tour report says that the German rural householders visited showed a taste in furnishing their homes 'that one would wish to see more widespread in France'. Even the political administration of the country clearly made some impression, particularly the initiative shown by the *Länder*, which demonstrated to the French the degree of local autonomy enjoyed by their neighbours.

Not all contacts arranged by the OFAJ are concerned with groups. Many associations, such as the *Bureau International de Liaison et Documentation* (BILD), to take one instance from among a multiplicity of existing bodies, are more occupied with individual encounters, often through the medium of the family. Innumerable glowing reports of such contacts can be found, to illustrate the warmth of the welcome, etc. Much of this may well be true but there has to be a note of caution here, since presumably it is those families who have a more international outlook already which extend their hospitality in the first place. The OFAJ, in assisting such encounters, seems rather to be exploiting existing goodwill than to be creating a new understanding, or arranging meetings between people not previously interested in one another.

Moreover, there is the additional matter in this connection of social class. Middle-class families are seemingly readier to take in a guest from across the Rhine than are those at a different point of the social spectrum, as BILD itself admits. Its own analysis of the young people it has dealt with for 1967–69 inclusive shows that youth from what may be called a working-class background (i.e. peasants, farm labourers and manual workers combined) was always under-represented in its programme. The percentage emanating from this milieu was in fact only twenty-one in 1967 and in the next two years fell to eight and twelve respectively. This led BILD to observe that a massive effort should be made to recruit youth from the 'more modest social milieus'.[37] When young jurists from both countries meet it is no doubt useful in the sense that they are the European leaders of tomorrow. But in the era of the mass electorate all sections of the community need to be involved.

Not all individual meetings, of course, are arranged through the medium of the family. Many activities, such as work camps, etc. are organised on a voluntary basis for young people, not necessarily in any youth association at all. A typical case meeting was the work camp for archaeological volunteers from both countries at Mont Bego where, despite the valuable socio-educational nature of the work in itself, the primary aim of the camp was to further Franco-German understanding.[38] Similarly, the OFAJ assists camps such as those arranged at the grape harvest, where students can earn pocket money during vacations and meet their foreign counterparts. This is not always an unqualified success, as some proprietors apparently regard the participants as cheap labour. In one case a German teacher accompanying some students complained that ten hours' work a day was too much for eighteen-year-olds, and expressed the hope that some local peasants should cease to regard them simply as cheap immigrant labour (*Gastarbeiter*).[39] No doubt the farmers were adopting the same attitude to French students, but this would have been surely of little consolation to the Germans. Even the differing attitude to the work by the students could cause problems. One German at a harvest camp in Burgundy reported not only how hard the labour was but how astonishingly diligent the French were: the only words heard all day were 'pass the secateurs'. There were no songs and no conversation. Hence actual social contacts tended to be minimal.[40]

It can be seen from the foregoing examples that the OFAJ has undertaken a vast and varied programme of exchanges, both on a group and individual basis. However striking this is at first sight, it needs to be further analysed in some respects in order to get some idea of the impact which they may have made, and how far the actual attitudes of the youth in both countries have to any real extent been modified by participation in these projects. In this connection, two sets of statistics will be offered. The first analyses OFAJ exchanges in a given year (1967) in order to bring out more clearly exactly who does participate. Secondly, the results of public opinion polls taken among French and German youth in 1968 and 1970 will be shown, in order that these may be compared with those of 1963, when the office was first inaugurated. This gives an idea as to whether five to seven years of reinforced contact has made any apparent difference in attitudes.

As early as 1967 the Administrative Council of the OFAJ decided to carry out a statistical enquiry regarding what sort of young people were taking advantage of its projects; the total number of these latter was 7,031 in that year, of which about two thirds were actually included.[41] The remainder were omitted either because of the time factor, i.e. they had been carried out too early in the year to be properly surveyed, or because of their type. Students' courses and individual visits, stays in holiday camps, were not included. Nonetheless, the survey comprised 160,000 young people, or over half of those assisted by the OFAJ that year.

The first category of analysis was by region, from which the interesting fact emerged that whereas the four northern *Länder* in Germany had at the time one fifth of the total population, they formed the meeting place of only about one eighth of the events. The difference between north and south in France was even more marked, however, since Provence and the Côte d'Azur attracted 11·8 per cent of the meetings, with only 6 per cent of the population of France. As the investigator put it, this is explicable by the touristic attraction of the South of France (but of course the OFAJ is not supposed to be subsidising tourism).

Insofar as length of stay was concerned, rather over four fifths of the French enjoyed six days or more across the Rhine, the German duration in France being roughly similar. Not surprisingly, stays of longer duration were most likely to occur in those regions furthest removed from the home town of the participants, with the short sojourns frequently taking place in the frontier regions. In this respect the OFAJ clearly was doing a useful job, since its financial aid obviously helped to make visits longer than they might otherwise have been.

In terms of total participation, the Germans held a numerical advantage of roughly 15 per cent. This seems to reflect their greater eagerness to participate, as at 1 January 1967 there were actually more persons aged from fourteen to twenty-four in France than in the Federal Republic.[42] This could perhaps be linked with the preference shown for southern France, which adds to the suspicions of subsidised tourism. Incidentally, since boys tended to predominate over girls more markedly in Germany (five to three as against a proportion of four to three in France) the number of French girls exchanged was almost equal to the German total.[43] As far as age was concerned, there was no striking difference; the Germans were on average slightly older, attributable to the fact that they study rather longer on the whole.

The regional origins of the clientele were interesting, in that six *Länder* (Saarland, Bremen, Rhenish-Palatine, Hesse, Berlin and Baden-Württemberg) were over-represented in terms of participation, the remaining five falling below the national average, including North Rhine-Westphalia. This suggests that local initiative is more significant than tradition or geographical location in the Federal Republic, at least for youth exchanges in 1967. Hamburg, normally orientated towards the UK, was under-represented, it is true, but the presence of Bremen, with roughly similar traditions, among the regions above average shows that hasty generalisations about North Germany would be out of place (Berlin was above average too, in contrast to Catholic Bavaria, historically often allied to France). A similar impression is given by the regional participation in France which again defies a neat geographical pattern. Lorraine was below average, whereas distant Brittany was above. Only the presence of three south-western areas (Aquitaine, Midi-Pyrenees and Limousin) lend any credence to the idea of territorial remoteness affecting participation (Schleswig-Holstein was below average in Germany). It seems clear, therefore, that except in cases of extreme distance, local initiative among youth leaders is more important in determining response than is geographical location.

Yet another category of analysis employed was that of participants' origin by the size of their place of origin. Here a very clear difference emerged in that whereas the percentage of participants from the Federal Republic corresponded roughly with the total percentage of the population living in those communities, in France this was not the case, as villages and small towns were considerably under-represented, whereas for the really large conurbations the reverse was the case. This latter analysis should be brought into consideration with another, namely that of the profession or trade of the participants. Whereas slightly over 70 per cent of all the French taking part were either at school or students, in the Germans' case this was rather smaller.[44] Although the Germans showed a somewhat higher proportion of working class youth it can be said that there was undoubtedly a middle-class tinge to the exchanges. This impression is heightened by a glance at the profession/trade of the participant's father. Where A=working class in both countries and B=middle to lower-middle class, the ratio of A to B was 34 : 64½ in France and 28 : 69 in Germany. (Some family origins were not given, hence the fact that the figures do not add up to 100.)

In sum, 1967 participants were on average eighteen years of age, were more likely to be German than French, certainly more probably male than female, and did not usually come from a region a long way from the neighbouring country. In social origin they were overwhelmingly middle class, and if French, much more probably emanating from a large city than from a rural area. The average length of stay was some three weeks, and was more likely to be spent in the south of the neighbour's country than in the north. In view of the large proportions in both cases still in full-time education, this geographical bent might lead to a certain feeling that the OFAJ was, at least to some extent, engaged in a large-scale programme of subsidised vacations.[45]

This impression was unfortunately heightened by the publication of a highly unfavourable article on the OFAJ in the Federal Republic in 1967.[46] Some quite sharp criticisms were made by the author, relating to five alleged weaknesses in the execution of the exchanges. Firstly, the diversion of funds away from contacts of a multilateral nature: the rhetorical question being posed 'Aren't relations with the Dutch, Poles and Swedes, etc. also important?' (i.e. from a West German standpoint). Clearly, this has some validity, if it is accepted that more funds in one case must entail fewer for others. This is pertinent for the Federal Republic, which has land frontiers with nine other states, not one. We shall deal with multilateralism as an issue in Chapter 9.

Secondly, there was criticism of how the OFAJ allocated its funds, of which nearly half went on such traditional events as a dance group visiting Auvergne, whilst yet another 12 per cent went on purely sporting activities.[47] The author alleged that French students of baroque art could spend fourteen days in

Bavaria on such a trip and have fewer conversations with the locals than could be counted on the fingers of one hand. Similarly, if a Catholic association in Germany wanted to arrange a youth camp all it had to do to get public funds was invite half a dozen young Frenchmen, arrange two or three 'discussion evenings' on French literature and promptly claim from the OFAJ. The French might be there only six days out of ten, but this was immaterial.

Thirdly, the question of young workers who spent a year across the Rhine was accepted as excellent in principle, but quantitatively inadequate in practice. Again, from the 1967 analysis already given, this judgement is factually impeccable. Fourthly, the scheme known as *Connaissance de la France* and its equivalent for Germany were said to be good in principle but stood or fell by the quality of the leader. An example was cited where leadership was allegedly so poor that many of the French participants became quite annoyed, as the course leader seemed to be evading awkward problems and questions.[48] Of a course at Cap d'Ail it was alleged that a German youth psychologist had rendered so adverse a report that it was never subsequently published and he himself was never allowed to investigate any further OFAJ functions. The lack of psychological insight shown by the OFAJ itself was the fifth line of attack. The author suggested that even if the OFAJ spent 5 per cent of its budget on psychological investigation it would at least ensure that the remainder would be used to the maximum possible benefit.

Almost as soon as this article was published the OFAJ itself commissioned a public opinion poll among youth, carried out simultaneously in both countries.[49] The results, coming after journalistic criticism and the 1967 analysis of shortcomings, were of little comfort to the OFAJ after five years of endeavour. In 1968 French youth had a less favourable opinion of its neighbour than when the treaty had first been signed, placing West Germany seventh on the list of preferred countries, rather than sixth as before. The Germans, it is true, had raised France in their estimation, but it still lay only third, behind Austria and Britain. As against this, they had little idea of France's industrial efforts. On both sides of the Rhine, English was held to be the most important foreign language rather than the neighbour's.

In terms of character traits, five years of exchanges had achieved virtually nothing. For the Germans, the French were 'friendly and gay' but 'superficial, proud, lazy and pretentious': the French felt 'pride and pretentiousness' to be among German characteristics, as well as 'seriousness, severity and diligence'. As in 1963, both groups frequently appropriated the same failings to themselves as they attached to the other, thus completing the general picture of stereotyped thinking on both sides of the Rhine, not apparently diminished by the OFAJ. However, quantitatively at least, some improvement had been made, in that the percentage of those questioned in France and the Federal Republic who had visited the other's country had risen to nineteen and thirty respectively (the Germans still showing themselves to be more travelled). The obvious corollary of these statistics is that the overwhelming majority of Franco-German youth still had not visited one another's countries. Under these circumstances the OFAJ could, of course, have claimed that the solution lay in an even bigger, and therefore costlier, programme (which presumably would have diverted even more funds away from exchanges with other countries).

In fact, both French and Germans showed a keen desire to visit the other's country. It is interesting to note that of those hoping to do so, only a small minority in both countries were counting upon achieving this as part of a youth exchange. This helps underline that youth contacts and the exchange work of the OFAJ are not synonymous. One third of all Germans, for example, simply wanted to make an individual visit. Well over four-fifths of those questioned said that they would like to meet young nationals of the partner country in their own land, as well as travelling to see them in theirs.

When these facts are taken into consideration with the point about finance just raised, the whole concept of youth exchanges at an official level is brought into question. If, in order to be effective, youth exchanges need to be heavily subsidised at a time when most young people are willing to travel by private initiative anyway, why bother with an official programme at all? The governments are faced with three choices; either all visits get aid, or none do, or some do. The OFAJ had been following the last of these, and assisting a minority of contacts, but indiscriminately, i.e. a minority of each type of contact. Logically it might have been better to have concentrated all available resources on courses, such as *Wir entdecken Deutschland*, and to have left such events as dance groups in a twin town framework wholly to private enterprise. That the OFAJ was becoming aware of this itself was seen in 1968.

Anyone who generalises so widely that he can seriously call a whole neighbouring people 'lazy' or 'brutal and warlike' can have little real acquaintance with them. In saying this we are aware that the way in which questions are put in polls can in itself produce generalisations. That these opinions were held five years after the OFAJ came into being, especially in view of current criticism of the Office, was a challenge to its policy. It should be said that some disquiet had reigned in official circles even before 1967. Three years previously there had been talk of putting more accent on quality, and helping young workers and peasants especially.[50] It was perhaps accumulated dissatisfaction which came to a head in 1967–68.

The result was a conference of interested parties including academics, civil service and youth leaders which was called to discuss the situation at Paris in November 1968.[51] The Secretary-General in his opening address referred to the reports and analyses already described here, and pointed out that about 2 per cent only could be taken as the maximum figure for youth participating annually in OFAJ exchanges, as the combined average for both countries. Since many young people had availed themselves of the OFAJ three or four times, it was highly probable that even to regard 10 per cent of present Franco-German youth as having been affected would be illusory. Thus even the scale of OFAJ activities was officially accepted as unsatisfactory.

The discussions which followed were even franker. The conference set up, it should be made clear, three study groups—one for each of the following questions: (a) what were the current political problems of Franco-German relations and how did Franco-German youth see them, (b) how was the OFAJ work influencing international encounters in general, and (c) how was it affecting society in France and the Federal Republic. As far as the first was concerned, the OFAJ was criticised for its apolitical approach, i.e. its policy of giving subventions to all possible youth functions, and avoiding all politics. As a consequence, no political questions were ever discussed. It was suggested that such themes should not in future be excluded. This does not seem to have occurred, since in 1971 the left-orientated German press was violently attacking the OFAJ for its neglect of politics, and in particular for its apparent policy of concentrating on scouts, Catholic and business associations, to the detriment of left-wing organisations. Equally, it was held still to be following a 'taboo' policy regarding important political problems.[52] To a certain extent this type of criticism mirrors that of Wilfert already discussed. The newspaper remarked that it must be clear that family meetings, winter sports etc., were one thing, but comprehensive information about a neighbouring country quite another.

The OFAJ was conscious of this apparently continuing weakness raised at the conference by many speakers. Certain practical difficulties would, however, arise in this respect. Academics or journalists can easily demand serious discussions on political problems, but a youth office with one eye always on the respective governments and their reactions to any publicly subsidised criticism of their own policies, has to be very wary.[53] All that can really be said of the OFAJ policy of an apolitical approach is that it must inevitably vitiate serious discussion, and therefore bring into question the whole idea of furthering understanding. If you can't discuss your neighbour's current political problems, what can understanding mean in the final analysis? In this respect, the establishment of an official exchange programme as such, hemmed in by its own political considerations, could be interpreted as a positive disincentive to understanding.

Over and against this criticism, the point has to be made (as it was very clearly at the conference by the study group for the political question) that the participants themselves showed no interest in serious discussions about current questions (of which they appeared mostly to be apparently shockingly ignorant). But the reporting committee stated quite clearly that in its opinion the 'apolitical approach' of the OFAJ itself was at least partly responsible for this anyway. Three members even demanded that no political debates should in future ever be forbidden or stifled, if OFAJ assistance had been obtained for that particular function. Similar opinions came from other members, who suggested that in future the OFAJ should adopt certain priorities. One such possible classification would be to place all encounters in one of three categories, viz. non-political, e.g. sports meetings, semi-political (presumably study courses such as *Connaissance de la France*), and fully political contacts, where current problems were discussed. It was further held that events of the first type should have less chance of OFAJ assistance than had so far been the case. In other words, where funds are necessarily limited, then insist on quality before spending them. For the remaining encounters the presence of qualified monitors as discussion leaders was accepted by study group members as essential; as these were in short supply, then the OFAJ must use resources to train the necessary numbers, perhaps through the medium of the universities. All in all, a re-orientation of OFAJ policy towards quality was demanded, especially in a political context. The OFAJ should, it was stated, make it clear to the two governments and the press that the accent had now ceased to be purely on quantity in exchanges.

There is no doubt that the conference has exercised in this particular connection a considerable influence upon subsequent OFAJ policy, which has been to some extent modified along the lines suggested. The best evidence for this is the document issued in 1969 by the OFAJ giving the policy guidelines to be followed.[54] The criteria in respect of assistance are clearly delineated here by the statement that 'the organisers and the participants should be conscious of the fact that the Office has not been created to finance tourist activities, superficial encounters, or holidays pure and simple'. Claimants are told that they must have a good programme of activities drawn up, of which participants are fully informed in advance. Above all it is made clear that a good programme implies a good leadership team.

In this respect too, conference suggestions have been influential. In the section on 'principles' it is now underlined that the OFAJ recognises the importance of technical-academic aid to further international youth understanding, and therefore itself promotes the collaboration of sociologists, educators and psychologists in the investigation of new methods and techniques in this field. The OFAJ also assists now in the preparation of youth leaders not only for its courses, but for private encounters which it subsidises. Language, pedagogy and general information on the neighbour's country are included in preparatory courses.

The second study group discussed what influence the OFAJ might be exercising on international encounters in general. It was reported that on the whole some prejudices seemed to have been swept away in the larger cities of France and West Germany. This could not be said, however, in regard to the smaller towns and rural areas, nor among the less well educated sections of the two peoples. Here the study group was merely reflecting the facts of the exchanges, with their urban, middle-class colour which we have already reported.

The third group dealt with the possible repercussions which the

work of the OFAJ may have had on the social structures of the
two countries involved. To begin with, it was accepted that youth
contacts had had some influence upon adults, particularly parents
and school teachers, by what was described as a sort of 'osmosis'
or 'contagion'. By this it meant that accounts of meetings given
to them by younger people had tended to create a social model of
international amity capable of being imitated by the elders. The
OFAJ should therefore exploit this possibility by encouraging
more systematic reporting by participants to parents and teachers.

The study group further accepted that encounters between
young people of similar backgrounds, for example students and
young workers, helped very much to create a kind of 'community
of problems, interests, and aspirations'. It realised, however, that
this applied to participants only, and that there was some difficulty
in extending such effects of exchanges to society as a whole. It
suggested that perhaps some sort of 'after-visit' programmes
could be built up, whereby participants should attempt to stimu-
late the interest of friends and colleagues to undergo similar
experiences. Members of the group dealing with this theme felt
that the OFAJ should pay special attention to this point where the
participants were likely to be among the future leaders of their
countries. These exchange visits should be longer, six months to
two years being suggested. The youth coming from the milieu
of the existing elites in both societies should also be particularly
furthered by the OFAJ programme.

Apart from future leaders, however, young workers and
peasants as such should also get more attention than formerly
from the OFAJ. It was held that the relative neglect of these in the
past had been less due to financial considerations than to lack of
OFAJ contacts with youth association leaders and public administrators. The OFAJ should in future play the part of middleman
and animator much more than previously for the type of contact.
Above all, it should take the initiative in trying to get a common
approach to the problem adopted in both France and the Federal
Republic. This would imply not merely directly linking organisations concerned with professional and technical education, but
even where necessary modifying existing legislation in order to
harmonise, not merely holiday conditions, but vocational training
as well. It might perhaps be commented here that if the OFAJ
could work in this field it would indeed be an exciting development, but it is difficult not to feel that the group was demanding

rather too much. Problems like the harmonisation of education and conditions of work are after all political, and would seem more appropriately dealt with at governmental level.

As far as student exchanges were concerned, the study group favoured direct relationships between specific universities, and the OFAJ again might take the initiative in this respect. Visits concerned with studies of special problems should also be encouraged, and financially assisted. This particular group also drew attention to the need for more drastic criteria to be adopted in deciding whether projects should be subsidised or not. Problems of urbanisation and regionalisation were mentioned in this connection as being especially worthy of support.

As can be seen, the various study groups had produced some searching criticism of the OFAJ, and some worthwhile suggestions, some of which would have placed some strain on funds. It should be pointed out, however, that the third group saw this, and advocated tapping new financial resources to cover this, by which it meant private industry and trade unions. On the whole, it could be said that as far as the OFAJ's first five years were concerned, they were held to be a partial success. Apart from the points made about the OFAJ as such, it had also clearly been accepted that society was changing quickly and structures and attitudes in both countries with it. Even had the programmes of the OFAJ been suitable in the past, therefore, they would have to be adapted to meet changing needs, in particular the fact that youth in both countries was becoming more similar in its outlook anyway and less narrowly nationalistic. This fact alone reinforced the demand for a close study of specific socio-political questions in common, rather than just mass tourism.

There is no doubt that the OFAJ itself, as a result of its own research and of public criticism, had become aware of its own deficiencies. This was reflected in the new guidelines for 1969 already described, and in its own publications. If it had been over-optimistic initially, and some of its officials had been,[55] it could anyway plead that it was not alone in this respect. In what it called the 'After-Adenauer-Phase' the arrival of political differences had led to a more realistic approach to the treaty of 1963 in all its aspects and its functioning in practice. The OFAJ, however, accepted that young workers had been overlooked to some extent in the past and now wished to put more emphasis on them in the future, but pointed out simultaneously that it was a middleman only, whose job was to awaken interest in others, rather than initiate its own actual activities; this point has to be taken. If, for example, rural youth was less well-organised in one country than in the other, the OFAJ could hardly be blamed. The further point has to be made here about the role of language and its effect upon international encounters among the less-educated. The percentage of French agrarian participants in 1967 who knew German well was 1·4, whilst 83 per cent knew none at all: figures for young French workers and for German workers/ peasants were very similar.[56] This whole question will be discussed in detail in a later chapter, but the obvious influence which a lack of knowledge of the partner's language exercised at this end of the social continuum on exchanges must be borne in mind when criticism for neglecting such young people is expressed. Incidentally, efforts are now being made to intensify the exchanges between young artisans (*Handwerker*) in both countries, in which the OFAJ collaborates with the relevant vocational chambers. As future self-employed craftsmen these young people are not, of course, strictly describable as workers.

Before any general balance sheet is drawn up, it may be as well to insert as a preface the aims of the OFAJ, and to consider, in their light, the results of the latest opinion poll, taken on its behalf in Paris and Munich, among 1,200 secondary school (*lycée/Gymnasium*) pupils in each city in 1970.[57] This, it is hoped, will form a useful prelude to any summing-up of the OFAJ's first ten years, in view of its given objectives, viz. 'to strengthen the ties uniting the youth of both countries, reinforce their mutual comprehension, and to this end provoke, encourage, and, where necessary, bring about (i.e. directly) youth encounters and exchanges'.

Obviously the OFAJ has quantitatively achieved some success in the last activity: has it apparently strengthened ties and mutual comprehension? The 1970 poll seemed not to suggest that. Neither national group questioned placed the neighbouring people in a privileged position in their estimation: for the Germans, France came in second behind the UK and for the French the Federal Republic followed the US and the UK. That history still played some part in not according the neighbour a higher place in the French sentiments is deducible from responses on both sides of the Rhine in the name of the other country. Two thirds of all Parisian scholars spontaneously mentioned German history before the war in response to the word 'Germany' as such: almost as many thought of the war itself. When Munich students were given the word 'France' only 3 per cent mentioned the war. Two other points emerge from what might be called the word-association test. For 90 per cent of the Germans the word 'France' evoked tourism and folk-lore, more precisely, French cooking, museums and art galleries, even the tramps (*les clochards*) of Paris. This type of image occurred to only 58 per cent of Parisian scholars in respect of Germany. France thus appears to risk being seen as a kind of curiosity country to Germans at least to some extent, rather than as a modern society (although admittedly just over two thirds of the Germans referred to the French economy). On the other hand, 61 per cent of Germans questioned also associated 'politics' with France, but a closer examination of this particular response showed it concerned almost completely with personalities—above all, de Gaulle.

In terms of national characteristics the same old clichés emerged, both in the picture of the neighbour and of themselves. Some good qualities were ascribed to the other in greater degree than he attributed it to himself. In sum, without repeating the results in full, it can be said that lack of concrete thought manifested itself in both young people's groups about their counterparts.

This was partly due to simple ignorance. Less than half of all French questioned could even name five West German cities: 87 per cent of the Germans, asked a similar question about France, were successful, but when asked to estimate the population of the neighbouring land were much less accurate. An interesting sideline here is that, in both cases, those learning the other's language tended to over-estimate the neighbour's population, whilst the reverse tendency was shown by pupils not learning the language. Not too much should be drawn from this, however, as the representatives of neither national group were very well-informed about the size of their own country or its leading political personalities. Equally, the economic products of one country known to the other's youth tended to be stereotyped: wine, cheese and clothing in the case of France, and cars and beer in the case of West Germany.

All in all, it can hardly be maintained that either group was especially informed about his neighbour, so that the 'reinforcement of mutual comprehension' desired by the treaty seemed not to have taken place to any great degree. The OFAJ itself could only advance three hypotheses as a result of the enquiry: firstly, Parisian pupils were more pragmatic, especially as far as learning German was concerned, than their Munich counterparts, but that some old resentments still lingered on from the war. Secondly, the Germans had a frankly touristic approach to France, which represented, as far as they were concerned, food, wine and sunshine: they were open and well-disposed towards their neighbours. Thirdly, the Germans were better-informed, had more desire to visit France, and knew more about politics, economics, art, geography, etc. in general. The OFAJ itself attributed this to the far greater use of mass media in the Federal Republic: the Munich pupils questioned read more newspapers and looked at TV more often than did those in Paris. But the main impression left to the reader is really how stereotyped the thinking was on both sides, and how much remained to be done to achieve a better mutual understanding based on knowledge of the other's problems.

What can be said, in the light of these results, about the OFAJ and its work? Firstly, the euphoria of the first five years has now given place to sober reality.[58] Anyone who thought that the French and the Germans would really get to like one another as a result of the OFAJ is now prepared to settle for understanding. This is partly because youth in West European countries is becoming increasingly similar in its approach anyway, so that reconciliation is now less important partly because the honeymoon phase of the de Gaulle/Adenauer period of Franco-German relations is over. There seems now to be a much more realistic air to the whole concept of exchanges and more emphasis on young workers and peasants. By January 1973 the former had come to constitute over one third of all current participants.[59]

The inherent difficulties involved in all exchanges are seen more clearly now. There are so many factors to be taken into account when arranging contacts at an international level that the importance of training leaders, planning carefully, the significance of the place and time of encounter, the disposition and previous experience of the participants are being emphasised by the OFAJ. This latter point ties in with the fact that there are still more Germans participating than French, and that they often have motives for visiting the South of France totally remote from those desired by the OFAJ. The French have a 'drive to the sun' too, but for them that means Spain and Italy, not West Germany. This means that qualitatively French visits across the Rhine are probably more valuable than those in the reverse direction, since they are much more likely to be motivated by genuine interest in German life.[60]

As far as political discussions are concerned, there is the problem, not so much of differing viewpoints to any one problem, but different educations and backgrounds which make such contacts difficult to realise in practice. German problems are more issues of foreign than of domestic policy, and cannot be solved by her alone. This is reinforced by the fact that the present West German state grew from an occupation zone with limited sovereignty, to which young Germans are now accustomed. French political questions are rather more of an internal nature, and French youth is not so accustomed or prepared to discuss them with outsiders.[61] To this fact must be added the high Communist vote in France, almost non-existent in West Germany. This diversity in approach is not likely to aid the OFAJ in any way at all.

Even harder for the OFAJ is that, in the political field, not everyone wants it to exist at all. This was made clear almost at the outset in the Federal Republic among SPD circles who wanted a European office and not a Franco-German one. The fear seems also to have existed that precisely because the OFAJ would sweep awkward issues under the mat, it would become a pillar of the establishment in both countries. Here one can only balance this valid point against the fact that the OFAJ was founded in 1963 and had to tread warily only eighteen years after the war (cf. the poll reactions to 'Germany' in Paris even in 1970). However, what was an excuse then is no longer quite so acceptable now that understanding takes priority over reconciliation.

This ultimately must be the final question to face here; in view of recent developments, particularly in mass tourism, does the OFAJ play any appreciable role at all, granted that large-scale contacts will take place anyway?

In this connection it should be pointed out that its budget has recently (1 June 1972) been further reduced, to the tune of 7 per cent, again by the French government. This inevitably meant programme cuts and produced another conference on the OFAJ future, at Strasbourg in November 1972. The OFAJ seems to have decided that students must bear the brunt of the new restrictions, in line with the need to concentrate on workers and on cadres. As students and schoolchildren have other facilities for making visits abroad, this seems a wise decision. Nonetheless, the OFAJ still devotes considerable resources just to purely bilateral exchanges (some £5 million annually). This is far in excess of what either government spends on bilateral youth contacts with any third country. The UK government in 1968, for purposes of comparison, apparently spent officially the equivalent of £50,000 (at current exchange rates) on subventions to bilateral youth contacts.[62] This does not include contributions from local authorities. In 1964, before financial cuts, West Germany devoted four times as much money to the OFAJ as to its youth exchanges with all other countries combined.[63] Even if one accepts bilateralism in principle (which we shall discuss later) this was disproportionate. Under these circumstances it is hardly surprising that official euphoria about the OFAJ was not always reflected in the private conversations which we have had.

It would be fair to say that this interesting experiment in international relations arouses very strong feelings in both countries. Some have called it the best part of the 1963 treaty, others refer to it as subsidised tourism. Initially this latter view had undoubtedly a strong factual grounding. Clearly, if any country spent the equivalent of £2½ million annually on youth exchanges with every other major state the expense would be intolerable. A degree of selection is obviously called for, as the OFAJ itself now sees. It seems to us that two classes of exchange are useful. Firstly, those between the future leaders of the country, young officials, businessmen, trade unionists, etc. These must surely aid further integration in the EEC. Secondly, in an era with a mass electorate surely some aid might be given to those young people who would not otherwise travel, in particular apprentices and young workers, whether in agriculture or industry. And we further suggest that all current political topics should be discussable at these encounters; if they are left out for fear of friction, what could understanding possibly mean? Ten years of experience have in fact shown in practice that understanding of the neighbour, rather than coming to like him, is probably all that we can aim at as a legitimate goal.[64] Polls appear to demonstrate that Franco-German youth had no greater preference for one another in 1970 than when the OFAJ was founded. But if the youth of one country can get at least to know its neighbour's problems, then in our view a foundation for progress has been laid in Europe. We feel that the courses like *Connaissance de la France* are useful, and might well be imitated in other countries. A selective programme of official youth exchanges would be our recommendation on the basis of the Franco-German experience.

In all fairness to the OFAJ we must point out that it was a pioneer in the field of mass exchanges. Mistakes have inevitably been made and are now in some respects being rectified. In June 1973 after the summit meeting between the political leaders it was announced that the administrative structure of the OFAJ was being altered and centralised, and further, that there would be a different policy in the future regarding the type of event to be subsidised. This is public recognition of the need for change, and the ability to learn from errors in the past.

But we must emphasise how strewn with pitfalls is the whole concept which the OFAJ embodies, and how hard it is to arrange successful (in the fullest sense) encounters between young people of differing cultures. The historical, administrative and psychological obstacles are legion, as has been shown. In this respect the far greater response shown by German youth to OFAJ proposals highlights the difficulty of the task; there is a whole complex of factors behind this difference. On the other hand, one hopeful pointer for the future is that the difficulties in removing prejudices on both sides of the Rhine have been greatest among the least-educated. This suggests that as the standard of living and education rises in Western Europe integration will become progressively easier. Moreover, youth on both sides of the Rhine is now sharing increasingly a common urban Western culture based on the 'Admass' society. National variations are declining.[65]

As a postscript to the foregoing we ought to mention very briefly the contacts between France and the GDR. The scale of youth exchanges has been minimal up to recent years.[66] In addition we have been told that in many cases the French have been disappointed with their sojourn in East Germany, as the propaganda has been too obvious. Serious rivalry between the two German governments for the winning of French youth to their side does not appear very probable for the foreseeable future.

Notes

1 Unless otherwise stated, the information given here on the actual structure of the Youth Office is taken from *L'accord portant création de l'office franco-allemand pour la jeunesse*, published by the French Government.

2 The first Secretary-General, M. Altmayer, was a Frenchman. *Le Monde*, 13/14 Oct. 1963. In 1969 he was succeeded by Herr Krause of West Germany, the incumbent until late 1973. *Correspondance*, no. 142, 1 Feb. 1969, p 12.

3 These financial details are from *Office franco-allemand; Taux des subventions*, pub. by Conseil des Communes d'Europe, see also *Stages de longue durée en Allemagne fédérale* etc. OFAJ.

4 For an account see A. Grosser, *Germany in our Time*, London, Pall Mall Press, 1971, pp 50*f*, and 'Deutsch-französische Zusammenarbeit nach 1945', *Deutschland-Frankreich*, vol III, p 17*f*.

5 *Allemagne*, no. 36, Apr./May 1955.

6 Ibid., nos 91–3, Sept./Dec. 1965.

7 *Frankfurter Allgemeine Zeitung*, 15 Jan. 1964.

8 H. Ott, *Handbuch der internationalen Jugendarbeit*, Cologne, Europa Union Verlag, 1968, pp 24*f*.

9 H. Barth, 'Jeunesse: coopération franco-allemande'. *Documents*, no. 5, 1963, p 47.

10 *The Guardian*, 17 Sept. 1963.

11 For a summary of the differing forms of organisation as a result of recent history see J. Rovan, 'Les relations franco-allemandes dans le domaine de la jeunesse et de la culture populaire', *La Revue d'Allemagne*, vol. IV, no. 3, 1972, p 675*f*.

12 These comments are based on *Aus dem Tätigkeitsbericht des Deutsch-Französischen Jugendwerks 1963–1968*, French Embassy, Bad Godesberg, Bulletin no. 44, 15 Jan. 1969.

13 J. Rabier, 'Préjugés français et préjugés allemands', *Revue de psychologie des peuples*, no. 2, 1968, p 186*f*.

14 These results are summarised in J. Rabier, 'Vorurteile gegen Völkerverständigung', *Documents*, no. 24, 1968, p 353*f*.

15 See 'La jeunesse française et l'Europe', *Documents*, no. 3, 1963, p 46*f*., and 'Connaissance de la France—ein Modell für die Jugendarbeit', *Documents*, no. 19, 1963.

16 *Le Monde*, 22 Apr. 1964.

17 H. Linnerz, 'Eine Umfrage zum Jugendaustausche', *Documents*, no. 20, 1964, p 178.

18 The statistics were 143,446 against 135,641. *Le Monde*, 7 Nov. 1964.

19 *La coopération franco-allemande*, pp 46–8.

20 Ibid., p 52.

21 Ibid., p 52.

22 *Allemagne*, no. 22, Dec. 1952/Jan. 1953 gives details of such a course for French and Germans run by an organisation called 'Peuple et Culture'.

23 Details from J. Rovan, 'Connaissance de la France', *Documents*, no. 19, 1963, p 189.
24 See 'Bericht einer Teilnehmerin des "STAGE"' etc., in *Mitteilungsblatt für die Deutsch-Französischen Gesellschaften*, no. 26, Mar. 1968, pp 115f.
25 F. Altmayer, 'Psychologie des Jugendaustausches', *Documents*, no. 23, 1967, p 262.
26 *Cinq Ans d'Echanges franco-allemands*, pub. by Education et Echanges, pp 45f.
27 *Aus dem Tätigkeitsbericht* etc., op. cit., p 11.
28 Ibid., p 21.
29 Ibid., p 11.
30 *Le Monde*, 28 Apr. 1966.
31 Herr Heyer, Chief of the OFAJ Paris, Press and Information Bureau, in a personal interview.
32 *Cinq Ans d'Echanges*, op. cit., pp 50f.
33 Ibid., pp 53f.
34 See *Mini-Kurier*, pub. by Arbeitskreis der deutsch-französischen Gesellschaften, Dec. 1970, pp 6f.
35 *Cinq Ans d'Echanges*, op. cit., p 57.
36 Ibid., p 59.
37 Ibid., p 27.
38 *Correspondance*, no. 202, 15 Mar. 1972, p 11.
39 *Le Monde*, 2 Oct. 1971.
40 F. Altmayer, 'Psychologie des Jugendaustausches', op. cit., p 262.
41 P. de la Roncière, 'Une année de rencontres franco-allemandes', *Documents*, no. 24, 1969, p 64f.
42 Roughly 8,400,000 against 8,100,000. H. Ott, *Handbuch der internationalen Jugendarbeit*, Cologne, Europa Union Verlag, 1968, p 162.
43 *Une année de rencontres* etc., p 69.
44 Ibid., p 72: it must be pointed out that whereas only 12·3% of French participants were under 15 years of age, 38% were described as school-children: most of the school-children must have been 15 or over, which suggests perhaps a middle-class slant again. In the case of the Germans, the difference between age and occupation was greater still.
45 In fact, as early as 1964 the Secretary-General himself was writing frankly about the 'pull towards the sun' shown by those taking part. F. Altmayer, *Das Deutsch-Französische Jugendwerk*, op. cit., p 302.
46 O. Wilfert, 'Harmonie allein genügt nicht', *Frankfurter Hefte*, July 1967.
47 The accuracy of these figures is confirmed by the OFAJ's own budget analysis, *La coopération franco-allemande*, p 52.
48 Wilfert, op. cit., p 455.
49 Published in a bilingual version in Sept. 1968, the German title was *Einstellung der deutschen und französischen Jugend zum deutsch-französischen Jugendaustausch.*
50 See *Le Monde*, 4 Feb. 1965.
51 The proceedings are published in a bilingual version, 1968—*Kongress DJFW—Colloque OFAJ* by the OFAJ.
52 *Frankfurter Rundschau*, 4 Apr. 1971.

53 It was pointed out in 1964 that the French Union of Students was not represented at the OFAJ, as it was felt to be Left politically. *The Times*, 7 May 1964.

54 Issued in a bilingual version: the German title is *Richtlinien des Deutsch-Französischen Jugendwerks*.

55 For example, one was claiming in 1964 that the Office was working to everyone's satisfaction, and that all categories of youth were receiving equal treatment. *Le Monde*, 7 Nov. 1964.

56 P. de Roncière, 'Une année de rencontres franco-allemandes', op. cit., p 76.

57 *OFAJ Dossier*, Versailles, 1971, OFAJ Bureau de Presse et d'Information.

58 Herr Heyer, head of the OFAJ Press and Information Bureau at Versailles talks of two phases, the first 'vague and emotional' up to 1968: then 'sober and concrete' afterwards: personal interview.

59 *Correspondance*, no. 218, Jan. 1973, p 11.

60 Vide F. Altmayer, 'Psychologie des Jugendaustausches', op. cit., p 263.

61 Ibid., p 264.

62 H. Ott, *Handbuch der internationalen Jugendarbeit*, op. cit., p 75.

63 *The Times*, 7 May 1964.

64 A 1964 poll showed only 48% of young French visitors to West Germany who were favourably impressed, a lower percentage than in the case of those who had been to Spain or Italy. *The Guardian*, 27 Mar. 1964.

65 As pointed out by Willy Brandt, when he said that nowadays one cannot tell the difference between young people in Britain, France or West Germany. Quoted in M. Salomon, *Faut-il avoir peur de l'Allemagne?* Paris, Robert Lafont, 1969, p 88.

66 The figures are in S. Reime, op. cit., pp 97*f*.

Chapter 3

Franco-German Academic Exchanges and their Educational Collaboration

One of the most important provisions both in the 1954 accord and the actual treaty nine years later was that dealing with educational co-operation. Historically there had been some influence exercised by one country upon the other even before those dates. German success in 1870, for example, led to the belief in some quarters in France that educational superiority had been its keystone, and that the French should organise their own system along similar lines.[1] The 1954 agreement foresaw more than mere imitation, rather a close, direct collaboration in order to strengthen the ties between the two peoples. This necessitated a certain administrative structure which ran into the usual snags of differing traditions.

In the first place there is no national Minister of Education in the Federal Republic, as each region has its own system co-ordinated by a standing conference. The Germans therefore had to install a special office to negotiate with the French for the *Länder* insofar as the treaty provisions were concerned. This plenipotentiary (*Bevollmächtigte*) also has to work hand in hand with the German Foreign Office. Successive occupants of the post have been Kiesinger, Alfons Goppel, Kühn and Filbinger, each of them the Minister President in his own region at the time of appointment. It is interesting, but probably coincidental, that not one has come from North Germany. To assist the Commissioner and the French government, there are various mixed committees, which meet regularly to discuss different aspects of educational co-operation. The initial one was the joint University Rectors' conference, which began its sittings in winter 1957–58, followed by a commission to deal with relations between technical colleges in both countries. The *Bevollmächtigte* himself meets the French Minister of Education bi-annually. Joint study groups have been set up to deal with the different particular issues involved.

Thus a whole administrative mechanism has been brought into play to co-ordinate efforts in the educational field. It faces a formidable task, as the attitudes are markedly divergent in the two countries, to compound administrative variations. A typical example of the latter is the lack of exact correspondence between the offices of *Recteur* and *Rektor*, which does not make for easy collaboration (a *Rektor* has university surveillance only as his task). Since 1968 the French equivalent to this office has been *Président de l'Université*. Moreover, the German view of education as the development of the 'whole man' tends to be at variance with the French concept of laying most stress on the purely cognitive aspects. A further difference is the rigid separation of Church and State in France which does not apply in the Federal Republic, where religion is still on the curriculum. At the higher level there are considerable organisational differences, for example more German students change from one university to another in mid-course than is the case in France. Proportionately France has had more students during the period under review.[2] Moreover, inside Germany itself there are considerable regional variations sometimes apparently of denominational origin: in 1960 Roman Catholics formed 45·5 per cent of the total population, but had only 35 per cent of the students.[3] In general, however, the Federal Republic spends a lower percentage of its GNP on education than France, or indeed Italy or Britain. A recent OECD report on the whole system in Germany was sharply critical of the prevailing situation.[4] This is not to say that everything in France is far better, as we shall see; we merely wish to draw attention to inherent differences in practice which hinder smooth collaboration. As a final word of introduction, we should point out that both countries are concerned about their respective positions in education, and are engaged in internal reforms, of which the major items began in France in 1959. Clearly, in the short term at least, this does not facilitate co-operation.

This seems to presage a gloomy picture of collaboration, or its absence, in the domain of education, but in fact by goodwill and energy fruitful work has been accomplished. Firstly, there has been considerable co-operation at the level of universities and technical colleges. Both governments give study grants for professors, or students, from the neighbouring country. To this end, the *Office National des Universités et Ecoles Françaises* works closely with the *Deutscher Akademischer Austauschdienst* (DAAD), which has had a Paris bureau since 1963. Obviously, contacts had commenced before that time, with exchange visits by faculty members. In 1955, to choose one illustration, twenty-eight of the Sorbonne staff were invited to the University of Munich.[5]

Additionally there are grants to students to enable them to pursue their studies in the neighbouring country, over three hundred being given by the French Government in 1967. These grants tend fairly obviously to be dominated by Romanists in Germany and by Germanists in France, as a knowledge of the partner's language is required to enable them to follow the course. The DAAD, for example, has a special yearly programme for two hundred Romanists who each spend six months in France. We have been told that demand for these places tends to exceed supply. Since 1967 the DAAD has run a programme with the OFAJ specially for Germanists who, after undergoing a certain time at a French university, may then proceed to four months at one in the Federal Republic, in order to extend their knowledge of contemporary Germany and its language. In 1972–73 forty-five students from the University of Paris at Asnières had the chance to enrol for these courses at any one of eight universities in the Federal Republic.[6] All this seems to us to be excellent, as quite clearly any student who specialises in the language and literature or contemporary society in the neighbouring country will benefit enormously from a stay there at university level, even if it does only last a few months.

Before we leave this point we should mention that although language students dominate the courses numerically, nonetheless those in other disciplines do participate to some extent. The DAAD runs 'a five-week language course as preparation for science students who wish to study in the other country, organised in conjunction with an institute at the Sorbonne. In 1967 about one third of grants given by the French government went to non-Romanists in Germany.[7] The authorities are aware of the relative monopoly of exchanges by language students and would like to change this but there are obstacles, of which clearly the question of a knowledge of the partner's language is one. Equally we have been told that science and technology students in the Federal Republic tend to be USA-orientated, no doubt a reflection of the latter country's current reputation in these disciplines.

As well as grants for students and assistants there are opportunities for research at the neighbour's universities; these are from two to four months in duration. Even faculty members may pass some time on the staff of a university in the partner's country; the scale remains frankly limited, however. In 1966 there were only three French professors so engaged in the Federal Republic.[8]

It is worth pointing out whilst we are dealing with education how much interest is now being shown at university level in *Germanistik* in France. Departments of German studies are flourishing, especially in the north and east of the country. At Rheims the local university's German department works closely with a trade promotion organisation called ARDELA in furthering contacts with German-speaking countries. There is a well-established centre for German studies at Strasbourg University, which among other activities has made a special study of the German-language press, in order to come to grips with contemporary Germany.[9] In Paris University (Asnières) similar attention is devoted to current affairs across the Rhine, rather than to more traditional aspects of culture on which Germanic studies in France used to be based. This qualitative revolution has been accompanied by a quantitative one. When a special association for French Germanists in higher education was formed in Strasbourg in 1968 there were 120 of them present. In 1939 there were only 19 at all French universities combined, including Algeria.[10]

Side by side with the apparatus of grants and special courses another aspect of contact at higher educational levels has been developed, that of university or college partnerships. The Franco-German Rectors' conference worked out in 1962 how such a link should be formally established in administrative terms, and Cologne and Clermont later became the first two universities to set up a formal connection.[11] Since then partnerships have become the order of the day. Late in 1962 Kiel and Rennes signed a similar accord, then came Bonn and Toulouse. The association organises visits by delegations, research projects in common, joint seminars and consultations, as well as student/staff exchanges. Sometimes, as in the case of Bonn and Toulouse, books have been donated by one academic library to another. How intensively the relationship is cultivated varies between different universities. By 1973 seventeen partnerships had been established.

It does not follow that all links of this nature are at university level; teacher-training colleges have opened up relationships as well. They carry out exchanges lasting four to six weeks between their students with the object of widening their horizons in a personal sense. This has nothing to do with any formal national treaty, and is not confined to language students. In 1967 there were sixty-five future German primary school teachers on exchange in France against over double that number of French in Germany.[12]

Even more fruitful collaboration has taken place in other areas of higher education. At least seven partnerships had been established by 1963.[13] Eventually a permanent liaison committee was set up to regulate the consultations between the *Grandes Ecoles* and the *Technische Hochschulen* in general. As an example of the sort of work carried out, we can take the 1969 two-day meeting of the office in Paris. The first subject on the agenda was the divergence in the teaching of mathematics in the two countries, although a study suggested that under the influence of modern mathematics they were coming closer together in method. It was confirmed that a German student in possession of a certain diploma (*Vordiplom*) would be permitted to study from three to six months at a *Grande Ecole* if he so wished, with reciprocity for French students. Agreement was reached that the study options available in each country for engineering students should be compared with each other. Next, the question of joint management courses was discussed, in an attempt to work out the necessary administrative details for the type of course envisaged. Among subsequent issues raised at the conference were reforms in the two countries, publicity for examinations, the joint production of brochures to compare the two systems with each other and the problem of language in exchanges.[14]

From the foregoing it is quite obvious that these discussions, which take place quarterly, are anything but a mere empty gesture. They are concerned with real co-operation at the level of practical day to day reality. All this seems irreproachable in both conception and execution, and demonstrates how initial differences in organisation and approach can be overcome by way of genuine collaboration. It is obviously only fair to point out that technology is in itself international, so that the basis for discussion already exists. This does not, however, affect our main point, namely that a bilateral approach has tied the bonds even tighter in this case. Incidentally, the joint management course discussed in 1969 had already begun to function three years later. Designed for graduates of technical colleges in both countries with a minimum of three years' practical experience, it lasts eight weeks, divided into two separate monthly courses in France and Germany, with a return to the individual factory in between. The staff are mixed as well as the students. Again, it is hard to fault a joint programme of this nature and we can only hope that the scale will be increased. If we wanted to present an exemplary case of real co-operation, this would be it, in that the results of bilateralism have been concrete, rather than limiting themselves to pious intentions, or mere expressions of mutual goodwill.

Before proceeding to contacts at secondary level, we should make two further points. Firstly, not all co-operation between students, especially in 1968, was necessarily of a similar nature. When in May 1968 French and German students planned to storm the frontier together in order to force across Cohn-Bendit, the German-born student leader, this was collaboration too, however much resented by the establishment in the two countries.

Secondly, contacts with German studies departments in French universities have also been set up by the German Democratic Republic. Grants similar to those offered by the DAAD are available to French students, but on a more modest scale: in 1968–69 there were thirty. So far exchanges have been one-sided: no East Germans have come to France. Faculty contacts have been very limited, sometimes due to political action. In 1961 the French government refused permission to all French professors invited to the 150th anniversary of the Humboldt University in East Berlin simply by not granting leave of absence. Nonetheless several French academics have participated in joint conferences on Franco-German problems held in the GDR. This does not imply their acceptance of the Pankow regime; doubtless they had solid professional reasons for attendance. It will be interesting to see how academic relationships develop now that East Germany has achieved official recognition.[15]

Close contacts have been made between the French and West German authorities at secondary level, as well as at that of higher education. This has nothing to do with cultural accords, etc. as such, as teacher and assistant exchanges are now widely practised throughout Western Europe in response to a UNESCO resolution in 1950. Indeed, a look at the statistics supports the contention made to us that the bilateral activities have been little affected by the treaty. Whereas in 1964–65 there were just over four hundred German assistants in French schools, by 1966–67 there were rather fewer and the figure seems to have remained more or less constant. In 1972 it was back to the 1964–65 number, with similar statistics for the French equivalents in Germany. In France there are said to be two applicants for each post, which seems to suggest that more could be achieved if the grants were made available.[16] Again, the majority of assistants are Romanists or Germanists perfecting their knowledge of the partner's language and way of life.

The exchanges of teachers and assistants have been in operation since before the First World War, although initially on a modest scale. In 1932 there were fifteen German assistants in France; when the exchanges were resumed in the post-war years they went from eighty Germans and sixty-four French in 1952–53 to 275 and 186 respectively eight years later. However, this expansion has not been maintained, despite the excess demand already referred to in France.[17] Apart from longer stays, there are also what are known as *Hospitationen,* where the assistant stays only three weeks in the other country, with no teaching responsibilities.

As far as the exchange of practising teachers is concerned, two forms are employed. In one scheme the applicants simply take one another's job for a certain period, in other words one finds a direct partner. Otherwise it is rather a question of finding a vacant place. In both cases there are problems in bilateralism, as fewer French teachers wish to visit the Federal Republic than there are Germans anxious for a stay in France. No doubt the currency exchange rate plays a part, as teachers just get their normal salary whilst seconded, clearly more advantageous for Germans in France than vice-versa. Under the direct-partner system there is the further point that when promotion or transfer occurs one person has to let the other down at the last minute. It is not, under these circumstances, surprising that teacher exchanges are far more modest in scale than those for assistants. In 1954 there were ten personal exchanges of place, in 1970–71 fifty, usually lasting three months.[18] This does not sound in any way impressive, especially as little increase has been shown in recent years, but at least it exceeds similar German contacts with any other single country. As in the case of assistants, teacher exchanges are usually confined to those teaching languages, already orientated towards the other country. Incidentally the official organisation for teacher-assistant exchanges is the same in France as for academic ones, but in Germany the secondary equivalent to the DAAD is the *Pädagogischer Austauschdienst* (PAD).

Careful preparation is given to assistants in the Federal Republic before they leave, in order to help them to bridge the cultural gap between their country and their future hosts, since once abroad they come to represent Germany. Despite this kind of planning, difficulties do arise, other than financial, which it would be foolish to ignore in our account. These come mainly from the differences between the two countries regarding not merely pedagogical methods but even what the goal of education as such should be. The first ever teacher exchanges after 1945 are said to have gone well, when in the immediate post-war era the Germans were open and eager to learn from the neighbours from whom they had been largely shut off since 1933.[19] This period has long since passed and German teachers or assistants now visiting France frequently end with mixed emotions over their visit, and often a good deal of criticism, expressed in a wealth of written reports.

Firstly, they have often deplored the distance, not merely between teacher and child, but even in the staffroom between the teachers themselves.[20] One German could even report that during a stay at one school only eleven out of seventy teachers even spoke to her.[21] The distance between teacher and child is felt to be partly due to French tradition, partly because French *lycée* teachers have only one subject and tend therefore, as it were, to concentrate on that rather than on the children as such; they are, in other words, subject-orientated. This tendency is clearly increased by the organisational procedure whereby discipline is in the hands of others, the *surveillants*: hence a French teacher often fails to get personally involved with the pupils. All too often it appears to the Germans that one man lectures and the children simply copy down his words of wisdom. Linked with this is the French emphasis on the cognitive side of education, often seemingly to the detriment of other aspects of the human personality such as music or games. It sometimes seems to the Germans that the cultivation of the 'whole man', a concept in Germany since the time of Wilhelm von Humboldt, is being overlooked. The French in reply might, of course, point to their attention to philosophy, and the concentration given in their schools to training in rational thought. But what the Germans appear to find striking is the relative neglect of what might be termed the other dimensions of the human spirit.

This is intensified by the lively spirit of individual competition which the French school fosters. Many still run a weekly *tableau d'honneur* showing the class position of each child, now a thing of the past in the Federal Republic. In many schools there is still an institution known as the *Carnets de Correspondance* which contains all the observations on behaviour, subject marks, etc. bestowed by the teacher, which the pupil has to take home to show to his parents. The corollary of all this competition is the tremendous workload imposed on the child, far greater apparently than in Germany. Under these circumstances, the French pupil tends to regard his school in no way as a second home, but simply as the place where he attends for a certain period of his life with the object of getting the qualifications necessary for his later career. As German observers have pointed out, French education appears to be governed by functional ideas, in order to fit the pupil into French society, and overlooks personality development as such.[22] The pupils need to be individually successful, and the pressures on them from French society and the family circle make it hard to produce any spirit of co-operation in the class. A subsidiary point here is that nowadays many French schools are larger than those in the Federal Republic; a German assistant arriving at an educational institution designed for 1,800 pupils and which now holds 2,300 no doubt feels overwhelmed. The absence of a more intimate atmosphere no doubt makes a certain psychological impression and adds to the sensation of strangeness.

Up to now we have stressed the negative side of the exchanges, and their impact. It must be emphasized, however, that another, more positive, aspect exists in French education. Many Germans have been impressed by the high standards of achievement in French schools and their frequently superior discipline in comparison with their own. Even the specialised teaching is seen as playing a certain part in producing better attainment by teachers and pupils alike. A further point to be borne in mind is that in all Western countries there is probably more discussion and reform in educational practice than in any previous era, as we strive to translate economic development into what is now called a better quality of life. This applies especially to France, after the up-heavals of 1968. Indeed, most Germans who have been on exchanges would say that now one has to speak of before and after 1968, as a considerable transformation has taken place since then (although not necessarily in all schools equally).

Of special interest here is the account given by one assistant who visited the same *lycée* in 1970 as she had in 1961, for a three-month stay.[23] The difference brought by the time span was impressive, not necessarily in a complimentary sense. Gone were the silent, obedient files of pupils, which had reminded her in 1961 of a barracks. Now it was a very different situation: only the smallest wore the formerly universal smock, many pupils smoked openly (although theoretically it was forbidden), exercise books were no longer in the same ideal condition, copying from class-mates was practised. Before, it had been a question of honour not to do such a thing (apart from which there was the fear of being expelled). Similar reports have emanated from others who had been on exchange in recent years. All this must not be exaggerated, as similar conditions are obviously not to be found everywhere; nonetheless the wind of change is blowing quite hard through the French educational system. It may well in the next decade produce a scholastic administration less dissimilar to that of Germany than France has had in the past. We must record, however, that some German teachers seem to have felt that the changes were being introduced rather too hastily in some cases, possibly due to too high a degree of conservatism in the past. As has been said, it is the fear of reform which precipitates the French into revolutions.[24]

We cannot leave this section without stressing that the school exchanges as practised are highly beneficial to the participants; however critical the Germans may be, that is something on which they are all agreed. In the first place they receive an insight into French life and beliefs scarcely obtainable by mere tourism. Secondly, they improve their knowledge of French (they are vir-tually all Romanists). Thirdly, they have the chance to compare the two educational systems, as we have seen, not always to the advantage of their own. This applies especially to their conviction that Germany could do with stricter discipline in its schools. It is also found that the French teacher's relative freedom from administrative routine has the advantage of permitting him to concentrate on his academic instruction.

The main thing which, prior to 1968 at least, struck French exchange teachers was the disciplinary problem in German schools. Some have even been known to tell visiting Germans in France that they would never return to teach in the Federal Republic after their experiences there. Next to this the relative democracy, insofar as relations between the headmaster and his staff are concerned, has made an impression in one case at least.[25] Equally, German insistence on personality development as an integral part of education is seen as being in marked contrast to French practice. Perhaps it is even superior, a sentiment revealed in the comment, 'They (the pupils) have the time not only to learn but also to bloom' (*s'épanouir*).[26] On the other hand, certain aspects of the German system are less attractive to French eyes, in particular the relative lack of opportunity for poor children, which means that classes in a *Gymnasium* are less mixed in terms of social origin than would be the case in a French *lycée*. The OECD report already referred to supports this contention (see page 50).

This point leads us on to two others; firstly, this social difference may in itself account for some of the variations in discipline between the two countries. Germans in France have pointed out that secondary schools with a mainly working class intake have fewer problems in that respect than those where the pupils emanate from a more bourgeois background. The differences between France and Germany may therefore be at least partly ascribable to sociological rather than to purely educational divergences, or to those of a mysterious 'national character'. Secondly, we have to beware of generalising too much about Germany, as each region is responsible for its own school administration. What strikes a French visitor as praiseworthy in one place may not even exist in another. Similarly, reforms are going on in the Federal Republic as well as over the Rhine, and consequently any praise or criticism made by the French may already have assumed a certain historical tinge.

It is indisputable that the exchanges are of immense benefit on the whole to both sides; they are claimed as the largest in scale which take place between two countries having no common language. There are still some difficulties to surmount, for example the regional preferences on both sides.[27] Many French participants want to exchange with a partner living near the French frontier, and rather shun Lower Saxony and Schleswig-Holstein. Germans would prefer the South of France or Paris. What also gives rise to problems is the fact that the emphasis lies in selecting a professional counterpart, not in choosing the school where he works; this may be unsuitable for foreigners, but has to be accepted if no exchange-partner is available at a better one. This is particularly unfortunate when a German from a comparatively small school gets sent to a mammoth comprehensive, as we have seen from the reports previously cited. There are still also minor administrative problems involved in the exchanges. The respective school years do not begin at the same time, and the German school has yet another difficulty when it accepts a visitor from France. He can teach one subject only, but is replacing a German who teaches two, which means a revised timetable. When all these points are taken into consideration it appears all the more praiseworthy that the exchanges have been effected at all. It demonstrates again the fund of goodwill on both sides. Even disciplinary variations have not proved an insurmountable obstacle. A Frenchman from a rural area arriving on exchange in a German city may abruptly acquire the impression of becoming a lion tamer instead of being a symbol of authority in a system where everyone gets precise instructions from above and simply has to execute them.[28] Discipline is still the number one problem in the exchanges, but, as we have indicated, French developments may alter this in time.

We would like to end this section with the observation that exchanges have to be prepared with extreme care in bilateral contacts, as so many potential hazards and organisational variations do exist. The Franco-German experience shows that they can be overcome. Finally, we wish to draw attention to the enormous benefit for a Romanist and Germanist, and subsequently for his pupils, in visiting the partner country. This applies especially to his language skills. There seems no real reason why every such teacher should not be given this chance, not once but regularly in his career.

An important by-product of the exchanges has been the foundation of an association consisting of former 'exchanges' on both sides. This commenced in France in 1956 under the name of *Association des Anciens Lecteurs, Assistants et Boursiers Français en Allemagne* (ALFA). Its parallel organisation in the Federal Republic is known as the *Carolus-Magnus-Kreis* (CMK), which has its headquarters at the *Deutsch-Französiches Institut* in Ludwigsburg.[29] Their common tasks are to act as a meeting point for members in each country, where information may be exchanged of value to Romanists and Germanists and also to maintain Franco-German links via conferences, etc. held jointly in either country. In addition, ALFA welcomes new teachers and assistants in France who come from German-speaking lands, and CMK does likewise for French Germanists on the other side of the Rhine. Inter-family exchanges are also arranged in the school holidays. Particularly interesting are the annual ALFA/CMK conferences, held on a different theme each year. Sometimes these are literary, as in 1965 at Caen, sometimes on political subjects such as post-war Franco-German relations in 1957, sometimes on the history and problems of a region, both Württemberg and Aquitaine having been treated in this way. We should emphasise that ALFA is under the patronage of the *Office National des Universités* and the French Embassy in Bonn, and cannot therefore be regarded exactly as an example of purely private activity. It works closely with the OFAJ and language teachers' associations and is another interesting example of how a variety of institutions have gradually been built up in the framework of Franco-German relations since the war. Incidentally, Germans appear to have dominated numerically in the annual joint congresses; at 1963 two thirds of the participants were German, although the event was held in France.[30]

One of the most interesting innovations in the realm of educational contacts in recent years has been the foundation of a joint secondary establishment in Saarbrücken; whether it is by definition a *Gymnasium* or a *lycée* is a fine point, but we shall call it the latter for the purpose of brevity. There was a *lycée* founded in the city as a result of the French occupation in 1945 and a German school as well in the same building.[31] After the Saar opted to return to Germany there was a period of co-existence,which later turned to closer co-operation. The basis which made it possible was the presence of French diplomats in the city, which entailed a number of children of school age of both nationalities simultaneously in one place. The concept of taking this opportunity to build up a joint establishment is said to have originated with M. Peyrefitte, the Education Minister, although apparently it found little response in educational administrative circles. He then went to the *Bevollmächtigte* direct, and eventually the German government spoke out decisively in favour. The project was accepted at the eighteenth bi-annual Franco-German political conference in February 1971.

The actual school, still in two distinct national sections, had already realised the need for some synchronisation of effort. By 1970 the decisive stage of drawing up joint programmes had been reached. The new political decision meant that what would have been collaboration in practice could now be raised to the formal level of a joint institution, bi-lingual and bilateral. To make one such *lycée* from two national schools is, of course, easier said than done, and illustrates yet again what administrative obstacles await authorities on the path of international collaboration. To begin with, French children go to primary schools from six to eleven and then spend seven years in a *lycée*, whereas in *Gymnasien* the pupils commence at ten and remain until they are nineteen. This necessitated the installation of a preparatory class (*Vorstufe*) for the German pupils of two years, later reduced to one. By careful planning of this it became possible to inaugurate the joint school officially in September 1971, nine months after the political decision. There are now some thousand pupils in all including just over four hundred in the *Vorstufe*; of this total just over three hundred were French in 1972, or about 30 per cent. The German intake comes from all parts of the Saar, even in some cases from other regions. Their counterparts are either the children of French families in Saarbrücken, or those from families which have returned to the mother country, but had once been in the Federal Republic. In both cases the children are liable to have some knowledge of German; the same does not apply in reverse, as local primary schools do not teach French to German pupils.

Another obstacle to smooth harmonisation lies in the differing concepts of a curriculum in both countries. In France less attention is normally paid to music, to drawing and to PE than in German schools; the latter include religious instruction, forbidden in France. This has resulted in a compromise solution at the Saarbrücken *lycée*. Religion is included in the normal timetable for the German pupils, who can be exempted at parental request as in England. French families have to demand RI for their children if they wish, as it is not included in their curriculum. This takes place with priests invited from outside, but not during the pupils' normal working hours. All this requires careful organisation and planning, more than in a purely national school.

It should be emphasised that the joint *lycée* is by no means merely an institution for improving foreign language skills alone. A full normal routine is followed in both sections, but obviously there is rather more emphasis on the partner's language than one would normally find. From the fourth class onwards geography is taught in French in both national sections, whilst German is the medium of instruction in history. Further plans are now envisaged which will enable music lessons to be given in German and later chemistry, while art will be taught in French and eventually biology as well. This will take time to realise, as it clearly demands bi-lingual teachers, not easy to come by in the natural sciences. In the joint *baccalauréat* now instituted, all pupils are expected to take as a subject the civilisation of the partner country, and the contribution made by both to European culture in general. The common *bac* was taken for the first time in 1972 by twenty-three German and thirty-four French pupils, and it affords entry to all French and German universities.

The whole experiment is interesting, and has even been seen as a pilot scheme for multilateral establishments, a breakthrough in national education systems in Western Europe.[32] We are unable to share this opinion. The Saarbrücken school shows again how careful organisation and goodwill can overcome national differences, which alone may make it worthwhile in terms of Franco-German relations. But even its headmasters do not deny the difficulties which have been experienced in the process of the harmonisation of varying viewpoints. Moreover, the *lycée*, which is financed by the French Foreign Ministry and the *Land* of the Saar, is a costly experiment; the existence of two headmasters simultaneously is an illustration of this. Cost per pupil is certainly above the average of that in purely national schools. But over and above this is one compelling reason why the idea cannot be applied on a wide scale, namely the absence of permanent, mixed populations in either land. Without the presence of French families in the Federal Republic or Germans in France there simply is no source of supply. Of course, boarding schools could be organised to overcome this. They would then be either so dear as to become socially exclusive, not a popular idea nowadays, or governments would be faced with heavy subsidies, again probably unacceptable. We cannot feel in these circumstances that the Saarbrücken experiment, however fascinating in itself, can really become a kind of European model.

This does not imply that it cannot be repeated anywhere else at all. At the award ceremony following the first *bac*, the Minister President of the Saar spoke of plans to widen the experiments: the current *Bevollmächtigte*, Filbinger, specifically mentioned six other possible places at the same ceremony.[33] A similar project for Freiburg has reached an advanced stage of planning, although not complete. Preparations have included intensified language courses and common excursions by the future pupils. Munich and Metz have been mentioned as other possible venues. In the latter city the council has already passed a unanimous decision calling for a bilateral *lycée*, said to be justifiable by the geographical situation, close to the frontier. This would make it particularly appropriate to train the future leaders of Europe.[34] Incidentally if all these do come to fruition they will be slightly different from Saarbrücken, as they will be joint *lycées* from the beginning and not just the result of a merger between two existing national schools. Nonetheless, they will have the Saarbrücken experience to draw on. The whole concept of future European leaders receiving a joint education is an exciting one in principle, but we must reiterate that the scale is likely to remain limited.

Quite apart from these conscious efforts at bilateralism there are a number of French schools in Germany and a lesser number of similar German institutions in France. The French troops and their families are a decisive factor in determining the difference (their presence accounts also for the choice of the second joint *lycée* at Freiburg). German pupils can also be enrolled in these establishments but the response is not impressive. In 1967 there were said to be only one hundred German pupils in the sixty French schools in the Federal Republic.[35]

A more interesting aspect of educational collaboration is the work performed since the war regarding the revision of school textbooks. As we all know, prejudice is easily implanted by a nationalist version of history. Some priority has been given to this in recent years in an effort to avoid the impression of false stereotypes on children at an early stage in their education. Attempts at international co-operation in this field have a long history; Franco-German teachers founded an international institute at Amsterdam for textbook revision in the cause of peace as long ago as 1926. In 1935 there was a bilateral meeting at which forty joint recommendations were produced; obviously the war intervened before any real action in the matter could be undertaken.[36] After 1945 revision of textbooks in general was undertaken in the occupation zones of Germany. Under the British authorities the task was entrusted to Professor Eckert of the

Pädagogische Hochschule, Brunswick.[37] The idea spread to teachers in the other western zones, so that Brunswick became the focal point of revisionism in post-war Germany.

The work assumed a bilateral nature in 1950 when French and German history teachers met for the first time in fifteen years. Twenty Germans and fifteen Frenchmen worked for two weeks on various themes of Franco-German history. In May 1951 a group of eight Germans went to the Sorbonne to meet a French commission, including such historians as Pierre Renouvin and Jacques Droz. The results were encouraging and in the following October a French group went to Mainz.[38] The encounters became an annual event, later biennial. In 1951 a joint agreement regarding revision was hammered out between the two respective teachers' professional associations at Stuttgart. A commission was to be set up inside these organisations to examine primary and secondary textbooks currently in use in both countries, with specialist groups for the various subjects.[39] One of the most important aspects was the treatment of various delicate themes in the histories of the two countries, such as the question of the alleged French attempts at natural frontiers in the east at German expense. Among other modern history problems to be jointly examined was the annexation of Alsace-Lorraine; more attention should be paid in German books to the protests this aroused in those regions. French textbooks were considered to exaggerate Pan-Germanism as a political movement and those in the Federal Republic to underestimate resistance in France to the Boulanger coup. Various other themes needed to be dealt with and as a general recommendation it was added that more attention might be given in the future to the periods of peace between the two nations, rather than a perhaps undue insistence on the record of their conflicts. It should be emphasised that agreement was not lightly won over certain aspects of Franco-German history, as one member of the French delegation has subsequently testified.[40] At one point during the 1951 negotiations it seemed as though the views of Gerhard Ritter and Pierre Renouvin were so far apart on the question of pre-1914 German society and its trends that common ground could not be established. Eventually, however, a formula was reached.

As examples of the kind of work which has been rendered we can refer firstly to a German view of a schoolbook on French history for French children, in order to bring out more clearly the kind of objections which may be raised against an apparently misleading picture. Firstly, it was felt that not enough space had been devoted to the cultural interchanges between the two peoples. More particularly, doubt was expressed over the use of sentences such as the following: 'Among all the peoples who envied Roman Gaul the Germans were the most miserable in the sad, foggy, barren and marshy land'. This was followed on the next page by uncomplimentary remarks about German warriors' adoration of Odin and their belief in a paradise where they would pass the entire night in drinking from the skulls of their slain foes. Somewhat later in the book the transformation of Berlin from a town *petite et misérable* to a rich capital was ascribed directly to the work of Huguenot refugees from France after the revocation of the Edict of Nantes. The description of the policies of the Weimar Republic seemed to the German reviewer greatly in need of revision; Locarno, Stresemann and Briand were not even mentioned in an account of the era. These are only a few of the points put to the French revision group by Professor Eckert. Several were accepted as valid, and certain corresponding alterations to the text suggested.[41]

We are not implying here that revision has been one-sided. German textbooks have also come under fire for phraseology which may be interpreted as giving too partial a view of German history, at least to French eyes. For example, a 1953 work contained the words *'Indogermanen'* to describe the forefathers of Europeans of today. As one French reviewer indicated, surely *'Indoeuropäer'* would have been more apt, as obviously not all modern Europeans are of German descent. The same book was held to over-simplify the role of the monarchy in France, and among other passages open to question gave Strasbourg as an example of an old German name; no one denies that it is, but to choose as an illustration a place in another country is unfortunate. When these objections were passed to the German author he agreed to make the recommended alterations in several places to achieve greater objectivity.[42]

All the foregoing demonstrates how very easily prejudice can be created with no real intention to do so, sometimes by phrases which may be offensive to one's neighbour, however harmless they sound to oneself. However, this is a story with a happy ending; by 1962 revision had gone so far that a Franco-German historians' conference could declare itself satisfied that new French textbooks had been produced in accordance with the recommendations made. Of current German ones a British observer has said that they are the most objective in Western Europe.[43] Franco-German historians and geographers have not even met regarding revision for the last five years, so complete is the work felt to be. Incidentally language manuals have been scrutinised for prejudice, as well as others. As early as 1954 the associations for language teachers in the two countries were meeting to discuss the criteria for ideal textbooks.[44] These encounters became an annual institution and are another illustration of fruitful co-operation in the realm of the battle against national prejudice.

So far we have been writing of direct revision, but apart from that there have been many conferences and courses held since the war for French and German teachers and academics, which no doubt have helped to produce a clearer picture of the neighbour in the minds of the participants. As this in itself presumably leads to more objective schoolbooks it might be called indirect revision in itself. A typical instance of such events was the course attended by forty Romanists from Bavaria, held in France in 1964, with five French *créateurs* including Camus and Cézanne as the object of study. The opportunity was also taken to learn more about France as a totality and Provence in particular. Sometimes meetings have been jointly arranged to deal with some outstanding topic or other. Representatives of the two national teaching professions met at Frankfurt in 1969 and issued a subsequent communiqué calling for at least four years in higher education to be given after the *bac* (or *Abitur*) in both countries. On other occasions the subjects discussed in common have been purely academic, as in the case of the joint colloquium arranged by the University of Strasbourg in November 1971. This sort of event, it is only fair to point out, has not always been crowned by success. A study meeting was convened in Dijon in 1969 on the theme of contacts with Eastern Europe, by two German organisations; those invited included academics and leaders of adult education. The conference fell through because although many Germans enrolled 'there was only a slight response (*Resonanz*) on the French side.'[45] The ostensible reason was a lack of accommodation in Dijon, which is hard to accept, as it obviously had not deterred the Germans.

Among other types of contact the visits of official delegations have been useful in promoting a Franco-German dialogue in education. Sometimes these have been regionally arranged, as when the local primary schools' association in Schleswig-Holstein invited a French group in 1949 for a week's discussion. Equally interesting was the tour of inspection by twenty-three school inspectors in Germany, which impressed them with its decentralisation said to be reminiscent of Switzerland. The part-time system of education for apprentices was also noted with approval.[46] Thus at many levels the exchange of views reaches impressive proportions. Even all these contacts, however, have not been able to overcome completely a very thorny academic problem, that of the recognition of the professional qualifications of one country in the other; we shall refer to standardisation under the general word *équivalences*.

The French showed themselves very anxious to proceed in the matter. When the Education Minister, M. Faure, met the then *Bevollmächtigte*, Herr Goppel, in 1968 the question of *équivalences* was raised. M. Faure spoke of initial bilateralism as merely a step on the road to creation of a kind of intellectual Common Market. By this he meant that if the French and Germans could both accept examinations taken in the one country as sufficient qualifications to ensure attendance at a course of studies in the other, then the idea could be spread inside the entire European Community. Legal provisions regarding the recognition of foreign examinations in this respect had already been made in France itself. As far as university studies were concerned the question was handled by the joint Rectors' conference, which then made its recommendations to the authorities. In October 1969 the West German Education Ministers' standing conference accepted these on behalf of their government; the necessary ministerial decrees were passed in France in the same year. It is now possible for students in both countries in possession of certain qualifications to undergo a course at a university in the partner's country, as his examinations are officially recognised in both. This applies to a certain number of disciplines, such as philosophy, *Germanistik*, biology, physics and chemistry; in the course of time the list will be extended.[47] This is undoubtedly an important step towards free circulation in the academic world and may well serve as a European model. The *Grandes Ecoles* are working along similar lines to the universities with the *Technische Hochschulen*. All this is clearly of great value to students.

When it comes, however, to allowing them to teach at school or further education level in another country, once qualified, the position is less satisfactory. The procedure for obtaining joint recognition is long drawn out, since every discipline has to be handled separately. A further drawback is the frequency of internal reforms, which may change the course of studies in France or Germany after the old ones have already been accepted as a qualification in the other country. In recent years the French in particular have been concerned to make certain changes in their own university qualifications, in some cases re-defining them, and as a consequence had to break off negotiations. In sum, little real progress has been made in this area; we have been given an estimate of the time needed to harmonise the titles of West Europe in this respect as twenty to thirty years. It is still difficult for Germans to teach in France, for example, except on short exchanges, as already described. M. Guichard, then Education Minister, has expressed the opinion that it should be possible for any teacher to obtain a post in another country without sacrificing his career, but the day is still a long way off; language difficulties are an added drawback here.

Whilst we are dealing with *équivalences* in general we should stress that attention is also being paid to the matter in terms of non-academic professions as well. In 1968 Faure and Goppel were discussing the training of engineers in both countries and ordered a study group to examine the problem and make recommendations regarding common procedures to be adopted by 1 April 1969. Once made, these were adopted by the two governments, another contribution towards European harmonisation, which in this case will clearly make economic collaboration far easier in future. Here again, recent national reforms of technical education in both countries have rendered further progress in standardisation of vocational training difficult to achieve in practice. This does not imply that all attempts have been abandoned; at the 1971 meeting in Stuttgart between the *Bevollmächtigte* and Guichard the matter came up again. A study group was set up to compare the systems of vocational training in both countries and to recommend what could be effected in the way of co-ordination. Work is continuing in this sphere but concrete results will not be achieved overnight.

When one surveys the whole field of Franco-German academic and educational contacts it seems clear that any general balance drawn up would be largely favourable. At university level, partnerships have been brought about, exchanges are carried out, and, even more satisfactory, *équivalences* in respect of study periods arranged in some disciplines. There are relatively few teacher exchanges although those that do take place are of undoubted value, which also applies to those for assistants. At Saarbrücken, and eventually in a few other places, interesting experiments in what may be called bilateral education are taking place. Our praise of these must be tempered by doubts as to whether the same concept would be possible on a wider scale. In the long term the revision of history, geography and language textbooks may well exercise a far greater influence on Franco-German relations, as the mass of school-children in both countries will receive a more favourable heterostereotype as a result (and a less partial auto-stereotype). Although the progress made in the realm of *équivalences* for teachers, academics and professional people has been on the whole less satisfactory, it has to be borne in mind that this is a difficult question. In any case, the very fact that the two countries are seeking standardisation is surely in itself an indication of a change in attitudes for the better. Of course, contacts between teachers and other aspects of collaboration took place before the war too, albeit on a lesser scale. Again, perhaps the real difference between then and now is the membership by both France and Germany of the European Community. This allows not merely for a bilateral relationship of a possibly more lasting nature, it also implies the possibility of co-operation between the two partners serving as a European model, a concept which we shall examine later.

Notes

1 See Flaubert, 'L'instruction supérieure a fait vaincre la France', quoted in W. Krause, *Gesammelte Aufsätze zur Literatur und Sprachwissenschaft*, Frankfurt-on-Main, V. Klostermanns Verlag, 1949, p 440.
2 In 1965–66 France had over 130,000 more students than Germany had even in the following year. 'Données statistiques sur l'enseignement dans les pays de la CEE', *Problèmes économiques*, no. 1157, 5 Mar. 1970, p 10.
3 *Documents*, no. 3, 1964, p 61.
4 *Correspondance*, no. 202, 15 Mar. 1972, p 3 for a summary.
5 M.-J. Durry, 'La Sorbonne à Muniche', *Revue des Hommes et des Mondes*, no. 27, 1955, pp 105–10 for an account.
6 Private information from Asnières German studies section.

7 *Correspondance*, no. 138, 15 Nov. 1968, p 24.
8 O. Wilfert, 'Harmonie allein genügt nicht?' *Frankfurter Hefte*, July 1967, p 456.
9 *Allemagne*, no. 94, Jan./Feb. 1966.
10 *XV Jahrestagung des Arbeitskreises Deutsch-Französischer Gesellschaften*, Mainz, 1970, p 55.
11 G. Hindrichs, *Kulturgemeinschaft Europa*, Cologne, Europa Union Verlag, 1968, p 53.
12 H. Neumeister, 'Der Austausch von Lehrern und Schülern mit dem Ausland'. *Auswärtige Kulturbeziehungen*, no. 4, 1967, p 298.
13 *Correspondance*, no. 27, 30 June 1963, p 10 for the list.
14 Ibid., no. 150, 1 June 1969, pp 15*f*.
15 This paragraph based on Reime, op. cit., pp 99*f*.
16 The figure of two candidates per post for 1971–72 is in *Correspondance*, no. 204, 30 Apr. 1972, p 15.
17 The statistics here are from G. Neumann, 'Deutsch-französische Austauschbeziehungen auf pädagogischem Gebiet'. *Bildung und Erziehung*, Heft 5, 1961, p 296, Office National des Universités etc. in private correspondence, and *Das Studien-Seminar* Band XII, 1967, p 34. See also G. Neumann, 'Internationaler Lehreraustausch', *Internationale Zeitschrift für Erziehungswissenschaft*, vol. VI, 1960, no. 4, pp 443*f*.
18 *Der Pädagogische Austauschdienst*, printed by PAD, Bonn, p 321.
19 For a report *Allemagne*, no. 35, Feb./Mar. 1955.
20 The following impressions are gained from reports of individual teachers on their exchanges in France made available to us by Herr Neumeister of the PAD, Bonn. See also G. de Bruyn-Oubuter, 'Erfahrungsbericht über meinen dreimonatigen Frankreichaufenthalt' etc., *Die neueren Sprachen*, Heft 3, Mar. 1970, pp 142*f*. R. Brüggemann, 'Bericht über mein Jahr als deutsche Lehrassistentin' etc., *Das Studienseminar*, 1967, no. 12, pp 35*f*., and K. J. Ehlers, 'Ein französisches Gymnasium', *Die Höhere Schule*, Oct. 1968, pp 249*f*.
21 On the other hand many get overwhelmed by invitations, so that individual experiences are not necessarily typical. But in general staffroom atmosphere seems cold in France.
22 For criticisms of this nature see Ehlers, op. cit., p 253 and Bruyn-Oubuter, op. cit., pp 146–50. The former even uses the phrase 'children without childhood' to convey his impressions.
23 L. Dietzelfelbinger, 'Deutsch-Französischer Lehreraustausch 1970'. This is a reprint of a conference report of her experiences augmented by extracts from R. Brechon, *La fin des lycées*, Paris, Grasset, 1970.
24 Quoted in ibid., p 6.
25 Y. Lucas, 'Rapport concernant mon séjour à Karlsruhe dans le cadre des échanges culturels franco-allemands', *Die neueren Sprachen*, Heft 8, Aug. 1970, p 390.
26 Ibid., p 386.
27 G. Neumann, 'Der deutsch-französische Lehreraustausch', *Deutschland-Frankreich*, vol III, p 257*f*. for the administrative difficulties outlined here.
28 Ibid., p 267.

29   The information which follows is from private correspondence with ALFA, Paris, unless otherwise stated.
30   *Allemagne*, nos 80–2, July/Dec. 1963.
31   Unless otherwise stated our account is based on personal interviews at the respective cultural departments of the two Foreign Offices, and with the joint headmasters of the lycée itself, M. Jordy and Herr Rasch.
32   R. Schlagintweit, 'Bonn-Paris: Modelle für Kultureuropa', *Aussenpolitik*, May 1972, pp 269–72. Herr Schlagintweit is in the cultural department of the German Foreign Office.
33   *Süddeutsche Zeitung*, 30 June 1972.
34   *Frankfurter Allgemeine Zeitung*, 3 May 1972.
35   O. Wilfert, op. cit., p 454.
36   O. E. Schüddekopf, *History teaching and history textbook revision*, Council for Cultural Cooperation of the Council of Europe, Strasbourg, 1967, pp 18*f*.
37   For much of the information in this section we are indebted to Professor Dr Eckert himself in a personal interview.
38   E. Bruley, 'Les rencontres entre historiens français et allemands', *Les Dialogues*, July 1952, pp 235–43.
39   The text of the accord is in G. Eckert and O. E. Schüddekopf (eds), *Deutschland-Frankreich-Europa*, Verlag für Kunst und Wissenschaft, Baden-Baden, 1953, pp 69*f*.
40   J. Droz, 'Zur Revision des deutsch-französischen Geschichtsbildes', *Deutschland-Frankreich*, vol. II, p 90.
41   The criticisms and reply are in *Deutschland und Frankreich im Spiegel ihrer Schulbücher*, Internationales Schulbuch Institut, Brunswick, Verlag Albert Linbach, 1954, pp 105*f*.
42   Ibid., pp 50*f*.
43   E. H. Dance, 'Bias in history teaching and textbooks' in Schüddekopf, op. cit., p 76.
44   See *Allemagne*, no. 34, Dec./Jan. 1955 and nos 68–9, May/June 1961.
45   *Frankfurter Allgemeine Zeitung*, 9 Oct. 1969.
46   *Documents*, Mar./Apr. 1967, pp 107*f*.
47   For the official list as at March 1971 see *Equivalences Universitaires Franco-Allemandes*, pub. jointly by the DAAD and the Office National des Universités etc. in both languages.

Chapter 4

The Problem of
a Common Language

The treaty of 1963 required that both signatories should facilitate in their educational systems the teaching of their partner's language. There was a clear recognition of this as a necessary instrument in mutual understanding. Traditionally, exchanges in this area have been very one-sided, in that French has enjoyed a prestige in Europe which the German language has never known. In the animal fable 'Ysengrimus', as early as the twelfth century the refined animals spoke French, but the donkey and the brutal wolf used German.[1] Later the importance of France politically in the seventeenth and eighteenth centuries, and the glory of the Sun King, made its language paramount on the continent. By the time of the Treaty of Nijmegen in 1678 it had become the recognised diplomatic medium. Of Frederick the Great in the next century it was said that he only spoke German to his horse. Inevitably, the French have become proud of their tongue, because of this historical prestige and because it serves as a carrier of French culture. The linguistic work done by the Académie Française is familiar to us all. Indeed the language has tended to assume the status of a symbol, the touchstone of national identity, rather like the Royal Family has done for many people in Britain. If in this chapter we are devoting more space to the promotion of French than of German it is simply a reflection of the greater efforts made by the government of France to further its language internationally.

Characteristic of the importance still attached to this is a recent article by a French civil servant, tracing the historical progress of French and stating openly: 'The spreading of French is of great concern to us'. The language is shown as enjoying great international standing through the creative works of those who have chosen it as their medium, and Senghor's description of it as a 'sun which illuminates outside the hexagon' is cited in support of these claims.[2] It is not then surprising to find M. Pompidou declaring in 1971 that his government would make it its business to secure a legitimate place in Europe for the French language.[3] Official concern has been paralleled by private activity. The *Cercle de Presse Richelieu* to defend French against misuse (in France) was founded in 1952; there is even a '*Ligue de défense de la langue française*', and an international association of universities whose teaching is all, or partly, in French (AUPELE).

Unfortunately, for various reasons French had become somewhat eclipsed in German schools even before the war. The extreme nationalism of the Hitler regime was partly responsible, because of a prejudice against anything foreign. French, hitherto obligatory in higher schools, was reduced to an optional subject. After 1945 came a foreign occupation of West Germany exercised mainly by English-speaking peoples, as the French zone was relatively limited in size. Consequently, when political power returned some 80 per cent of schools in the Federal Republic had adopted English as their first foreign language.[4] This had already caused some uneasy stirrings in France, where it was suggested that the dissemination of French was necessary in the interests of Franco-German reconciliation.[5]

A reaction of this nature to the retreat of French was perfectly understandable, since the French themselves had taken the decision to promote German in their country as early as 1945. In the summer of that year the French Minister of Education called on parents to let their children learn German, which would remain the language of a neighbouring country. The French began to feel that they were not getting justice linguistically.

Their doubts were resolved at least in principle with the signing of the 1954 cultural accord. Article seven of the agreement quite specifically laid down as a goal the furtherance of the partner's language on both sides of the Rhine. A joint cultural commission was set up to assist contacts in general and the question of each language was to be included in its sphere of activities. Adenauer is said to have assured Mendès-France personally in writing that the German government would secure for French language and literature the same place in the Federal Republic as German already enjoyed in France. Despite the Education Minister's efforts in France, the German language had not, in fact, caught on particularly at the time. English had come to predominate to such an extent that even French teachers of English were trying to encourage German, just to reduce the numbers in their own classes. In 1952–53 about one fifth of French schoolboys in secondary establishments were learning German, against three fifths learning English.[6] Before the war the proportion for German had been about one third greater.

In other words, in both countries English had come to be accepted as the first foreign language. The position for French was rendered more difficult still as even Latin was being favoured at its expense in some schools. Equally the differing structures in the two countries made any implementation of Adenauer's promise hard to achieve in practice. France has a centrally-organised system, but educational administration in the Federal Republic is left to the individual *Länder*. However, to ensure some degree of co-ordination between them there is a standing conference of their Education Ministers, which meets periodically to discuss policy matters for West German education in general. What this type of organisational background could mean in respect of the 1954 Accord's clauses on language was made abundantly clear in the following year.

For in early 1955 the conference, meeting at Düsseldorf, produced its own internal agreement in regard to foreign languages. Henceforth in modern language grammar schools (*neusprachliche Gymnasien*) English would be obligatory from the fifth year, but French only from the seventh, with effect from 1 April 1957. This decision not unnaturally caused consternation in France.[7] A French language teacher on a professional visit to Munich called it 'disagreeable news', a graphic illustration of how the French feel about their language.[8] In this instance annoyance was perhaps justified by the fact that the agreement was plainly at variance with article seven of the 1954 Accord. Moreover, at the conference's meeting, the Accord had apparently not even been mentioned.[9] The situation was thus that the German government had sworn to further French, and now saw itself unable to implement its desire. As one French commentator ironically pointed out, this was the fruit of post-war French opposition, for political reasons, to a centrally-governed West Germany.[10] Another fact which annoyed the French was that whereas in their system the parents could choose which language their children should study, the Düsseldorf agreement left it to the school's discretion.

There is no doubt that the conference decision was a setback to French in practice as well as in principle. As far as *Gymnasien* were concerned, by 1962 there were actually fewer young Germans learning French than had been the case three years previously (although in other secondary schools the situation was less unfavourable). The position was actually similar everywhere; in Berlin it was especially bad. Even Latin was pushing out French in many cases. As the teaching of German in France was booming, by 1960 the French felt that apart from any other consideration this gave them a lever to bring pressure on the Germans. No doubt the increasing economic role of Germany in Europe was an incentive to French parents to decide for its language.

Thus the background situation to the 1963 treaty, insofar as language was concerned, was undoubtedly the relative world predominance of English. In 1957, for example, nearly half of all the works published in the world were in that language, the proportions for French and German being approximately one eighth in both cases. In terms of translations English also held sway over any other language, providing one third of all publications issued in this way in 1965.[11] What impression this was making in Germany can be seen from an investigation three years before among advocates of European collaboration in the Republic. Whereas 63 per cent hoped that the future mother tongue on the Continent would be English, only about one in six plumped for French (and even fewer for German).[12] What sort of task confronted the French government when the January 1963 treaty was signed is evident from a public opinion poll at the time; whereas one German in five claimed to speak English, only half that proportion could make a similar statement about French.[13]

The treaty obviously gave a new impulse to efforts to establish French on a more secure footing. The existing regime in the Federal Republic was quite ready to meet French wishes halfway. Only a few weeks after the treaty had been signed Adenauer emphasised to the heads of regional governments that concrete measures needed to be made to increase the number of German schoolchildren learning French, in accordance with the new agreement. Yet again the central administrations in both countries ran into the old obstacle of German federalism. The standing conference had by February more or less implied that the Düsseldorf

Accord would be kept in force. An interrogation of individual *Länder* Ministers showed that most would still be giving priority to English. Possible exceptions were the frontier territories of Saarland, Baden-Württemberg, and also, curiously enough, Berlin.[14] Ultimately, only the first of these areas did actually place French as the first foreign language. Thus, despite the recommendation of the joint cultural commission in June 1963 to the effect that French should be far more favoured, regionalism prevented any progress.

It would have been surprising if the French, in face of such decisions, had remained mute. As early as February 1963 they made their presence felt in North-Rhine-Westphalia. When the regional Minister President stated that the last year at school in the area should linguistically be devoted to an intensive study of English, the French Consul-General called to protest against the treaty violation. Some concession was obtained from the *Länder* in October 1964, when at Hamburg it was decided that any region could henceforth make French the first language if it chose, and even introduce it into primary schools. This new arrangement represented the wishes of the then Federal *Bevoll-mächtigte*, Kiesinger. The national governments had won some ground. There seems little doubt that the meeting between Kiesinger and the then French Education Minister Fouchet in March 1964, at which the whole language question was discussed, had been responsible for Kiesinger bringing new pressure on the *Länder*. In fact, the Plenipotentiary tried to arrange a meeting at Stuttgart between Fouchet and the regional Education Ministers. That only five turned up seemed sufficient commentary on their attitude.

French pressure did not slacken with the initial concessions made in the Hamburg agreement, although it has to be said that these did bring some progress. The authorities in Baden-Württemberg made use of them in 1965 in order to introduce French in their primary schools, as apparently parents in Baden had been demanding it in place of English.[15] Some advances had been made in other *Länder* by now, notably in respect of French as a second foreign language. Evening classes were also coming to show some re-orientation away from English in favour of French. In 1969 a Certificate of French was created, putting it on a par with English, for which a similar diploma had been instituted two years previously.

By 1968 there had been a steady growth in the number of French pupils learning German, which enabled the French to bring more pressure. The new *Bevollmächtigte*, Goppel of Bavaria, showed appreciation of their desire to reinforce the position still further in the Federal Republic. French propaganda against any possible common language in the new Europe continued (by common language English was certainly meant). Typical of their general line was the speech by M. Guichard, Minister of Education, addressing the standing conference at Freiburg in 1971. He stressed the need to learn the language of any people in order to be able to comprehend its culture, and that the road to authentic cultural unity in Europe lay through linguistic diversity. The Minister then attacked English more directly, by saying that if M. Dupont and Herr Schmidt conversed in that language it was in effect the betrayal of both their cultures. Similarly, the French cultural attache in Germany pointed out that it was a sorry state of affairs when a schoolboy in Kehl or Landau (near the French border) could not learn French as his first foreign language. He disclaimed all intention of attacking English as such. What the French were allegedly afraid of was that a kind of polyglot tongue, ostensibly English, was threatening the position of both German and French in the world. A colourless argot, useful in business and various emergencies, would come to replace them both as a medium of communication.[16]

Public speeches were accompanied by political pressure. At the April 1971 meeting between M. Guichard and the current *Bevollmächtigte*, Herr Filbinger, the complaint was again raised that not enough French was being taught in the Federal Republic, as it had not yet reached parity with English. This was alleged to be against the letter of the 1954 agreement and the spirit of the 1963 treaty (which, of course, was true). Guichard was quick to claim to the press in Stuttgart that one sixth of all French secondary pupils were learning German as a first language and a further 35 per cent as a second. All this produced the right result in the form of new pressure on the *Länder* to revise the Hamburg agreement, even from Brandt himself. Filbinger had publicly attacked the arrangement even before, in October 1970. The fact that the Hamburg Accord was due to expire shortly no doubt played a part in the 1971 pressure exercised by Filbinger on the *Länder*. As Minister President in Baden-Württemberg he had already introduced French as the first foreign language for that region, and at the July 1971 bi-annual conference of political leaders it appears that it was by now understood on the French side that their language would receive a further push towards parity.

In October this hope was fulfilled when the *Länder* representatives, meeting at Kiel, signed a new agreement. From now on, French or English could be chosen anywhere by the parents as the first foreign language for their children. At a subsequent meeting M. Guichard expressed his satisfaction with the new arrangement. It should be pointed out that the parity now attained is theoretical only; in practice, as the French well know, most parents will choose English.[17] For this reason, the Kiel agreement is seen by them as a first step, not the last, in the promotion of their language. In this connection, their officials point to the fact that whereas in France ten pupils wishing to learn German are sufficient in principle to guarantee a class, in the Federal Republic twenty-five children are held to be the minimum necessary to start a French class. Under these circumstances we may expect that they will continue to make every effort to spread French—a perfectly understandable decision in view of the traditional prestige that it has enjoyed in Germany.

In the struggle to obtain parity for French, the government of France has found useful allies in those Germans who teach it professionally (Romanists). Their support has been given either through a language teachers' association, the General German Modern Languages Association (ADNV are the German initials), or through the medium of private Franco-German societies of which many Romanists are members. Their agitation on behalf of French began before the 1963 treaty, as they naturally saw in the Düsseldorf agreement of 1955 an infringement of the bilateral cultural Accord.

At their Easter conference of the same year, the Romanists' association sent a memorandum to the authorities protesting about the Düsseldorf decision. Apart from the importance of French they were concerned about the sequence proposed in German higher schools, namely English first and then French as a subsidiary. Romanists maintained that this had been shown as unfavourable to language-learning in previous experience. They claimed that it was easier for Germans to learn French first and then English, rather than the other way around. There were, in other words, solid educational reasons for putting French first, quite apart from its intrinsic importance.[18] By 1957 their feelings had crystallised sufficiently to enable them to publish a book on the subject, *We learn French again*, produced under the auspices of the Franco-German Society of Berlin.

Romanists' concern about the position of French was heightened by internal reforms in the educational system, made to simplify the examinations for the *Abitur*. These introductions had the effect, in general, of further disadvantaging both geography and French. Thus in the classical *Gymnasien*, Latin and Greek took precedence, in those orientated towards mathematics and science English was the first foreign language, followed by French or Latin. Even in modern languages *Gymnasien*, French sometimes had to be content with third place, behind English and Latin. This meant that in the German equivalent of the upper sixth (*Oberprima*) French was simply dropped by the pupils, in order to concentrate on other subjects.

By 1963 the Franco-German Society in Berlin had managed to secure first place for French in some Berlin schools. Moreover, Berlin Romanists had been active in drawing the attention of their colleagues in other regions to the possibility of promoting the language, even within the framework of the Düsseldorf agreement. In May 1962 the Circle of Franco-German Societies, which included many Romanists, sent a general resolution to the standing conference, which it claimed had resulted in many *Länder* ministers making an intensive study of the position in their own region.[19] Optimistic reports were rendered, which seem not to have convinced the ADNV in any way. At their conference in Wiesbaden in 1963 concern was expressed as to whether the situation was as favourable as the *Länder* wished to present it. In particular, fresh reforms aimed at a more unified national procedure could again have been harmful to French. Under these circumstances Romanists in the Franco-German Societies Circle urged their fellow members to do everything possible to further the language, seen as a means of reconciliation between the peoples. It was suggested that apart from resolutions the Societies should work through parents, who possessed the right of decision as to which kind of school their children should attend. A new edition of *We learn French again* was produced as added ammunition.

Despite all good intentions the struggle for French was long and hard. In effect, there were three obstacles. Firstly, the general predominance of English. Secondly, traditional attachment to

Latin as a cultural foundation in general, and finally, the popularity in Germany of the school reforms. These seemed to promise more unity in a country where educational administration showed perhaps too great a diversity. This was especially important to parents obliged to move to another region, where the system was probably different from the one to which their children were accustomed. Consequently, not too much progress was recorded until 1971, except in Baden-Württemberg, when the Hamburg Accord was due to lapse.[20] As this coincided with new curriculum recommendations which could have been dangerous, the Societies became especially active in that year.

The Franco-German Societies Circle produced a memorandum on the subject, underlining the point that any new disadvantage for French would clearly be in contravention of existing bilateral agreements. French was advocated in economic terms, since France was now so important a customer of the Federal Republic. In any case, what Germany was said to need was a liberal languages policy, rather than the quasi-monopoly which English allegedly held. In other words, the Circle was aiming at parity for French as a first language, at the parents' discretion.[21] At the Circle's yearly congress, held in 1971 at Caen, the President was able to announce that hopes had been fulfilled, in that a modification of the Hamburg agreement was to be ratified (i.e. the one at Kiel previously mentioned). He pointed out that the task of the Circle now lay in ensuring that parents made use of their option for French, otherwise the new regulations would be a dead letter.

This was the heart of the matter. However many resolutions the Circle might pass (even those which the government accepted), ultimately the parents would decide. As one newspaper put it, French was waiting for enthusiasts.[22] However, as far as the Romanists and the French government were concerned, at least theoretical parity with English has been attained. How the parents will, in reality, exercise their choice remains to be seen. This is an area where trade will certainly play some part, since the commercial exchanges between France and West Germany have reached a level which makes this an important factor in the promotion of the neighbour's language. How this situation will be affected by British entry into the EEC only time can tell. That the French drive to establish their language at a European level is, however, primarily a matter of prestige is certainly accepted in Germany.

As far as the furtherance of German is concerned, the Federal Republic has shown itself somewhat less anxious than its neighbour, partly because of its low profile in cultural terms after the war, partly because it now sees co-operation as more important than the promotion of national culture as such. Nonetheless, it is recognised that language serves as a key in assisting the understanding of any people's way of life.[23] The German government does not seem, however, to have made any especial attempts to spread its language in France since the two bilateral Accords of 1954 and 1963. This stems partly from the fact that in France the choice of first foreign language has been at the parents' discretion for the period under review here. The Germans appear to accept that the majority will choose English in this case.[24]

Nonetheless, there had been some increase in the number choosing German as the first language, which doubled between 1958 and 1968. By 1970–71 about 850,000 school-children in France were learning German altogether.[25] This is a national generalisation, since the statistics varied according to region; in the north the percentages tended to be high, as in the border regions.[26] In the latter areas trade and simple geographical contiguity were doubtless the main factors. It would seem that the role of the economic miracle in general, and French exportation to Germany within the framework of the EEC, have tended to create interest in German across the Rhine. There are now, incidentally, some 750,000 German children learning French.

Two more interesting experiments in linguistic collaboration have been produced in recent years, both capable of expansion. The first concerns the teaching of the partner's language in infant schools in both countries. A beginning was made in 1965 in Bordeaux, on local initiative; a German Froebel-trained teacher was invited by the educational authorities in Aquitaine to spend some time there at an infant school to teach German to children aged six. Three years later the then French Minister of Education, M. Peyrefitte, proposed to the German *Bevollmächtigte*, Herr Goppel, that this experiment might be extended. He suggested an exchange between twenty infant teachers in each country. To facilitate the process, the Germans should be sent initially to Alsace and the French representatives despatched to Germany would be themselves Alsatians. This was intended to help them learn the partner's language prior to teaching their own. It was hoped to raise the numbers to 400 quite soon.

The scheme was confined at first to Bavaria and Bordeaux, the former being Herr Goppel's own region, By 1972–73 this had been extended to cover several other *Länder* in South and West Germany, and the numbers exchanged had risen to 100 from each country. This took place despite some initial difficulty, again due to the differing administration regulations in France and the Federal Republic. The former is well-advanced in respect of infant schools in general, which are State-run, whereas in Germany they are private. Inevitably the French teachers are professionally qualified in the normal way, whilst the German staff are volunteer helpers. From experience they know how to deal with children but they usually have no training in education as such. Also, the French although qualified teachers in general are not really language specialists. This remains an unsolved problem at the moment, so that only some fifty thousand children in both countries together are enjoying this early introduction to their neighbour's tongue.[27] A further obstacle is the lack of German volunteers who speak French, so that in 1971–72 only seventy could even be recruited.[28] It is an interesting experiment in the teaching of the spoken language and may be extended when administrative handicaps are overcome.[29]

Equally intriguing is the concept of bi-lingual secondary schools, which the two partners have also launched in collaboration, at the suggestion of the joint cultural commission. The idea is simply to teach certain disciplines, notably music, drawing and physical education in the partner's language. Altogether about nine hours' instruction weekly is given in this way, apart from actual French or German lessons themselves. History and geography are sometimes included in the subjects taught in this manner; even biology has been mooted as a possibility.[30] By 1969 the first of such classes had been instituted in France, and in February 1972 further extensions were being announced by the new *Bevollmächtigte*, Herr Filbinger. These would be in addition to the thirty or so then existing in each country.

Yet again we have to point to structural differences in the two systems which preclude this experiment from being on a far greater scale. The chief obstacle this time is the lack of French teachers, who are trained to teach one subject only at secondary level, unlike Germans who have two disciplines normally. As the Frenchman cannot instruct both in history and in German it becomes difficult to implement the idea. It appears to be hard to get French assistants to aid the scheme in the Federal Republic, so that what is described as 'ideal' in theory tends to be difficult to realise in practice. What is said to be an admirable experiment qualitatively remains unfortunately limited in scope, but as in the case of the kindergarten, at least the pilot schemes have turned out well, and the concept has been accepted in principle on both sides.

Considerable attention has been paid in recent years to extra-scholastic linguistic teachings, especially through the medium of the Youth Office (OFAJ). The Office had to be interested in a common language since its contacts were found by experience to be far more valuable when the participants could converse readily. Consequently as soon as February 1964 it was speaking of language courses as an essential preliminary to youth exchanges.

Previous experiences in the field of modern linguistics led the OFAJ to choose audio-visual methods as the best means, using a language laboratory at Vichy among others. The courses are run in conjunction with various youth movements and educational associations. Said to be hesitant at first, by 1968 36 national and 155 regional organisations had taken part in such courses.[31] The number of participants annually was about eleven thousand during the first years, most of whom were from the educational sector themselves, either teachers, students or school-children. Needless to say, young workers and peasants were again under-represented, forming about one eleventh of the total.

An analysis of the motives impelling young people to attend these sessions showed considerable variation. Reasons varied from a desire to complete one's general culture to a professional need of the partner's language and preparing for a visit across the Rhine. But since most participants are middle class it would appear that the courses are in a sense supplementary to normal, scholastic media. No doubt they are qualitatively of value in this respect, but wide sectors of the population who would not normally learn the neighbour's language are not really being reached. This impression is only strengthened by statistics: in 1967 only 7,505 young people attended the sessions in Germany.[32] By the following year just over 7 per cent of the OFAJ's financial resources were being devoted to linguistic promotion.[33] It is hard to avoid feeling that more funds spent on this and less on 'camp fire' type meetings would be advantageous. This is especially true as so many of the people attending are already teachers who can profit from a *stage* of this nature in the partner's country, which will obviously make them better French or German teachers at home. But observations such as this only raise the question as to whether it would not be better simply to give the money directly to the school authorities in both countries anyway. There are already holiday courses in German schools for foreign children; over half of these in 1970 were for French children alone.

Several other media for language promotion are now employed. In France there is the *Alliance Française*, founded in 1883 by de Lesseps; this has the aim of promoting French civilisation, and especially the language. The headquarters are in Paris, where courses, subsidised to a limited extent by the state, are offered to foreign students.[34] About twelve years ago as many as a third of all enrolled learners came from West Germany, but today the proportion has fallen to around one tenth. This disquieting diminution is attributed to competition from the English language. However, German officials and foreign correspondents in Paris say that the main reason is probably the growth of the German economy, so that secretaries and typists have such a relatively high standard of living they are no longer willing to become au pairs. As three-quarters of the German students at the *Alliance* are girls, this sounds very probable. But it must be discouraging to see Germans losing interest in France at a time when there is so much talk of collaboration. Incidentally, the *Alliance* now maintains 1,200 committees in other countries, none in Germany, apparently because the treaty assumes that linguistic promotion will be achieved via the normal scholastic channels. This makes the loss at Paris doubly hard.

Another organisation disseminating the partner's language is the Franco-German Chamber of Commerce, which affords commercial courses to businessmen. Obviously the scale here is relatively small but in view of the size nowadays of Franco-German trade the importance of this should not be under-estimated. By 1972 the respective Chambers of Commerce in Paris and Düsseldorf had come to an agreement recognising translators' diplomas by both associations. The Düsseldorf president pointed out that France was the best buyer of German goods and her biggest supplier too. He regretted that French had not received more consideration in Federal schools in the previous decade.[35] Speeches of this nature by businessmen may well be a better guarantee of a bright future for French in Germany than any formal treaties.

Finally, there is another form of teaching to be considered, that undertaken on the mass media. ORTF has daily radio courses (except Sundays) for its German listeners. Equally, thanks to French centralisation, it can guarantee reaching the whole of France with its German courses, prepared under the aegis of the Ministry of Education. In the Federal Republic itself considerable time is allocated to French lessons.

In retrospect it would appear that the 1963 treaty has made little difference to the language situation in each country, particularly as the parity now acquired by French in the Federal Republic is theoretical only.[36] Presumably there are two practical reasons for having a language in common, of which the first is commercial. It is true that this is compelling for businessmen dealing with France, but after all Germans export to more than one country, as do Frenchmen. If it is really necessary for a salesman to learn French in order to sell in Paris, then he has to know Dutch and English to export to Germany's second and third best customers, Holland and the USA. Where does he stop? Similar considerations arise in the matter of using their language as a key to understanding another people's way of life, which is the second motive for learning. Granted that in Bergsonian terms it is absolutely essential, in order to *s'installer dans le mouvement* of another culture, to acquire a knowledge of its language first, again where does one draw the line? This question arises particularly in the case of the Federal Republic, which has frontiers with eight other states (not counting the GDR). There is such a degree of linguistic diversity in Europe that it would be quite impossible to learn all the languages necessary, if it were accepted that genuine understanding could only be attained in this way.

Under these circumstances what can be done? Either the French and the Germans decide to favour some neighbours especially (which the treaty of 1963 in effect did) or they adopt a third language as a medium in their contacts. As this would be English it is an unacceptable choice, on one side of the Rhine at least. This leaves the furtherance of the partner's language, as the treaty foresees, but simply overlooks the points raised above. Neither the argument from culture nor the one from economics can really justify a concentration on one language, unless the economy and the way of life of the people it represents are really dominant at international level. This is not true of any West European nation. It might be possible to come to some definitive agreement in the

EEC that the same two or three languages would be promoted in all school systems, but this is a matter to be dealt with in a later part of this book.

Notes

1   H. Krause, *Französisches Kulturbewusstsein und deutsch-französische Begegnung*, p 34.
2   'Hexagon' denotes France because of its hexagonal appearance on a map. J. Basdevant, *Das Zwanzigste Jahrhundert—das Jahrhundert der kulturellen Beziehungen?*, French Embassy, Bad Godesberg, Bulletin, no. 44, Jan. 1969. M. Basdevant was General Director of the department for cultural relations at the Quai d'Orsay.
3   Quoted in K. O. Nass, *Gefährdete Freundschaft*, p 78.
4   According to Herr Schröder of the Cultural Department of the German Foreign Office in a personal interview.
5   See *Allemagne*, no. 2, June/Aug. 1949.
6   W. Bökenkamp, 'Der heutige Stand des Deutschunterrichts in Frankreich', *Deutschunterricht für Ausländer*, 1954–55, vol 4, no. 2, pp 32*f.* These figures do not include the educational areas of Strasbourg or Algiers.
7   *Allemagne*, no. 36, Apr./May 1955 referred to it as a 'disastrous decision'.
8   M.-J. Durry, 'La Sorbonne à Muniche', *Revue des Hommes et des Mondes*, 1955, no. 27, p 110.
9   According to *Allemagne*, op. cit.
10 A. Grosser, *Germany in our time*, London, Pall Mall Press, 1971, p 100.
11 *Correspondance*, no. 150, 1 June 1969, p 18, and no. 74, 22 Sept. 1965, p 18.
12 *Documents*, 1962, vol III, p 338.
13 *Correspondance*, no. 35, 1 Dec. 1963, p 6.
14 *Le Monde*, 10–11 Feb. 1963.
15 *Correspondance*, no. 67, 12 May 1965, p 16.
16 R. Cheval, 'Die deutsch-französischen Kulturbeziehungen', *Dokumente*, 1969, no. 25, pp 32*f.*
17 As we were told at the French Embassy, Bad Godesberg.
18 H. Rheinfelder, 'Das Memorandum der deutschen Romanisten zur Reihenfolge der neueren Sprachen an den höheren Schulen', *Deutschland-Frankreich*, vol II, pp 373*f.*
19 *Mitteilungsblatt für die Deutsch-Französischen Gesellschaften*, no. 16, Oct. 1963, pp 26*f.*
20 In 1966, for example, 2·4 million pupils were learning English as against only one quarter of that figure French, *Frankfurter Allgemeine Zeitung*, 14 July 1971.
21 *Memorandum des Arbeitskreises Deutsch-Französischer Gesellschaften zum Französischunterricht in der Bundesrepublik Deutschland*, Wetzlar, Feb. 1971.

22 *Frankfurter Allgemeine Zeitung*, 14 July 1971.
23 'Kulturabteilung des Auswärtigen Amtes', *Jahresbericht*, 1970, pp 37*f*.
24 Which 82% did in 1970–71. *Mitteilungsblatt für die Deutsch-Französischen Gesellschaften*, no. 35, Oct. 1971, p 61. The corresponding figure for German as first foreign language in France was 17%.
25 According to Herr Schröder of the Cultural Department of the German Foreign Office in an interview.
26 Information from M. Gossot of the Cultural Department of the French Foreign Office in a personal interview.
27 Schröder interview, op. cit.
28 Gossot interview, op. cit.
29 For an account of Munich–Bordeaux exchanges see Dr E. Mauser, 'Zweck und Durchführung des deutsch-französischen Erzieherinnen-austausches', *Pädagogische Welt*, 1969, vol 23, no. 8, pp 453*f*.
30 Information from Mlle. Fischer, French Embassy, Bad Godesberg.
31 'Cinq années de promotion linguistique à l'Office Franco-Allemand pour la jeunesse', *Education et Echanges*, Bulletin du Comité de coordination des associations d'échanges internationaux, Paris, 1969, p 6.
32 *Süddeutsche Zeitung*, 25 Sept. 1968.
33 *Aus dem Tätigkeitsbericht*, etc., op. cit., p 10.
34 The subvention for the headquarters is approximately 5% according to M. Brueziere, director of the school, in an interview with the authors, on which this section is based.
35 *Handelsblatt*, 16–17 June 1972.
36 It is interesting to note that the Secretary-General of the Alliance has recently expressed his satisfaction with the position of French in the world except in West Germany, where he felt still French to be menaced, despite the treaty. *Correspondance*, no. 222, 15 May 1973, p 13.

Chapter 5

The
Development of Franco-German
Economic Ties

It should not have come as a surprise when in 1968 it was announced that France and West Germany were now one another's best trading partners. The two countries already enjoyed a long post-war record of profitable trading relations. Whereas in 1953 France drew one tenth of its imports from its neighbour, by 1958 the proportion had risen to approximately one sixth, and three years later to 22 per cent.[1] This was partly due to the EEC and its role in re-orientating external commerce. In the case of West Germany its exports to other EEC countries rose from 27·3 per cent to 34 per cent of its total foreign sales between 1958 and 1962, with imports showing a similar trend.[2] The latter year was a bumper one for Franco-German commerce, as both countries increased their sales across the Rhine by about one sixth.[3] It would seem that the EEC was a more efficacious motor for the French economy than for the German; whereas between 1952 and 1958 the former grew at an annual rate of 4 per cent in foreign trade, for the period 1958–64 the yearly increase was as high as 10 per cent. The German growth rate over the latter period scarcely changed, in fact its export rate slightly diminished.[4]

Superficially the two economies were similar at the time of the 1963 treaty, except for one or two areas where one enjoyed superiority, coal mining in the German case, agriculture in the case of France. In reality, the French suffered some apprehension as to whether they could compete with the land of the 'economic miracle' once the last tariff barriers in the EEC were removed. After all, in 1965 the Federal Republic had 38 per cent of the total production of the Six, and a close survey showed that in many sectors it enjoyed a superiority, due often to the sheer size of German concerns in comparison with their French counterparts. Linked with this was their apparent capacity to make bigger profits: additionally, the chronic labour shortage had pushed German firms into rationalisation, and high productivity resulted from this process. A 1965 examination of the two economies by certain sectors showed the French as superior only in aviation and petroleum refining, with the Germans leading in construction, the chemical industry and metallurgy, with car manufacture and the electrical goods industry comparable. It should be pointed out here that in both countries there was heavy US investment in all the areas named above.[5] If the size of the enterprise is a crucial factor in modern industry then the Germans had an undoubted advantage; in 1963 not one French concern figured in the list of the ten largest in the Common Market, no fewer than four of which were German. Of the fifty greatest three years later, over half were German, against eleven French. In sum, the dynamic German economy appeared quite capable of overwhelming the French, especially as not merely its individual firms, but also its working force were so numerically superior. This applied particularly to manufacturing, which in 1964 employed in all branches almost twice as many persons on one side of the Rhine as on the other.

This disequilibrium produced two consequences, the first being a deficit for France in its trade with the Federal Republic. For example, for the four years 1962–65 inclusive, it only once had a credit balance, and even then it was minimal. Not surprisingly, by the latter year the attainment of an equilibrium was set as an objective in French export policy. This was not immediately realised, however, indeed post 1965 the balance was increasingly deficitory for France, even after the devaluation of the franc in 1969. The situation has remained, amounting to over 1,000 million DM in 1971.[6] That devaluation has apparently failed to work in this instance seems due to the qualitative superiority of German industry in some respects. In 1971 French businessmen were quoted as saying that German machinery was so much better than that of its competitors that they would buy it even if it were twice as expensive as theirs.[7]

This leads to the second consequence of the imbalance referred to above, viz. the relative dependence of France on her neighbour. Whereas Germany gets 12 per cent of its purchases in France, the German share of French imports is 20 per cent (1971 figures).[8] Dependence is particularly pronounced in respect of machinery and capital goods; in 1968 France imported three times as much of these from the Federal Republic as it sent to Germany.[9]

However, the picture in recent years has been by no means completely one-sided. Firstly, France enjoys an agrarian advantage to offset industrial handicaps: in 1963 it had nearly half of all the agriculturally-employed land in the Six, against Germany's one fifth. Secondly, an examination of its export pattern to Germany shows a growing proportion of its sales coming under the heading of finished goods, rather than just raw materials or foodstuffs. Whereas in 1958 the respective percentages of foodstuffs and finished goods (in total French exports to Germany) were 14·6 and 21·8, ten years later they stood at 21·4 and 41·4.[10] In other words, France was selling more foodstuffs, but the augmentation in the sale of industrial products had been much greater. This trend still continues; in 1970 almost exactly two thirds of French sales to Germany consisted of finished goods, the share of foodstuffs now being less than one fifth.[11] Too much should not be made of this, as German exports still showed a far greater concentration on finished products, which formed over four fifths of sales to France in the same year. But we should not overlook the fact that France is transforming itself with great and accelerating rapidity into a modern industrial state. The effects of this will be felt in her future trade, and perhaps in her whole relations with Germany.

Indeed, it is hard now to remember that German industrial superiority was openly feared as recently as 1967, when a newspaper article could carry the title *Marianne and the Wolf*, when it dealt with French apprehension about tariff reductions. The French were then allegedly scared of being eaten up.[12] Even in 1971 Pompidou spoke of German economic superiority, but added that he did not feel it would last. It would be premature to say that the events have shown this opinion to be correct, but undoubtedly the French economy appears set for long-term expansion. The country is now the world's third largest exporter and has enjoyed an annual growth rate of 5·9 per cent since 1960, compared to the 5 per cent figure for Germany. Despite lingering backwardness in the tertiary sector France is far better placed than her neighbour in the long run, at least in terms of GNP, due to demographic factors. By 1980 there will be a working force 12 per cent greater in the country than in 1968.[14] In Germany the population trends are currently markedly less favourable: in the few months of 1972 there was actually a surplus of deaths over births to the tune of 10,300.[15] Moreover France still has a larger proportion of its working population in agriculture; this presumably affords it the chance to increase its industrial labour force even more markedly than can the Federal Republic for the foreseeable future. The next decade will be interesting in the field of Franco-German trade relations.

Apart from direct commercial exchanges the question of an investment policy in the neighbouring country has been in the forefront of Franco-German economic links. By 1968 over 700 German enterprises had established a branch in France, the corresponding figure for French firms in Germany being some 400 implantations.[16] (Many other concerns are represented as well as having an actual branch of their own; in 1965 over 15,000 German enterprises had established some link in this matter.)[17] In 1966 alone 58 German businesses set up a French branch.[18] This sounds statistically impressive at first, but when comparisons are made with the investment record of other countries in both France and Germany, a better perspective is obtained. The number of French firms establishing subsidies in the Federal Republic in 1969 put that country only in third place among foreign countries in Germany; even the Netherlands, with a quarter of France's population, set up half as many firms as did the French.[19] At the end of 1970 total French investments in Germany put her in sixth place among foreign investors. The German stake in France at the same time amounted to a modest 2,125·8 million DM, which set the Federal Republic third among investors from abroad.[20] It seems fair to say that activity has lagged somewhat behind expectations insofar as investment in general is concerned. This appears still to be the case. In the first quarter of 1973 West German investments in France represented only a small part of those placed abroad in general. The Netherlands was the most favoured recipient in absolute terms, and even in Spain German activity was more marked than in France.

The high number of German subsidiaries in France is in any case explicable by the differing export pattern between the two countries, at least up to now. As the Germans have traditionally exported heavy machinery and equipment, they need branches on the spot in other countries to deal with installation and servicing. The French export structure consists rather more of foodstuffs or consumer goods, luxury or otherwise, which can be sold through the normal distribution outlets abroad.

Before we examine why investment has been relatively low, we should indicate briefly in what sectors of the partner's economy the other country has acquired an interest. The Germans in France have tended to show most activity in chemicals, electrical goods and electronics, the metal industry, machinery and food-stuffs (other than unprocessed food). It is interesting to note that the same has also been true of the French in the Federal Republic. The chemical industry has been the biggest magnet in both countries, accounting for one fifth of German firms' investments in France between 1952 and 1972.[21] In fact, the sectors in which both concentrate are more or less the same in which heavy US investments have been made, as they happen to be the growth areas.[22] The logical corollary of this seems to be that since the Americans obviously dispose of far more capital, both the French and the Germans are not likely to exercise any decisive voice in the partner's economy in the foreseeable future.

The modest scale of activity until now has been partially determined by political factors and partially simply by legal and cultural differences. As far as the latter are concerned, the sort of obstacles which German businessmen may find in France have been graphically described in one article.[23] Often the representative of his company cannot speak French, and is, in any case, less flexible in negotiations. The Frenchmen he encounters frequently adopt a 'laws are made to be broken' attitude which he finds incomprehensible. It is alleged that French firms with whom he deals will find excuses for delaying payments, just in order to do so. They admire German discipline and methods, sometimes without desiring to imitate them. Advertising is also said to give the Germans trouble, as the style is different in France, and is said to display more imagination.

The French for their part have maintained a low profile across the Rhine when setting up branches. This may originally have been connected with the poor reputation which their goods had in Germany until recently.[24] As a result, French firms tend to be relatively unknown, do not seek much publicity, and in general make a less definite impression than their German counterparts in France. Consequently they have not provoked the hostility which the German impact sometimes brings about in France. In 1967, for example, agriculturalists in the Charente region demonstrated against the acquisition of land by German firms. As this was mainly extreme left-wing in nature, however, it may have had an ideological rather than a strictly economic background.

The two governments play an obvious role in the whole question of establishing subsidiaries across the Rhine. It has been alleged that de Gaulle's attitude towards foreign investments in general frightened off many German companies when he was in office.[25] Whether this was true or not the present administration appears open to foreign business activity and indeed welcomes it.

This is also true at regional level, as can be seen for example from the efforts being made in Champagne to attract German industrial implantations. A new organisation (ARDELA) has been founded and a programme of publicity undertaken to this end. In the framework of a German Week at Rheims, bankers and industrialists from across the Rhine were given information about the success enjoyed already by German firms in the region Champagne-Ardenne. Equally, through the University of Rheims, attempts are being made to integrate economic with cultural links between the area and German-speaking countries. Because the region lies between Paris and Germany it has already welcomed many German subsidiaries. Furthermore, in ten years' time, because of present communications schemes, Rheims will be at the centre of a crossroads of *autoroutes*, facilitating export to Germany among other things. The joint action with the university to train German-speaking cadres will therefore not only assist in the implantation of German subsidiaries in the area, but also promote the sale of French goods across the Rhine. All this is a mixture of private enterprise and municipal and academic initiative and collaboration; unlike some French regions Champagne receives no government regional aid.[26]

Unhappily the picture of welcome and co-operation is not to be found everywhere. In order to illustrate the kind of troubles which joint activity or foreign investments can cause we shall take two examples, that of a region in France and of an industry in Germany. With these instances we hope to show the pitfalls of international economic collaboration, and how hard a foreign investment programme can sometimes turn out in practice, because of legal, cultural or political obstacles.

The region we shall consider in France is Alsace-Lorraine, bordering on Germany's western frontier. Historical factors have played a big part in determining economic development in the area, as many business leaders emigrated in 1871 when Bismarck's annexation took place. This prevented Alsace-Lorraine from benefiting completely from post-1871 expansion in Germany.[27] The autonomy crisis in the 1920s was followed by a kind of economic Maginot Line mentality in Paris, according to which development in the border areas would be dangerous, since anything constructed might be lost in time of war.[28] In the post-war years there was a textile crisis in the 1950s, which played a part in retarding regional progress in Alsace.[29] Communications are also relatively poor; it has even been said that Frenchmen travelling from Colmar to Strasbourg use German roads to make the journey. Moreover, Alsace-Lorraine faces Baden-Württemberg, one of the most heavily industrialised regions in the Federal Republic (183 workers per 1,000 population in 1964). This makes Alsace particularly conscious of its relatively slow growth. Whereas the number of persons employed in the secondary sector of the economy rose by 43 per cent in Baden-Württemberg between 1950 and 1960, the increase for Alsace was 6 per cent only.[30] The dynamism of its neighbour creates a psychological problem for Alsace, which otherwise is by no means the poorest French region. It could obviously have attracted industry from other parts of the country in the governmental decentralisation policy; when 380 firms left Paris for the provinces between 1962 and 1965, however, only five went to Alsace. One other firm, Simca, which chose that region itself, was ordered by the government to go to La Rochelle instead.[31]

As domestic concerns did not help, appeal was made to foreign ones. That did work, in some respects only too well. Between 1955 and 1967 over half the new jobs created in Alsace were provided by German firms;[32] there were basically three reasons for this drive. Firstly, there was plenty of labour, the cadres were bi-lingual and there was an added attraction in the geographical position, since the whole area is at the heart of the EEC. Lorraine equally appealed for German investment, partly because of France's withdrawal from NATO. For example, the departure of Canadian and US forces entailed a loss of 3,500 jobs in the *département* Meurthe-et-Moselle.[33]

Quite distinct from the mass arrival of German firms in the

border regions, the local inhabitants were re-orientated in another way as well, viz. the higher wages and salaries in the Federal Republic. When the EEC was founded the reverse was true, and a French visitor could be struck by the low rates of remuneration in Germany. Devaluation of the franc and revaluation of the mark have radically altered this situation. At Hagenau a Frenchman can earn 1,000 francs monthly at Siemens, but if he gets up earlier and goes to a Siemens factory over the Rhine he can get 1,000 marks (=1,600 francs). By the beginning of 1971 there were as many as 40,000 trans-frontier workers living in France and earning their daily bread in Germany, of whom 80 per cent were either Alsatians or Lorrainers, in equal proportions. It is interesting that when a French worker was asked why he chose to do this, he gave not merely higher wages, but better working conditions as reasons.[34] In Wissembourg half the working population was dependent on Germany in one way or another in 1971.[35]

It would have been surprising if all this development had not occasioned some fluttering in the dovecotes, both in Paris and locally. After all, we are speaking of a region where many people still speak German, and which was formally annexed to the Third Reich some thirty years ago. In particular, some circles in Paris wished to distinguish between national and international regional policies in the EEC. The drawing of Alsace into the German orbit, thus making the whole middle Rhine into one huge economic unit across existing frontiers seemed perilously close to an international solution, which would in effect present Alsace to Germany.[36] A peaceful economic conquest would be followed by a political one. By 1969 there was already talk of a joint Franco-German university at Strasbourg, and of making the bilingualism already inherent in the region official.[37] French political concern was expressed in a speech by a Cabinet Minister, M. Guichard, to the Franco-German Chamber of Commerce in November 1968. He drew attention to the imbalance in German industrial and commercial activity in France centred around Paris and the east. He outlined governmental policy as based on working through the Chambers of Commerce to establish more French firms in the frontier regions and so achieve a better balance. In early 1969 the press representative for Chambers of Commerce in South Baden, referring to Germans in Alsace, said that the French were by now attempting to put German investments on a kind of quota (*Kontingentierung*) basis. He was presumably referring to the office which the French set up in Frankfurt in early 1969 with the object of diverting investment to other regions. In February 1970 a French official invited the Germans to invest more in the country, but in all areas, not specifically in Alsace-Lorraine alone. A Gaullist deputy from Alsace somewhat emotively called on the government to build a sort of economic Maginot Line for the region in the same year.

We must not exaggerate the importance of the German economic penetration in Alsace, as it clearly represents no serious threat to Franco-German friendship, but it does illustrate how fraught with problems the establishment of subsidiaries can be. There is no intention in France at the moment of stopping German investment in Alsace; the government wishes to balance it by encouraging French firms.[38] The difficulty here is their reluctance to settle near the eastern frontier. The problem is likely to continue as Baden-Württemberg industry is so dynamic and the steel industry in Lorraine is having some difficulties due to reconstruction, with 12,000 jobs due to disappear by 1977. Hence, no doubt, the visit of M. Pompidou in April 1972, when he promised Lorrainers a better infrastructure. Incidentally, communications in the Lorraine-Saarland area have become the object of joint study, as suggested by Kiesinger in 1969. This collaboration confirms that the possibility of friction over the border regions certainly should not be exaggerated. But a handicap here is the very existence of better wages in Germany, which will last for the foreseeable future, because of the favourable exchange rate for the mark; this has produced the influx of frontier workers into Germany, and the consequent loss of skilled men to the French economy. A survey by the Chamber of Commerce in Metz revealed that of 3,655 workers employed in thirteen firms in 1969 no fewer than 887 were working over the frontier in the following year (including some in Luxembourg).[39] Germans have not always been slow to suggest that French industries in the region needed state protection because they were inefficient.[40] Similarly, the alleged backwardness of French education in training managerial staff has beer cited by German businessmen concerned with Alsace as a factor in holding back French competitiveness.[41] These are strong comments, but we have to remember that in the fifties the French appealed for German investment in the area, and then in some quarters turned sour when it came. Some degree of indignation in Germany is therefore understandable.

Sometimes it was the Germans who showed themselves sensitive to French economic activity in their country. The petroleum industry is an instance here. The two countries originally co-operated quite happily in the realm of petroleum refining and distribution; two French refineries aimed partly at the German market were opened near Strasbourg in 1963. A French company, Total, signed an agreement to create a huge network of service stations in Germany with a German firm. The French were very favourably placed, due to their supplies of oil from the Sahara. Trouble came six years later when Total bought a 30 per cent stake in a German coal and oil company, GBAG, through the Dresden Bank. Allegedly under political pressure from Bonn, however, the Germans backed out of the deal; the veto was felt keenly in France, all the more as Hoechst, the German chemical combine, had just bought into a French firm, with no French objections. However, as Germany was in a position to refine only about one quarter of its oil imports, the government wanted to regroup its own industry first, without necessarily being against French participation in principle.

The president of Total's group (CFP) visited Germany, but was disappointed; the ban still stood. Failure on the private enterprise level was followed by political pressure, apparently with some force. Evidently the French had over-reacted, and one German official in the Economics Ministry was quoted as telling the press that he would not designate the French initiative as gunboat policy, but that it had shocked those well-disposed towards France. Kiesinger then apparently promised to take the affair in hand himself. Eventually the GBAG shares went to a German firm and the French CFP got a long-term delivery contract in compensation. It was also awarded a subsidy, as Sahara oil was so dear. Even this compromise was attacked. Strauss was apparently against the subvention, as German public funds would be bolstering a French concern (1969 was an election year in the Federal Republic, hence the objection). Equally, the German oil industry was not keen on CFP oil for various technical reasons.

What makes the affair interesting is the political reaction in France and then the inevitable German answer, which generated an unusual degree of heat. Firstly, it was pointed out that the petroleum industry was already three quarters under foreign control, so that German reluctance to lose some of the remainder should have been understandable. Some circles also pointed to the irony of the French government bringing this kind of pressure, when a so-called French solution had been applied in the past to keep foreigners from gaining control over some sectors of French industry. All in all, the capacity of economic interests to bring about political ill-feeling was still alive, some six years after the 1963 treaty.

Nonetheless, a good deal of collaboration has been carried out, both at official and at unofficial level. It would be quite misleading to concentrate on those cases where friction has been engendered in Franco-German economic relations. A whole mechanism of bilateral co-operation has been set up by the two governments to facilitate commerce in every possible way. In 1965 a joint committee was installed to further industrial collaboration. The aim was to smooth over existing legal or bureaucratic difficulties inherent in bilateral relations in any field, especially in regard to investment in the neighbouring country. Sub-committees have been set up to deal with particular obstacles, for example one is concerned with the suppression of administrative problems. A manual of information (bilingual) has been issued to assist the businessmen in both countries to work together.[42] This kind of help is vital in a Europe still largely based on national custom, even industrially, where, for example, toothpaste comes in three different product-type categories in Britain, France and Germany. The 1965 committee was followed three years later by another, composed of civil servants and businessmen. As far as the composition of the latter was concerned, the stress was rather more on private enterprise. The Germans serving represented various industrial sectors, plus banking and the retail trade, French membership being similar. Among the new commission's duties were tax harmonisation, joint research, patents and legal problems: all this was to further investment and technical co-operation. Another step was taken in 1970 when the commission decided to set up joint bureaux at Paris and Cologne to further bilateral action by individual enterprises.

It should be made clear that however efficacious these joint groups are, they are by no means unique. An Anglo-German bilateral economic committee has been in existence since 1956, consisting of officials from various Ministries, who meet twice yearly.[43] On the other hand, it does seem as though Franco-German co-operation has gone somewhat further in degree if not in principle. As early as 1964 it was announced that the Vth

National Plan in France would take cognisance of German economic development in its preparation, and that joint talks to this effect would be held. It is doubtful if bilateral relations are that close between either France or Germany and a third country.

A further organisation which facilitates commercial exchanges is the Franco-German Chamber of Commerce. In 1971 this was extended from Paris to include a number of leading cities in the Federal Republic, to assist French businessmen trading there. The main branch in Paris continues to issue brochures and information leaflets designed to ease bilateral trade. Apart from information and legal/administrative assistance, a vital factor in international trade is credit facilities for exporters; this domain has not been neglected. A joint group has been in existence since 1963, meeting bi-annually, consisting of officials from both countries. It covers the whole range of the financial aspects involved in bilateral trade and investment, and complements the work of a similar, but multilateral, credit co-ordination committee at Brussels.[44] Investment has been aided legally as well as by advice and credit guarantee. In 1968 it was officially laid down that henceforth German shareholders in French companies would receive equal treatment with French nationals. As early as 1956, a joint accord relating to the taxation policy to be followed in both countries in regard to firms establishing subsidiaries across the Rhine was adopted. The Franco-German Chamber of Commerce also helps to smooth out problems for industry and commerce caused by lack of standardisation in the two countries.

Co-operation at official level has clearly aided the joint projects or agreements made between individual companies. These have been occasioned sometimes by private marketing or production needs, but the part played by the governments should not be overlooked, as the US challenge seems to suggest that a bigger scale of enterprise is required in Europe to make its firms competitive. As Giscard d'Estaing has pointed out, Europe needs more giants, as in 1966 over half of the world's 240 biggest enterprises were American.[45] Despite this, actual mergers have been few and far between on the Franco-German front; it is not hard to see why. A survey showed in 1964 that although nearly half of French firms questioned said that they would give preference to a German company if it came to joint action, 84 per cent admitted that co-operation was easier with the Americans, because of their facilities and experience.[46] Similar considerations have been in play on the

German side; collaboration was limited before 1970 as so many firms had already signed agreements with US companies.[47] As in the case of capital investment, the shadow of multinational (usually US based) organisation lies heavily across Franco-German bilateral accords. Legal and administrative complications are an additional factor inhibiting mergers and restricting agreements.

Of course, a good deal has been done in the way of farming consortia, nonetheless, or exchanging technical information, or simply making production or marketing agreements. The argument here is that this would have probably been more extensive without prior arrangements with American firms. It is obviously quite impossible to list all cases where there has been a bilateral agreement between individual companies, but we can point to the huge petrochemical complex which has arisen in the Saar-Lorraine area, where private firms from both countries are happily collaborating. Similarly, a Franco-German consortium has been formed to build diesel engine factories in Hungary. Retail links have been forged as between cheese producers in France and a distribution company in Germany. In respect of general sales, two big retail chains, Paridoc (France) and Gedelfi (Germany), found apparently that tastes in the two countries are often different, yet another hazard in international trade relations. But despite all official encouragement it remains the case that collaboration has been relatively slight between individual firms; one source gives 151 purely bilateral contracts as at 31 May 1969.[48] Franco-German industrial leaders and politicians have spoken repeatedly of the need for more joint efforts, and more investments across the Rhine, but results have so far failed to match exhortations.

Intimately connected with this problem is the question of purely technical collaboration, and again US dominance, as a result of which both France and Germany have a deficit in the balance of payments concerning licences, royalties, etc. Both countries pay more to acquire technical expertise than they earn by selling their own. France seems to be in decline as an inventive country. Over the time span 1957–63 its rate of three new patents yearly per 10,000 inhabitants placed it eighth on the list of world rankings.[49] By 1970 the situation had changed little; of the roughly 48,000 patents registered in France that year fewer than 30 per cent were of French provenance.[50] In terms of pure research France appears to be slipping relatively, if Nobel prize awards constitute any criterion. Between 1945 and 1970 Frenchmen received only four, compared to Germany's eleven. To put this into relief, Britain got twenty-four and the USA fifty-seven over the same period.[51] In the case of Germany, the 'brain drain' has contributed to the holding back of technical progress. A Volkswagen Foundation report gave the outflow of doctors, scientists and technologists from the Federal Republic to the USA as 5,600 for the period 1949–65.[52] The net result is a huge payments deficit for technical exchanges, which in 1970 amounted to 494 million francs for France in international transactions (excluding those with the overseas franc zone countries).[53] Germany has been even harder hit: in 1971 it paid out 1,483 million marks and received only 546 million marks in exchange.[54]

It is in this context that the two countries have carried out technological collaboration in recent years, much of which has been concerned with atomic research. There was a trilateral accord between France, West Germany and Italy regarding an isotope-separation centre in France in the late 1950s, with potential military significance. This, in France, was apparently partly an aftermath of the Suez affair. In 1963 Siemens signed an agreement with the French nuclear authorities, aiming at building a joint nuclear centre. Nothing much seems to have come from this collaboration, however, but two years later it was announced that a reactor would be constructed jointly at Grenoble. This project proved more fruitful and the high-flux reactor began operating in late 1971.

Various other projects have been mooted from time to time, such as the A300B Airbus, Franco-German participation in an international observatory, and some military armaments in collaboration. This has often met snags, as in the case of a joint transport aircraft which ran into internal opposition in Germany because of the sales campaign carried by Lockheed for the Hercules C.130 and perhaps also because of the relatively high cost of the joint plane.[55] In space research the story has been happier, and joint satellites have actually been launched. But the scale is obviously nothing compared with Soviet or US efforts, and it is hard not to feel again that in this field bilateralism is simply not enough. This is especially true when one considers that US technical knowhow is often acquired merely through the size of the enterprises, rather than by pure invention as such. The logical answer seems therefore to lie in a European solution to the technological deficit, rather than in joint action by two countries.

A number of large-scale projects concerned with communications have also been undertaken at bilateral level. The Moselle and the Rhine have often been the object of joint public works, concerned with barrages, canalisation, etc. In the case of the first-named river a joint commission was nominated in 1956, with another for the Rhine eight years later. For works of this nature bilateralism is obviously the most appropriate form of organisation.

Additionally, the two countries have worked together to give aid to the Third World. Needless to say, a joint committee meeting quarterly exists to co-ordinate these efforts created in 1963.[56] The Germans are not entirely disinterested in this matter; in 1967 the Federal Republic was contributing one third of the total to the European Development Fund, but its firms were being awarded only 9·1 per cent of resulting contracts.[57] Most work given out was in the form of building projects, where a country like France, with ties to its former colonies, had an obvious advantage. Co-operation with its neighbour provides German industry with useful outlets. It is not then surprising that joint assistance has usually gone to Africa, for instance common aid in building up a West African textile industry.[58] Other African schemes have included a fertiliser factory in Senegal and a whole industrial and harbour complex (Operation San Pedro) in the Ivory Coast. A Franco-German consortium has built an oil refinery in Teheran, and other projects have been executed in Latin America; these range from a factory in Mexico (with Italian participation) and technical aid to Peru. There has been recent discussion about synchronising assistance even more closely in future. There seems no reason to suppose that a joint approach of this kind is not fruitful, both in helping the less-developed countries and as a practical exercise in Franco-German relations.

Before we summarise economic links and their significance for Franco-German friendship we should mention briefly that on private initiative there has been a good deal of contact between businessmen, both great and small. There was a summit meeting of industrial leaders in 1965, and later the same year they met again to discuss the EEC and its problems. These encounters have become a regular occurrence, since the first ever post-war meeting in 1950.[59] Leaders of smaller-scale enterprises have also established close links with their opposite numbers. By 1963, joint talks were in progress at Munich on various common problems, such as vocational training, works councils and adaptation to technical progress. In the following year the president of the German national federation of artisans (*Handwerker*) announced its desire to set up closer links still between individual chambers in the two countries. These ties proved fruitful and in 1965 nearly half of all existing German chambers (twenty-one out of forty-five) had a link with one or more of the corresponding associations of the ninety French chambers; this was enabling them to harmonise their professional examinations, among other forms of collaboration.[60] Official contacts since 1965 between Alsace and Stuttgart have led to many joint discussions, especially between young artisans on both sides.

What effect does all this have on political relations between the two countries, and on national stereotypes? As far as the first are concerned, it would seem that politics have usually taken precedence over economics in international relations. After all, Franco-German trade was booming in the period before the First World War. It seems safe to say that had the political atmosphere not improved, the two countries would not be in the EEC today, so that the present state of their trade is a consequence of friendly relations rather than a cause. Nonetheless, the recent industrial expansion in France is beginning to impress German opinion. Nearly a quarter interrogated in one poll as to what the word 'France' evoked for them mentioned industry, frequently citing car production.[61] The French economic miracle will change its people's image in Germany.

We should not in any case over-estimate the interdependence of the two economies. True, in 1972 France was the Federal Republic's best customer but its purchases expressed as a proportion of Germany's national income amounted to only just over 2 per cent. Two years previously, French sales to Germany were under 3 per cent of its own internal production. In other words, both countries could, if necessary, live without the other in terms of commercial exchanges.

Secondly, insofar as technical co-operation is concerned, and the building of consortia to meet the US challenge, we have to ask whether bilateralism is enough. On the evidence to date we feel bound to answer no. Of course, bilateralism is better than nothing, but the real solution is undoubtedly to create European companies, as the two partners already know.[62] The problem lies in building up large-scale enterprises, not easy in a Europe where national tastes, laws and standards all differ widely. Existing agreements with US firms by individual national companies do not help to facilitate a European solution to the technology gap. But it is only fair to consider Franco-German collaboration as a pioneer approach to the matter. In this respect, bilateralism can be seen as a stage towards multilateralism, rather than as an obstacle to it.

Thirdly, what is the future of Franco-German trade? There seems no doubt that the two economies are coming to resemble one another in terms of the trade pattern between them. French exports are increasingly composed of finished products, rather than merely of luxury goods or foodstuffs as formerly. This is bound in with the rapid transformation of the French economic scene in the last fifteen or so years; after the war the Germans had the chance of starting from their 'year zero' with new factories and equipment, but now it is the French who are seemingly modernising most rapidly; this is especially true of sectors such as chemicals and machinery where the Germans have had the advantage up to now.[63] This is not to say that they will necessarily overhaul the Germans completely, but it seems fairly safe to predict that by 1980 the gap between the two GNPs is likely to be smaller than it now is, as French manpower reserves are so much greater. This will not in itself transform Franco-German relations, but it will clearly affect them to some extent at least. A final note of caution needs to be sounded, however. We are speaking of a relatively better performance by the French in recent years, but there is still a huge gap to bridge. In 1970 West Germany's total GNP (682·8 billion DM) was vastly greater than France's at 820 billion francs, which at current exchange rates equalled only about 70 per cent of the German figure.

Before leaving the subject of trade relations we should point out again that there are two Germanies. In 1973 France concluded a long-term trade and technical pact with the GDR. It had been, the previous year, the third largest purchaser of East German goods among the Western powers, and its second greatest supplier. There is no reason, however, to suppose that augmented trade between the two will damage relations with West Germany.

Notes

1   *Correspondance*, no. 7, 27 July 1962, p 7.
2   Dresdner Bank Report, July 1963.
3   *Die Welt*, 9 Mar. 1963.
4   *Les échanges commerciaux entre la République Fédérale et la France*, Paris, Centre d'Etudes de Politique Etrangère, 1966, p 1.
5   For the survey see *Problèmes Economiques*, Paris, Institut national de la statistique et des études économiques, no. 934, 23 Nov. 1965, pp 1–7. Henceforth 'PE' will designate publications in this series.
6   *Statistisches Jahrbuch*, 1972, Statistisches Bundesamt Stuttgart/Mainz, W. Kohlhammer Verlag, p 305.
7   *Frankfurter Allgemeine Zeitung*, 28 Oct. 1971.
8   *Correspondance*, no. 191, 15 July 1971, p 20.
9   G. Ziebura, *Die deutsch-französischen Beziehungen seit 1945: Mythen und Realitäten*, Stuttgart, Neske, 1970, p 146.
10 *Les échanges* etc., op. cit., p 13 for 1958 statistics; Ziebura, op. cit., p 147 for 1968.
11 *Frankreich: Wirtschaft in Zahlen 1970*, Bundesstelle für Aussenhandels-information, Cologne, Sept. 1971, p 70.
12 *Die Zeit*, 6 Oct. 1967.
13 'Une comparaison des potentiels socio-économiques français et allemands', PE, no. 1323, 23 May 1973, p 13.
14 'Un point de vue allemand sur les possibilités de l'industrie française', PE, no. 1262, 8 Mar. 1972, pp 17*f*.
15 PE, no. 1323, op. cit., p 15.
16 *La coopération franco-allemande*, p 62.
17 *Documents*, nos 4–5, 1965, pp 192*f*.
18 *Correspondance*, no. 111, 30 June 1967, p 11.
19 PE, no. 1166, 7 May 1970, 'Les investissements directs étrangers en République Fédérale d'Allemagne', p 23.
20 PE, no. 1240, 7 July 1971, 'Bilan des investissements directs allemands à l'étranger et étrangers en Allemagne', p 11.
21 *Correspondance*, no. 215, 1 Dec. 1972, p 14.
22 See PE, no. 1166, 7 May 1970, op. cit., p 21.
23 K. W. Herterich, 'Les investissements allemands en France', *Documents*, Mar./Apr. 1972, pp 38*ff*.
24 This aversion is alleged in the *Frankfurter Allgemeine Zeitung*, 12 Nov. 1966.
25 *Die Zeit*, 6 Oct. 1967.
26 Information on this drive was supplied by M. Burguet, Secretary, Rheims Chamber of Commerce, and M. Flahault of Groupe Régions du Futur, undertaking the publicity at Paris, in personal interviews.
27 This is not to deny that some expansion, especially in textiles, took place. See M. Anderson, 'Regional identity and political change', *Political Studies*, vol XX, no. 1, 1972.
28 E. Juillard, 'L'Alsace va-t-elle basculer dans l'orbite économique allemande?' *Documents*, July/Aug. 1969, p 84.

29 J.-P. Sicre, 'Les allemands à la conquête de l'Alsace', *Documents*, July/ Aug. 1969, p 98.
30 E. Juillard, 'Un problème de déséquilibre économique sur le Rhin moyen', Brno, *Studia Geographica*, 20, 1971, p 227.
31 Sicre, op. cit., pp 101*f.*
32 'Investissements allemands dans l'est français', *Documents*, July/Aug. 1969, p 66.
33 *Frankfurter Allgemeine Zeitung*, 15 Aug. 1966.
34 *Die Zeit*, 21 Apr. 1972.
35 PE, no. 1206, 11 Feb. 1971, 'Les problèmes économiques des régions frontières à l'interieur du Marché Commun', p 13.
36 See 'Investissements allemands', op. cit., p 65, and Sicre, op. cit., pp 103*f.*
37 Juillard, 'L'Alsace va-t-elle basculer', etc., op. cit., p 77.
38 As pointed out by Couve de Murville in an interview in 1969, *Documents*, July/Aug. 1969, pp 105*f.*
39 *Correspondance*, no. 166, 15 Apr. 1970, p 21.
40 See *Die Zeit*, 25 Apr. 1969.
41 Sicre, op. cit., pp 95*f.*
42 *La coopération franco-allemande*, p 60.
43 *Englische Rundschau*, 7 Mar. 1963, reporting the fifteenth encounter.
44 *La coopération*, op. cit., pp 65*f.*
45 Giscard d'Estaing, 'Coopération et fusion des entreprises françaises et allemandes', *Politique Etrangère*, no. 2, 1966, p 140.
46 *Correspondance*, no. 58, 15 Dec. 1964, p 11.
47 J. Vernant, 'Perspectives franco-allemandes', *Politique Etrangère*, no. 1, 1967, p 25.
48 *La réalité*, vol I, p 206*f* for a fuller analysis.
49 *Le Monde*, 10–11 May 1964.
50 PE, no. 1279, 5 July 1972, 'La balance française des échanges techniques', p 17.
51 Ibid., p 17.
52 R. Gerwin, 'L'exode des cerveaux', *Documents*, Mar./Apr. 1968.
53 PE, no. 1279, op. cit., p 17.
54 *Handelsblatt*, 17 May 1972.
55 *Le Monde*, 12 Oct. 1963.
56 'Les organes bilatéraux des relations économiques franco-allemandes', Centre d'Etudes de Politique Etrangère, Paris, 1966, pp 5*f.*
57 *Financial Times*, 16 May 1967.
58 W. Handke, 'Deutschland und Frankreich in der Entwicklungshilfe', *Aussenpolitik*, June 1967, p 351.
59 *La coopération*, op. cit., p 62.
60 *Correspondance*, no. 73, 5 Sept. 1965, p 17.
61 Ibid., no. 221, 20 Apr. 1973, p 9.
62 The joint economic Commission was discussing this in 1968, *Neue Zürcher Zeitung*, 2 Oct. 1968.
63 See R. von Lilienstern, 'Der französische Markt und die deutsche Industrie', *Kleiner Almanach der Marktforschung*, Bielefeld, Oct. 1970, p 61.

Chapter 6

Relations Between the Workers in Both Countries

Apart from the contacts made by the employers of France and Germany, relations have been strengthened at another level also, that of the organised working class and its leaders, young or old. The instrument employed has usually been the trade union. It would be optimistic to suppose that the associations in both countries were similar; differences of history, and therefore of structure and attitude, complicate this example of Franco-German relations as they do in other fields of endeavour. One statistic is revealing in this connection. In 1964 the French economy lost some $2\frac{1}{2}$ million working days by industrial action; the Germans in the same year forfeited less than 17,000.[1] Clearly we are dealing with two differing industrial scenes, and to set the background for bilateral contacts we should first describe briefly how these divergences arose.

As far as the Federal Republic is concerned, trade unions, having ceased to exist from 1933 onwards (in any normal sense of the phrase 'trade union'), were re-constituted post-1945. Partly as a result of Allied insistence they were based henceforth on the individual sector of the economy, rather than on the worker's craft, as in Britain. So the whole reformed system in Germany is simple and functional, with only sixteen associations in all; these are all members of one federation, *Deutscher Gewerkschaftsbund* (DGB), which is neither denominational in the religious sense nor tied to any one political party. However, a minority of the DGB, with memories of pre-1933 Catholic unions, did break away in 1955 to found its own movement (CGB). Additionally there is a union for white-collar workers (DAG). As the whole workers' front is relatively unified the DGB has a large-scale membership amounting in 1970 to over six million.[2] This is by far the lion's share of enrolled workers, although in recent years it has declined slightly.[3]

The situation in France is markedly different. The first ever Confederation to be formed was Catholic-based, founded in 1887;[4] individual *syndicats* had existed long before then. Eight years later saw the start of the *Confédération Générale du Travail* (CGT), representative of differing political tendencies all under the same roof; in particular both Proudhonists and Marxists were in the federation together. Pluralism was intensified in 1919 when the scission between Socialists and Communists produced two corresponding workers' movements (the CGT and CGTU). The breach was temporarily repaired with a fusion in 1936, but in 1947 the CGT split again when the CGT-*Force Ouvrière* was founded. The picture is rendered more pluralistic still by a cleavage in the Catholic ranks which has given rise to one main association (CFDT), no longer really denominational, and a smaller one called CFTC *maintenue*. In sum, there is a Communist association, a Socialist one, *Force Ouvrière* (FO), and two other unions, (one denominational), which do not necessarily share the same political opinions. Figures for membership seem open to question, as different sources give varying statistics. The CGT's claim to 2,300,000 members has been contested, and we have been told that the real figure is about 1,750,000. Before the scission in the Catholic ranks some 700,000 workers were enrolled, and FO has about 800,000.[5] All in all, there are probably fewer than four million trade unionists in France, and their loyalties are divided, both in a political and in a religious sense. This obviously vitiates their effectiveness as pressure-groups. To take one example, workers in the electricity industry are grouped in three different federations, 55 per cent in the CGT, 17 per cent in the CFDT, while FO has 13 per cent.[6] Relations have been strained as a consequence of ideological divergence and of the bitterness which it engendered in the past. It would not be unfair to say that France presents a picture of division among workers' associations in comparison with Germany.

This is the first obstacle in Franco-German relations at union level. Secondly, there is the problem of divergent attitudes. Living standards in Germany are high; workers' net weekly earnings in 1972 were just over double those of ten years previously, the cost of living having risen less than 40 per cent. It may well also be that lack of militancy is to some extent inherent in German workers, at least in the present generation: the wage-restraint policy of the Third Reich may have played some part in this, as may memories of the terrible 1923 inflation, plus the post-1945 struggle for survival. But whatever the origins of the German attitude, it certainly exists. In 1952 two young Frenchmen who spent some time at a Mercedes factory were impressed by the discipline, and by the fact that the workers were not apparently envious of their bosses' greater wealth.[8] DGB's post-war demands have certainly been anything but revolutionary: in 1965 its pro-grammes consisted essentially in trying to obtain a better deal under capitalism, rather than in advocating a radical change in the existing economic structure. It is probably true to say that German workers tend to feel no particular opposition to the state as such, in which they consider they also have a place. Some political confrontations between unions and government have occurred since 1945, but on a limited scale.

Moreover in 1962 the DGB's newly-elected President, Ludwig Rosenberg, had been in exile in Britain after 1933 and was allegedly somewhat orientated towards that country. He was by political conviction reformist and not revolutionary. No doubt the fact that the DGB possesses considerable wealth of its own also determines its attitudes, and choice of leaders. Membership dues are high and the federation does not have to subsidise any political movement (there are state subventions for leading parties in Germany).[9] An additional point is that what is collected is not usually given out again in strike pay. Not surprisingly, German unions are rich. In 1960, the DGB itself (which collects 10 per cent of individual union receipts) had an income of 40 million marks; the metalworkers' union alone had a capital of 300 million marks in 1964.[10] Among union properties are the fourth largest bank in Germany, a housing construction trust, 150,000 dwellings themselves, and nine thousand retail outlets.[11] Trade unionism has a large stake in German capitalism, which must affect its view of society as a whole, and of management/labour relations.

As an illustration we may take worker-participation in German industry (*Mitbestimmung*), the process by which union representa-tives are given places on the management board of individual enterprises (this applies to offices of public administration as well as to private industry and commerce). This has become so much a part of the German scene that the whole concept has a regular journal devoted to its activities in practice. There seems little doubt that the delegation of responsibility by management to workers themselves, as far as possible, has aided production in the Federal Republic[12] (although workers actually elected to management committees simply come to be seen as part of management itself in a short time). This whole system, however, is rejected by many French unionists, who tend to see the Germans as associates of capitalism for accepting it. We are not suggesting here that the French are unique in this; Herr Vetter, the DGB president, has admitted that unions in other countries look on *Mitbestimmung* 'like the devil on holy water'.[13] The point that we are making is quite simply that such a divergence of views does not make collaboration easy at bilateral level. This becomes even clearer when one contrasts participation with the French concept of worker-control (*autogestion*), and the general anti-capitalist tone of syndicalism in France. This tradition firmly rejects the idea that participation can be anything but an illusion, and describes it simply as the acceptance of capitalism. This is not merely the viewpoint of the CGT; the CFDT subscribes to it with equal force. Much of the French movement is committed firmly to the concepts of either *autogestion* or public ownership. We must be careful, however, not to generalise too widely. There are considerable divergences of view between various federations, as well as within their own ranks, on this question. FO, for example, is firmly opposed to *autogestion* and demands rather a programme of selective nationalisation. Officially it holds workers' control to be incompatible with a planned economy. Moreover, some younger members of the DGB at its last annual conference seemed to be moving away from *cogestion* towards workers' control. Under these circumstances it would be unwise to conclude that views on the whole subject are either unified or definitively decided in either country, although the general tendency in France is still to reject *cogestion*. Nonetheless, this is still a matter for lively debate, for example in the CGT where the whole issue of *co-* versus *autogestion* is still under discussion.[14]

Ideological divergences are accompanied by those in respect of wealth. French unions are relatively poor by comparison with the DGB; limited membership is obviously the chief factor in the difference, plus losses through strikes. There appear to be discrepancies between numbers officially enrolled and actual payments, so that even the theoretically possible income is not attained.[15] Thus financially there is little comparison between French and German unions, with the former not in possession of an equivalent share of their country's economy.

Despite historical, structural and financial differences, however, both movements are in the final analysis the representatives of organised labour in their respective countries, and this fact has enabled barriers to be surmounted. There is nothing particularly new about this; even before the 1914–18 war there were contacts; the militants in Alsace-Lorraine sometimes served as inter-mediaries, the liaison in this area being continued in the 1920s.[16] After the Second World War DGB established links with the FO in the framework of their common membership of the International Confederation of Free Trade Unions; Léon Jouhaux of the FO played a leading role in this *rapprochement*.[17]

On the German side the immediate post-war contacts were aided by unionists such as Albert Preuss, who had been a political refugee in France since 1935. His personal friendship with French union representatives enabled contacts to be renewed at what was clearly still a difficult time for Franco-German relations. By 1948 the atmosphere had sufficiently improved to enable the DGB to set up its own bureau in Paris; this was only partly to help in contacts with French unions, the other reason being the need to look after the interests of German workers in France, of which more later.[18]

Ideological divergencies come inevitably to the forefront in determining with which French movements the DGB has subsequently co-operated most closely. In fact, the order seems to have been closest relationship with FO, rather less contact with CFDT or CFTC *maintenue* and comparatively little with the CGT. These are generalisations, as the DGB, with a membership of over six millions, comprehends a wide range of political views at least at rank and file level. The fact that some West German trade unionists attended a CGT congress in 1965 (according to *L'Humanité*) should not be taken to mean that this represents the official DGB line.[19]

Relations with the FO have been cordial, aided by common membership of the so-called 'free' unions in Western Europe (of which Rosenberg was elected president in 1964). The DGB bureau in Paris has facilitated contacts at bilateral level, although inevitably the existence of structural and financial differences weighs somewhat on the relationship. Nonetheless, there has been a constant exchange of views and information at confederation level, including the presence of fraternal delegates from each movement at the other's meetings. At a lower echelon there have been exchange visits between young leaders, limited in extent but nevertheless valuable. Yet again these have tended to be one-sided quantitatively. In 1963, for example, over twice as many Germans went to France as French to Germany (342 against 147).[20] At the meetings of the European 'free' unions both organisations have often adopted a common approach to EEC problems, which helps to create bonds between them. Both the FO and the DGB have advocated European integration, for example. Bilateral discussions have continued to take place over current European affairs, as well as those at European union level, for example on the issue of immigrant workers in both countries.

Incidentally, the negative attitude of the CGT towards the Common Market has impeded links between it and the DGB, as Herr Vetter made clear in 1970. A CGT leader, M. Krasucki, in reply said that his union wanted a closer relationship with the DGB but admitted that differences existed over some questions, including the Common Market.[21] In this connection it should be remembered that one member of the European Commission at Brussels, Herr Haferkamp, is himself a former DGB executive. This must make it difficult for the federation to work with any movement which is formally committed to opposition to the EEC.

Unlike the FO, the Catholic unions in France, CFDT and CFTC *maintenue*, are not members of the 'free unions' in Europe, which virtually means the social-democratic ones: the Catholic unions have their own international federation. This naturally makes it more difficult for the DGB to collaborate with them. Some contact has been established: for instance when a joint conference was held in Paris in 1953 between the FO and the DGB, the CFTC sent representatives to discuss matters like participation, the Schumann Plan, etc. and to exchange information over each one's own respective organisations.[22] Since then, however, contacts seem to have been slight, although there are some within the framework of such European institutions as the ECSC, where both federations have representatives.

A more promising partner for the Catholic unions in France is obviously their denominational counterpart, the CGB.[23] Both these federations were members of the European Christian trades union federation.[24] Nonetheless the two French unions have not succeeded in building the same relationship with the CGB as that which obtains in respect of the FO-DGB. There have been mutual exchanges of information, and in October 1965 the CFTC *maintenue* expressed a desire at its annual conference to forge closer links with the CGB, among others. But up to now contacts have tended to be at the level of individual unions, rather than between the federations as such; this has been true, for example, of the miners in the Saar and neighbouring Lorraine.[25]

Finally, there have been some bonds created between the two white-collar federations DAG in Germany and CGC in France. As early as 1953 discussions were held jointly on such matters as social services at factory level, participation and vocational training.[26]

Apart from contacts at top federation level there have been a number at that of the individual unions; in this respect the metalworkers on both sides of the frontier have been especially active. Here again differences in size pose a certain problem, as in 1965 the German IG *Metall* had nearly two million members, the French metalworkers (divided among CGT, FO and CFDT) about one ninth of that number.[27] The International Federation of Metalworkers (FIOM) has acted as an intermediary in facilitating contacts, however, which have taken place at union leadership level. Equally, contacts have been made between unionists in individual factories. Two examples here are those between Nord-Aviation and Bolkow, and those between Volkswagen and Renault.[28] There have been a number of exchanges between young metalworkers in both countries as well; young French unionists have been invited to IG *Metall* seminars.[29] Relations have now gone beyond the bilateral level with the formation of a European federation (to which no French Communists were invited). As well as the metalworkers, some other trades have established links with their counterparts across the Rhine at the individual union or factory level. This is true even of CGT members, whose local organisation for printing operatives in Alsace has put itself in touch with its opposite numbers in Baden.[30] Even at the level of capitalist enterprise the DGB has collaborated on a project in France, when its own bank went into association with a financial concern helping to develop the economy of Lorraine.[31]

Thus not all contacts involving unions have necessarily been in an inter-union framework. Sometimes adult education organisations have played a part in bringing workers, young or old, together. The Friedrich-Ebert Foundation has organised a number of seminars and conferences via its offices in Saarbrücken, near the frontier, for workers from both countries. Themes discussed have included vocational training at work, participation, the quality of life, the future of the craftsman in an industrial society, and trade unions and the consumer.[32] That these subjects can be discussed at all is a contribution to adult education in itself, but that they should be handled bilaterally seems to afford them a wider dimension still, as the current problems of our society are placed in an international context. This kind of event undoubtedly fills a gap in the 1963 treaty, with its emphasis on youth, academic and technical collaboration, none of which is strictly describable as furthering contacts among workers as such.

The unions themselves in both countries are alive to the question of adult education, and the need to exchange young workers and young trade unionist leaders. On both sides of the Rhine the federations have undertaken a good deal of education off their own bat, and whole organisational structures have been erected accordingly. Collaboration between the organs of popular culture in both countries preceded the 1963 treaty. As long as eleven years previously a study group of French experts had been set up to aid their German counterparts in the domain of bilateral contacts in adult education.[33] Nonetheless it has to be accepted that the treaty has enormously assisted by making OFAJ funds available to subsidise youth encounters and courses run jointly for younger trade unionists.

The closest collaboration in this field has probably been that between the DGB/adult educational organisation 'Work and Life' (*Arbeit und Leben*) and various French groups, notably the *Fédération Nationale Leo Lagrange* (FLL). In 1970 alone the last-named organised fifty-eight different functions with 'Work and Life' concerning youth contacts.[34] Other groups with whom the German office has worked include *Culture et Liberté*, which itself works closely with the FO and CFDT in France. Also important as partners are *Centre de Coopération Culturelle et Sociale* and the *Union des Foyers des Jeunes Travailleurs*. With all its collaborators 'Work and Life' carried out ninety-eight events in 1970, mostly in France, with Germans again being numerically preponderant. The programme of activities was varied, including language courses, seminars, and 'information journeys'. It should be made clear that 'Work and Life' has a regional structure, so that the responsibility for the meetings is not undertaken at national level. Some German regions seem to have been more active than others in arranging encounters in France, for example North-Rhine-Westphalia. Altogether, nearly two thousand young people participated in events of this nature backed by OFAJ money in 1970. Individual unions, such as IG *Metall*, have helped in the execution of these encounters, as well as the DGB as such. A further instance would be that of the German Postal Union, which aided eleven joint functions of one kind or another in the same year.

'Work and Life' has itself been represented on the Permanent Commission of the OFAJ since 1969, as have the DGB, the DAG, *Culture et Liberté* and the French trade unions FO and CFDT. In November 1970 a week-long seminar was carried out in Düsseldorf, by 'Work and Life', to which the French organisations sent representatives, the theme being 'Democratisation in the economy and society'. Needless to say, participation was again one of the subjects jointly discussed. Further events of this nature are being planned, so that practical experiences gained in both countries can be jointly analysed and evaluated, with a view to co-ordination of practice, and the improvement of conditions for the workers, as well as greater efficiency at factory level as such.

The joint seminar is probably the most effective means of collaboration in the educational field for young trade unionists. Here FLL is by far the most important partner for 'Work and Life'. These encounters have now been divided into three categories. The basis of the first is the participant's job itself, so that advantage can be taken on both sides of research and practical experiments which have been carried out in the other country. In the second category the workers may have different occupations, so that a certain theme is selected which can be discussed jointly. The third type of seminar is concerned with the education of youth leaders themselves, insofar as management and organisation is concerned. The details of the encounters of all three kinds to be held in France in 1970 were hammered out at a joint FLL/'Work and Life' leaders' meeting early that year in Mainz. The subjects dealt with included, in 1970, youth co-operation, the 1970s, and the probable developments in society which they would bring, youth problems both at work and during their leisure time, automation, and even the new foreign policy of the German government.[35]

It is hard not to feel that themes of this nature discussed in common must lead to a greater understanding on both sides of the problems of the other, as well as being of mutual benefit, in the sense that the organisation or experiments made in one country can be communicated to the other. It is then all the more regrettable that the numbers of participants are so limited; in 1970 only just over two thousand German young people took part. On the other hand, as those who do are often potential leaders of either unions or youth associations, quantitative deficiencies are perhaps redressed by the advantages of quality inherent in these exchanges of views.

There have been plenty of other contacts between the younger members of the working class in both countries apart from in the framework of adult educational programmes. As early as 1952 French metalworker apprentices visited Solingen factories and discussed participation among other things.[36] Similarly in 1961 a mixed group of French students and young union leaders went to Mannheim on the initiative of Catholic leaders. Here the background to the visit was primarily religious, but this did not stop current questions of society in the West being jointly discussed. These included trade union structures, the problem of under-developed countries, adolescent education, and inevitably worker participation. The French youngsters were taken on a tour of the poorer districts, and discussed the question of subsidised housing for workers.[37] Thus, in a framework of common religious belief, social problems contributed to the dialogue between French and German youth.

Obviously political creeds can also provide the basis of contact. In April 1965 the French branch of the European Union of Young Democrats, dedicated among others to the belief in European integration, arranged a joint discussion between young Franco-German youth leaders in Paris. Virtually all the German federations sent representatives, including even those of farm organisations and the employers' federation. The French list was similar, including both CFTC and FO.[38] Capital investment in Europe, and the workers' share in it, was discussed, including the role of foreign, i.e. extra-European, investments. The second session was devoted to migration by workers inside West Europe, and the problems it presents. In addition the divergences in the various nation-states concerning social legislation were noted, and the hope was expressed that such variations should disappear in the relatively near future. Economic planning provided the subject-matter of the third session, where the Germans defended participation. On the French side there was a desire to see a more democratic control of industry, which was linked with worker participation, but evidently in the sense of *autogestion* rather than the German concept of *cogestion*.

The whole conference was an excellent example of bilateralism, firstly, because important social, political and economic problems were jointly handled, and secondly, because it illustrated the difficulty inherent in bringing together two sets of persons who have grown up in different cultures. It is obviously wholly to the good that both sides should hear the other's point of view; indeed there could never be integration in Europe unless that happened. But the limits to comprehension were revealed as soon as the theme 'participation' arrived. The differing attitudes to it were quite plainly manifested. Because the German employers and trade unionists had to work together after 'year zero' to put Germany back on its feet, they have become accustomed to collaboration. This has not applied in France where the whole background to trade unionism has been different. As a sample of this divergent mental approach we offer the following experience. A young German schoolteacher on exchange in France examined the notebook of one of her class, in a school where elected pupils had the right to sit on a committee with teachers and parents (*Conseil d'Administration*). The book contained a leaflet which pupils had circulated, containing a classic French conjugation of the verb *participer*: *je participe, tu participes, il participe, nous participons, vous participez, 'ils' profitent.*[39] We are not trying to suggest from this one example that the French are all automatically against collaboration in industry or administraion, still less that all Germans are equally for it. We merely wish to say that there is a different tradition on one side of the Rhine from that prevailing on the other. Therefore, even when all due praise has been lavished on bilateral contacts, this divergence remains as a problem, one which can be resolved no doubt in time, but the existence of which must be taken into account when assessing Franco-German *rapprochement*. As we have said, participation has been the order of the day at endless Franco-German seminars, etc., but many French workers in the final analysis are still opposed to the German conception. There is a limit to mutual comprehension which history has created, and which only the passage of time can erase.

Incidentally, OFAJ funds have enabled the Young Democrats to continue as a forum in bilateral unionist encounters. In October 1966, for example, there was another Paris meeting, with DGB and FO representatives present. Unionism in the light of European integration was dealt with, and the harmonisation of purely national laws.[40] Contacts have also taken place between the youth leaders of different political parties, but here again organisational divergences have proved to be an obstacle. The upper age-limit for Young Socialists in Germany is thirty-five, but for the Young Socialist Federation in France only twenty-five. This discrepancy in criteria for the word 'young' does not facilitate the forging of links. Incidentally, the individual trade sometimes serves as an instrument in promoting encounters. Young printers in Strasbourg and Karlsruhe arranged a meeting in 1971 through their local branches.[41]

Just as not all workers' contacts have necessarily been in an inter-union setting, so the educational activities, especially of the DGB in France, have not been confined to union members. On many occasions it has carried out programmes of seminars and study-visits embracing persons from various walks of life. Between the Paris bureau's foundation in 1948 and 1967, as many as 38,500 people participated in such activities, including not merely union representatives, but also teachers, parliamentarians, students, representatives of churches and political organisations, and those from trade and the press. When all types of function for the same time-span are taken into account, the attendance in France by either Frenchmen or domiciled Germans amounted to not less than 450,000.[42] These events could take place on such a scale quite obviously only through the closest co-operation with municipal authorities and other French organisations. The claim has been made that apart from all activities the DGB bureau has often assisted in bringing about twin towning relationships. The themes of most conferences, lectures, etc. have been either bilateral or European. As financial patron the DGB itself spent over $2\frac{1}{2}$ million DM over the twenty-year period. From 1959 the German Foreign Office gave a subsidy, at first 25,000 DM yearly, which by 1967 had increased to 80,000 DM. This is nothing more than a plain recognition of what the DGB is doing in France for

Franco-German friendship, not merely in respect of unionism. It would scarcely be an exaggeration to call its work a reinforcement of foreign policy: indeed, this aspect was clearly visible even in the post-war years, when bilateral union contacts preceded an official foreign policy, just as did culture in another area.

Since 1967 the programmes have continued on a considerable scale, including even cultural events in the old-fashioned sense. Altogether in 1972, the latest year for which we have information, 337 events were arranged and attended by almost fifty thousand persons.[43] Themes included *Mitbestimmung*, educational reforms, vocational training and re-training, the development and harmonisation of European social policies. Not only union representatives but *Bundestag* deputies, officials from the EEC and municipal councillors have been among the speakers, at meetings including both adults and young people. Films have also been shown. As reports for earlier years show a similar pattern, it can be seen quite clearly that to a certain extent the DGB in France complements the work of the Goethe Institutes and their national cultural policy. There is thus another aspect to the DGB over and above the purely inter-union contacts which it assists.

As we have said, French and German unions have also been able to establish some contacts via the European federations, three in number, of which they are members. Apart from the purely bilateral exchanges in this framework, they have also been able to take part in multilateral actions at European level. These must obviously have had some influence on bilateral contacts in themselves, since participation in joint campaigns creates a feeling of solidarity. For example, both French and German unions condemned de Gaulle's attitude towards Britain and advocated an EEC open to democratic countries only. This surely helped to underline that the feelings and beliefs of various organisations need not be tied to the policy of their government, as anyone wedded to the concept of a national stereotype might suppose. Similarly, the discussion of such subjects as wages policy, working hours, the equalisation of rights for manual and white-collar workers, equal pay for women, etc. at European level, as frequently happens, must assist Franco-German solidarity as well.

This leads us on to the question of multilateralism in trade union organisation, as opposed merely to joint action between two countries. There seem to us to be two compelling reasons why the first choice is preferable to the second in contemporary

Europe. Firstly, union 'Europeanisation' is the logical corollary to the EEC, and efforts at political and economic co-ordination between nation-states, as one German unionist has indicated.[44] It is therefore understandable that national unions acting together at European level should produce a joint programme of demands including the right to union representation on the various EEC directing bodies. Europe obviously does not exist solely for politicians or employers.

Secondly, the shadow of the multinational firm falls heavily, and increasingly, across the whole industrial scene in the West. One international trade union official has predicted that by 1980 some two hundred companies will control three quarters of the West's capital assets.[45] These groupings enjoy many advantages denied to the unions, for example the use of tax havens and the capacity to switch production from one country to another. Again, the logical solution for the unions to multinationals is multinational union policies, even if the workers' associations do not actually integrate totally. One obstacle here is clearly the political-denominational split in the European federations, which in itself reflects national disunities.

Nevertheless, joint action has been undertaken against international companies. The policy of redundancy and short-time working adopted by Philips International (with 200,000 employees in Western Europe) was jointly opposed by the EEC unions, who appointed a Dutch representative as their common negotiator. In 1970 the same company was approached by a joint delegation, led by a German, in respect of international wage contracts; a similar case has been reported for Brown-Boveri. Sometimes action has been trilateral rather than wholly international; French, German and Italian unionists at Michelin have collaborated in a programme of joint demands. The CFDT and the DGB worked together in respect of the Clermont-Ferrand enterprise and at Cuneo the CFDT co-operated with an Italian federation. We can certainly expect this form of approach to multiply. The conclusion to be drawn from it as far as this work is concerned is that bilateralism at union level has already been overtaken by events.

This does not necessarily imply that there is no longer any need for Franco-German union, or young trade unionist, contacts. Here we must clearly distinguish between certain categories of endeavour. The answer to the multinational firm is certainly multinational union co-ordination, if not integration. But the sort of seminars which we have described here at bilateral level need not disappear, since they contribute to a wholly different aspect of contemporary affairs, namely Franco-German reconciliation. Between unions as industrial organisations and unions as agents of *rapprochement* there is a substantial difference. Because bilateral action is superfluous for one aspect of workers' associations does not imply that it is for another.

The real problem however remains that of differing structures in the two countries, and above all in differing attitudes to worker control and industrial action. In a sense the French currently have greater difficulties than the Germans, as France is really now becoming a modern capitalist country based on large-scale industrial concerns, a state of affairs long familiar in Britain and Germany. Undoubtedly, this is a factor in current French re-thinking in some union circles of their beliefs about workers' control. Syndicalism in its classic meaning is obviously easier in a land where the average enterprise is relatively small than in those where giant concerns have been established. Whether at least some French unions, under the impact of this new development, will move closer to the German concept of participation is difficult to say, as such a long tradition of militancy exists in the country. French trade unionism is still steeped in the spirit of the class-struggle. Hence the workers' leaders are bound to regard the Germans as assisting capitalism, rather than combating it. There is no doubt that German workers were docile by almost any-one's standards. As an illustration, between 1965 and 1969 the employers' share of the national income rose in the Federal Republic by 43 per cent, the employees' over the same period by 23 per cent only.[46] There is still a wide gulf between the French concept of unionism and one which will apparently accept this state of affairs. It nonetheless remains important that bilateral seminars should continue, especially for young unionists, indeed we are tempted to say that just because of this divergence they should go on.

Before we leave trade unionism we should mention two other aspects of bilateralism. Firstly, it has by no means been confined to France and West Germany. A considerable programme of exchanges has been carried out by 'Work and Life' with British institutions of adult education, as well as with those in France.[47] However, the scale has been far more limited, due to the availability of OFAJ funds for Franco-German exchanges. Here is a clear case where the 1963 treaty has been of positive value in assisting reconciliation.

Secondly, not all union contacts for the French have been with West Germans. The East German federation (FDGB) has enjoyed close relations with the CGT; this has been especially valuable as the latter has obtained so many leading positions in factory committees, etc. for its representatives in French industrial undertakings. Joint conferences which have been held have tended to deal more with political questions than with the more traditional union activities such as wages policy. Contacts between the CGT and FDGB began quite early, in June 1950, with an official agreement allowing for relations at factory level, or at that of regional organisation, containing phrases such as 'the common struggle of French and German workers in defence of peace', etc. Both federations are members of the Communist trade union international which facilitates their relationship. In June 1960 a CGT delegation visited Berlin in connection with the celebrations of the fifteenth anniversary of the German Democratic Republic, as well as of the tenth birthday of the CGT-FDGB accord. The two movements issued a statement pledging themselves to battle on against 'West German re-militarisation and the intrigues of American-directed monopoly capitalism'. A 1966 conference gave the opportunity to exchange views in the spirit of the 1950 agreement.

At local and regional level, the relations have assumed a rather more practical character, in respect of actual co-operation. Which side took the initiative is unclear, but one source suggests that it may well have been the FDGB.[48] There have been a number of information visits and exchanges of views by various delegations in both countries. The regional body for the CGT in the Somme area signed an agreement with the FDGB organisation for Halle in 1961, and twelve months later the district bureaux for Karl-Marx-Stadt and the Upper Rhine (in France) did the same. In the latter case a visit took place in September 1963. These accords have been followed by others at local level.

Sometimes a relationship has been attained between the unionists in individual enterprises. In April 1963 French representatives, the majority apprentices, visited Berlin on the invitation of the East Berlin TRO, an electricity workers' association. The French came from Sencma, a firm concerned with reactors and rocket construction. Individual unions have also occasionally made propaganda directly for the GDR in France, as in 1966, when various local unions in Alsace opened an exhibition, dedicated to East Germany, at Mulhouse.

Not surprisingly, a good deal of energy has been spent on building up contacts between young workers directly, by way of information journeys or holidays in the GDR. Four hundred young workers in a single group spent their August leave in East Germany in 1968. These events have been fairly one-sided, since not many East Germans have come to France.[49] The educational union in the GDR has played a considerable part in these activities by inviting French teachers, not all of whom are CGT members. For example, a delegation from the *Fédération de l'Education Nationale* spent eight days in Halle in 1964. These visits are used, however, rather more for internal propaganda than anything else; the glowing reports, allegedly made by the visitors, of the GDR's educational system are regularly reproduced in East German periodicals.

The FDGB has, from time to time, made propaganda against the West directly in France. In May 1962 seven French trade unionists were invited to a rest cure in the neighbourhood of Halle, in order to enable them to recover from 'the heavy injuries suffered by them on 8th February in Paris as a result of the brutal attack by de Gaulle's police'. The strife between workers' representatives and police on that occasion produced an FDGB telegram to Paris as well, expressing sympathy. A coal strike in France in March 1963 had a similar sequel. Holidays in the GDR have been offered to the families of strikers, for example to those in Lorraine. The FDGB circulates a number of periodicals in France: *Le Magazine* is sent monthly to all works councils. A German-language journal, *Wir*, goes to 46,000 German workers in France regularly.[50] For children's holidays the FDGB produces *Vacances joyeuses pour nos enfants*.

It is clearly difficult to estimate exactly what sort of effect these activities produce on the French public consciousness. We merely wish to say that another German state does exist. Now that it has been recognised it is not likely to diminish its drive to win friends and influence people in the Communist interest. Where unions are concerned the FDGB has an obvious outlet in the CGT, which we have to remember is France's biggest union. This must inevitably temper our judgement concerning bilateral contacts between the DGB and French workers' associations by putting them into a statistical perspective. Where unions in general are concerned, we cannot overlook the fact that the majority of French unionists are more likely to want to co-operate with the FDGB in the foreseeable future than with the DGB. Moreover, in a sense the relations between the FDGB and the CGT are deeper than those between, say, the DGB and the FO, just because there is a political belief in common in one instance which does not exist in the other. This whole situation can, of course, be seen in a sense as a challenge to the DGB; by intensification of its contacts in France it can try to show the French working class that the West German economic system has more to offer than its eastern competitor. Here again, the DGB can be seen as assisting in the West German foreign policy of friendship with France, just as it did in the post-war years.

Notes

1 *Relations entre syndicats allemands et syndicats français*, Centre d'Etudes de Politique Etrangère, Paris, 1965, p 1.
2 *Correspondance*, no. 150, 1 June 1969, p 1 (Econ.).
3 In 1970 to 6,200,000 against 250,000 in the CGB. *Le Monde*, 10 Feb. 1970. In fact, in 1951 as many as 39% of employees were in unions, but by 1968 this had declined to less than 30%.
4 J. Capdevielle and R. Mouriaux, *Les syndicats ouvriers en France*, Paris, A. Colin, 1970, for this section and *Relations*, op. cit. There had, of course, been many individual *syndicats* prior to 1887.
5 For full figures see *Le Monde*, 16 Oct. 1973.
6 Capdevielle and Mouriaux, op. cit., p 39.
7 *Stat. Jahrbuch*, 1973, pp 464, 476.
8 *Allemagne*, nos 20–1, Oct./Nov. 1952.
9 Union dues are one hour's wages per week for the hourly paid and 2% of salary for those paid monthly (except in the case of five unions which take 1½% or less).
10 *Correspondance*, no. 42, 15 Mar. 1964, p 12.
11 *Relations*, op. cit., p 1.
12 For sociological investigations on this subject summarised see *Correspondance*, no. 134, 15 Sept. 1968, pp 11f.
13 Quoted in *Neue Zürcher Zeitung*, 28 Sept. 1970.
14 For information on modern union views see Capdevielle and Mouriaux, op. cit., also *La CFDT*, Paris, 1971, Editions du Seuil and *Le Monde*, 16 Oct. 1973. We are also indebted to M. R. Degris of FO for a personal interview on the theme.

15 *La CFDT*, p 71.
16 *Correspondance*, no. 197, 30 Nov. 1971, p C.
17 *Relations*, op. cit., p 10.
18 Information from Herr Preuss of the DGB, Paris, in a personal interview.
19 *L'Humanité*, reported cited in *Relations*, p 16.
20 Ibid., p 19.
21 *Neue Zürcher Zeitung*, 28 Sept. 1970 and *L'Humanité*, 12 Nov. 1970.
22 *Allemagne*, no. 25, June/July 1952.
23 Although not all CFTC leaders necessarily wanted to see a Catholic union in Germany, some were even hostile, *Relations*, p 5.
24 The ETUC, founded in 1973, includes unions from outside the EEC and replaces the separate organisations which the Christian and free unions had in the EEC. The Italian CGIL has also joined although in late 1974 its joint office in Brussels with the CGT was still open.
25 *Relations*, op. cit., p 6.
26 *Allemagne*, nos 26–7, Aug./Nov. 1953.
27 *Relations*, op. cit., p 12.
28 For the first, ibid., p 13, and the second, *Allemagne*, no. 30, Apr./May 1954.
29 *Relations*, op. cit., p 13.
30 Ibid.. p 16.
31 *Le Monde*, 8 July 1970.
32 Information supplied by the convenor, Herr Rehfeld.
33 *Allemagne*, no. 19, June/July 1952. German adult education leaders had already visited France to study popular education in 1950, ibid., no. 6.
34 *Arbeit und Leben. Geschäftsbericht für die Jahre 1968 bis 1970*, published by Arbeit und Leben, p 30, on which our account is based.
35 These were the themes of all 'Work and Life' seminars with French partners, not merely those with FLL.
36 *Allemagne*, no. 16, Sept. 1952.
37 Ibid., nos 72–3, Dec. 1961 and Jan. 1962.
38 *Correspondance*, no. 67, 12 May 1965, p 19.
39 L. Dietzfelbinger, *Deutsch-Französischer Lehreraustausch 1970*, private conference report, Pädagogischer Austauschdienst, Bonn.
40 *Allemagne*, nos 97–9, July/Dec. 1966.
41 *Correspondance*, no. 199, Jan. 1972, p 17.
42 *Bilanz der Aktivität des Verbindungsbüros des DGB Paris von 1948–1967.*
43 *Bericht*, 1972, also printed privately by DGB, Paris.
44 Herr Brenner of IG Metall. *Frankfurter Allgemeine Zeitung*, 13 Mar. 1964.
45 *Daily Telegraph*, 22 Oct. 1970.
46 *The Times*, 8 Feb. 1971.
47 See *Arbeit und Leben*, op. cit., pp 47*ff.* for the details.
48 Reime, op. cit., *Die Tätigkeit der DDR in den nicht-kommunistischen Ländern*, vol. IV, *EWG Staatenohne Bundesrepublik*, p 73.
49 In 1969 5,000 French children spent their vacations in the GDR apart from apprentices' visits, ibid., p 78.
50 It does not make much impact according to Herr Preuss (see note 18 above).

Chapter 7

Twin Towning and
Contacts at Popular Level

One of the most interesting of post-war phenomena at the level of
international relations has been the institution of the twin town,
now an accepted feature of the West European scene. There are a
number of federations at international level which provide the
necessary framework for these activities, of which one is devoted
to Franco-German understanding. This is the *Union Internationale
des Maires* (UIM) (in Germany known as the IBU) founded as a
result of initiatives which began in the immediate post-war years.
In the winter of 1947–48, Karl Arnold, the Minister President of
North-Rhine-Westphalia, went incognito to Berne in order to
test the chances of establishing international contacts.[1] He got
in touch with two journalists, one German and the other Swiss,
both committed to Franco-German *rapprochement*. The latter,
Eugen Wyler, was invited to speak in Essen in early 1948 on the
theme of European unity, at an event led by the local mayor, Dr
Gustav Heinemann (the recent President of the Federal Republic). In April of the same year, the then mayors of Frankfurt and
Munich discussed with Swiss journalists how the local community
might be utilised to build bridges between the French and German
peoples. The two original publicists found a helper in the shape
of a French journalist and writer, and Wyler was eventually able
to invite Franco-German mayors in June 1948 to a joint conference near Geneva, attended by six French civic leaders and several
from still-occupied Germany.

The meeting began rather stormily but discussions proved
efficacious in promoting some degree of understanding. On the
proposal of a French mayor it was agreed to set up a liaison

office under Eugen Wyler himself. The well-publicised meeting found a favourable echo in the press, as well as among prominent politicians and intellectuals in both countries. A whole series of conferences followed to tie the links closer. By summer 1949 as many as thirty Franco-German mayors met at Lucerne to discuss communal problems in general, democracy, and the possibility of cultural exchanges, including those between workers and apprentices.[2] The following year saw an even more decisive step, when exchange visits between Montbéliard and Ludwigsburg took place.[3] The year of 1950 also saw the first Franco-German mayors' conference in the Federal Republic itself. A full organisational framework had now been created for bilateral contacts, which began to multiply as the bitterness of wartime memories faded, although progress was rather slow at first. By 1957 only twenty-seven partnerships had been created, although the rate of twinning began to increase quite sharply in the later fifties.

There is no doubt that the greatest spur to setting up formal relationships has been the 1963 treaty, since it permitted OFAJ funds to be employed for youth exchanges in a twin town frame-work. Moreover the whole idea came apparently to be seen as a weapon of foreign policy in respect of reconciliation. The German Ambassador in Paris was said to be canvassing in 1963 with lists of aspirant towns in Germany seeking formal links in France. Certainly it is true that whereas the period 1950–62 inclusive saw 126 twinnings, the next six years produced no fewer than 271. The rush continued so that by early 1973 there were nearly 700, either actually sealed or about to be. It is significant that of the French towns which had established a formal post-war partnership with another European one by 1972, five in every eight had the link with a German community as compared to one eighth which had twins in the UK.[4] There seems little doubt that current propaganda on Franco-German reconciliation, plus OFAJ subsidies, were the main factors in this considerable numerical disproportion. It is only fair to point out, however, that geographical proximity plays some part in the matter as well. This is clear from the geographical distribution of partnerships in Germany, which show regions such as Baden-Württemberg and North-Rhine-Westphalia at the head of the list, whilst Lower Saxony and Schleswig-Holstein together had concluded only fifty twinning arrangements with the French by 1971.[5]

As far as motivation is concerned, those towns which have

formed partnerships have provided an investigator with a variety of reasons for their action. Curiously enough, reconciliation is rarely among them, although understanding and the removal of prejudice often appear as motives, as do such aspects as exchanges of information and experience between the partners. In this respect the twinning is apparently seen as a means of assisting local administration as such, by opening it up to the views of others. Supporting the 1963 treaty is frequently given as the ground for partnerships established since that date, which shows how the decisions taken above can in themselves bring closer links at local level. In general it seems clear that there may well be a wide-ranging complex of reasons behind an individual twinning. In one case the war was directly responsible for a link, that between Tulle and Schorndorf. Some 100 hostages had been executed in the former town during the war; when a Schorndorf youth group went to a European folklore meeting in 1965 they made the acquaintance of the mayor of Tulle, who commissioned them to offer their community a partnership in view of the wartime events.[6]

Before we describe the actual activities carried out in the twinning framework, we should point out that not all are necessarily bilateral only. Because of this there are three separate federations dealing with community partnerships, two of which are not confined to Europe; one of these will be dealt with later when we discuss relations between French towns and those in the GDR. Nearly all West European twinning takes place under the bilateral cover of the *Union Internationale des Maires* (UIM) (known as the IBU in Germany), or of the pan-European *Conseil des Communes d'Europe*. As the chief aim of this latter body is to bring about European unity rather than merely Franco-German understanding, it will be discussed in a later chapter. It should be said that the UIM in France has now in any case fused with the *Conseil* although the IBU remains separate in West Germany. The variation in aims is brought out clearly in the differing formulas for the official oath-taking. In that of the *Conseil* there is a definite commitment to Europe, whereas the oath for the UIM/IBU refers only to Franco-German understanding.

The first point to be made about the actual events involved in the twin towning arrangement is that generalisations are difficult, as the quality of the programme varies so much according to the towns concerned. This is to a certain extent due to the personality of the leaders of the activities, either private or official council members. Sometimes the relationship tends to be confined to the town notables, and is simply a series of exchange visits by councillors, which may be of mutual benefit to them but does little to contribute to popular contacts on a large scale. Under such circumstances, any partnership is little more than an empty formality.

Incidentally, it should be pointed out that not all official partnerships necessarily come to fruition as a result of the local authorities' action. An empirical study of the Franco-German experience yields some interesting information in that respect. Of 202 such links examined, no fewer than 80 came into being through the medium of private contacts, sometimes individual, including mayors, sometimes groups or societies. Of course the UIM/IBU or the *Conseil* often themselves play a part in introducing towns but it seems to be a declining one. Between 1964 and 1972 these organisations were only responsible for the original approach to the towns concerned in less than a quarter of the cases actually examined in the study.[7] In recent years the tendency has been more and more for municipal authorities to take up contacts of their own accord without reference to intermediaries. This seems to suggest that the whole concept is now becoming an accepted practice at local level, so that a push from official channels above, as in 1963, is no longer necessary. This is surely an encouraging development. Even more so is the degree of popular participation frequently demonstrated.

For example, the delegations at the twinning of Neuilly and Hanau included educational leaders and businessmen as well as local officials. At Easter 1958 the Wetzlar visitors to the twin town of Avignon numbered as many as 300. Between Epernay and Ettlingen relations have become so close that a book has been jointly produced dealing with the links, and how the school and the community can act as instruments of reconciliation. In 1969 the exchange visitors from Blois to Waldshut included representatives of the local Lions' Club, sports clubs, the Fire Brigade, schoolteachers and the chess and philatelist associations; the Waldshut delegations in the same year were similarly composed.[8] Sometimes the chance is taken to run a Franco-German friendship week in the twin town framework, as in the case of Frankfurt and Lyon in 1960. In innumerable instances a whole series of links between various associations have been constructed within an inter-city relationship.   The Wetzlar-Avignon twin towning embraces no fewer than twenty-nine of these, ranging from schools to ex-servicemen's associations, all of which have been directly established between corresponding groups in the two cities.[9] It has been found that sports associations tend to be the most frequently involved inside the general activities, with choirs and musical groups coming second.[10] This we feel to be probably due to the limited part played by language in such contacts. There seems little doubt that the lack of a common language is a hindrance in forming more relationships at the level, for example, of professional or vocational relations. Simple gestures of friendship often, however, spring from a partnership, as in 1961 when the council of Weinheim issued an annual municipal calendar in French as well as in German, and sent a copy to its twin town Cavaillon. Commerce is frequently included in the exchanges; a typical example was provided in 1968 by Osterode and Armentières. The latter town produced a week-long exhibition of its local products in its German twin, with representatives of over thirty firms present.[11] Thus against a partnership background a whole scale of differing activities, including the commercial, is possible. School twinnings form a large part of the relationships, as do youth exchanges in general. Eighty-four communities which made some estimate of the total scale of participation in their partnerships in general gave the youth contacts as forming some 60 per cent of the total.[12]

Although on the whole the relations are probably better between municipalities with similar backgrounds, this condition is desirable rather than essential. There are numerous examples of flourishing friendships between rather oddly assorted communities. In fact, there are mixed views on this whole question; some towns which are badly paired for size have given this as a hindrance, for instance Fellbach and Tain-l'Hermitage. On the other hand, Freudenstadt and Courbevoie report a close-knit relationship, despite the fact that the French town is four times as large. Most communities which are very different, but nonetheless have established close links, attribute this to the effects of the old adage that 'opposites attract'.[13]

As an illustration of how given local initiative can be achieved by two similar cities, we shall take the Amiens-Dortmund relationship. Both of these are industrial areas, with similar climate and scenery in the immediate locality, which no doubt psychologically lessens the feeling of strangeness for the visitor from an equivalent ambiance. It might even be said that West-phalia and Picardy have the common historical heritage be-queathed by Charlemagne, as they both once formed part of his empire. As early as 1959, a lively partnership existed between the two cities, in a certain sense fostered by wartime memories. The mayor of Amiens in a speech in Dortmund pointed out to his German audience that he had twice seen his native city destroyed in wars, and that this must not be allowed to recur. The delegation accompanying him included representatives of all professions and walks of life in Amiens. Three years later, the two cities were exchanging over six hundred persons annually. School partner-ships had been effected as well as sports and drama contacts. There was even a contest between hairdressers in the two cities. Common discussions took place over youth exchanges, and French and German were introduced respectively as foreign languages in several local primary schools. By 1963 exchanges reached approximately a thousand people annually, half of them via youth organisations.[14] A close relationship has been built which embraces a large number of social activities, partly by local drive in both cases, mainly because the two cities are roughly comparable in the first place, which permits genuine contacts.

What applies at local level has similar validity regionally. Franco-German links are by no means confined to towns or cities, but to whole areas of each country which have established a relationship with a corresponding one across the Rhine. North-Rhine-Westphalia is linked with part of Northern France, Lower Saxony with Normandy, the Rhenish-Palatine with Burgundy. Of course, there is an immediate difference in status, in that the German regions are administrative organs in their own right, whereas Burgundy is a concept limited in effect to history and geography. In fact, supra-municipal partnerships have sometimes assumed an air almost of absurdity, as when it was announced that a link was to be brought about between the Black Forest and the forest of Rambouillet. Unless the two areas were similar in population and economic structure it is rather hard to see what the connection could possibly mean.

In other cases, however, the links have been more practically-based. That between the Palatine and Burgundy is an example; the step was taken in 1962, the respective capital cities, Dijon and Mainz, being already twinned. A Burgundian delegation visited Mainz, then celebrating its thousandth anniversary, and an official document was duly signed committing both sides to Franco-German reconciliation. The French occupation authorities had already begun this task in the post-war years; for example, the University of Mainz was reopened by them as early as May 1946. The Rhenish-Palatine as an administrative unit was created in the following year, and two years following a French Institute in Mainz. Mainz University set up a link with that at Dijon in 1953. In the same year two prefects and twenty-six mayors from Burgundy made a study visit in the Palatine. 1957 saw the foundation of an organisation *Amicale Bourgogne—Rhénanie Palatinat* to act as a counterpart to a similar friendship association in the Rhineland. The official regional twinning was the culmination of a long historical process, in which geographical contiguity also played a part.[15]

The large number of individual communes in both regions which are twinned anyway assists the regional relationship, which then in itself promotes still more local partnerships. As both regions have a considerable agrarian base, especially viniculture, to their economies, a common interest in trade facilitates contacts also. This is emphasised by the use of the regions as a whole, as an import-export transit area for Franco-German trade. The Palatine itself took in the first three months of 1970 nearly one quarter of all its foreign imports from France,[16] and is thus important as a consumer, too. Incidentally, a Franco-German national park, the first ever, comprising territory in the Palatine and north of the Vosges, has been created in the area.

The popular exchanges between the two regions have been varied and lively, including contacts between technical high schools and other educational institutions, professional conferences and seminars and simple family exchanges. Even the regional automobile clubs have established a relationship. One particular link worthy of mention is that forged by concentration camp victims, who have associations in both areas. The usual type of sports and theatrical events have also taken place, as one might expect.[17]

In addition to this particular regional partnership, Lower Saxony has established one with Normandy. In 1967 the two regions exchanged some six thousand persons at least (precise statistics were not apparently collected). Contacts were of the usual kind, with emphasis on youth, holiday camps, sporting events and family exchanges. This particular regional partnership, like that

between North France and North-Rhine-Westphalia, seems some-
how less convincing than that described above. Two important
connections are missing, geographical contiguity, and hence
common commercial interests, and the memory of post-war
French occupation and cultural work. Under these circumstances
the relationship is bound to assume a rather artificial colour.

The whole concept of twinning as an agent of international
friendship is relatively new, certainly on the scale which it has now
acquired. It is not perhaps surprising that a good deal of what has
taken place in many partnerships appears of little lasting value.
What effect it has on Franco-German relations is obviously hard
to say; no one can measure the influence which school partnerships and sports encounters really have as so many have been
concluded at bilateral level because of the 1963 treaty. As this
made OFAJ money available, it enormously multiplied the number of formal relationships, some of which remain formal. As an
example of how twinning became a cult in the sixties when reconciliation was on everyone's lips we can refer to Hanover. In 1958
the councillors wanted a partnership with a French city and chose
Rouen, a perfectly logical selection because of the Lower Saxony-
Normandy connection. As a result of a change in mayoralty in
Rouen, the idea fell through. Then it was decided to arrange a
link with Perpignan, a smaller place and right at the other end of
France. German municipal delegates received a moving welcome
and the partnership was sealed. Once the mood of euphoria had
passed, practical difficulties arose immediately. Firstly, the two
cities are 1,700 km apart, an expensive journey of two or three days
by road. Then, as English is the main foreign language in Lower
Saxony, the lack of a common language made itself felt in youth
exchanges; in addition, it was found difficult to arrange accommodation in Perpignan. When the Germans requested exchanges
permitting their pupils to spend a month in Perpignan schools,
this was turned down for administrative reasons. Three years
after the partnership had been founded, it was conceded that
certain obstacles still existed which must be overcome.[18] However
in 1966 Hanover did sign up for another twinning, this time with
Rouen.

Formal relations of this nature are full of pitfalls, as can be
seen. We suggest that relations are successful only when carefully
thought out in advance; as those experienced in the matter would
say, there are a number of points to be borne in mind. Firstly, it

should be more than just a series of encounters between officials and should seek to include all sections of the respective populaces. The logical corollary of this is to arrange ties between places roughly similar in size and economic structure, otherwise there is little basis for contact. Rheims has a link with Aachen which functions well; it also has one with Canterbury, the results of which have been rather less positive. But this may well be because Rheims is a large industrial city, and Canterbury a small town with little industry. Equally, distance plays a part in determining relations, as smaller communities which are linked need to be fairly close, because of travelling expenses, which weigh heavily on municipal rates and on OFAJ subsidies alike.

There are a number of other conditions which must be fulfilled if a partnership is to have any real significance in fostering Franco-German reconciliation. Visitors should be assured of accommodation *en famille* so that their stay helps them see what family life is like in the neighbour's country. Linked with this is the need to encourage spontaneous contacts as far as possible, to escape from the world of official receptions. Young people should be encouraged to participate as much as they are able; equally, there should be some practical point to the activities wherever that can be arranged. The promotion of commercial exchanges is a case in point. Because of the foregoing, a proper delegation or committee needs to be set up to deal exclusively with the twinning, including representatives of youth, local administration, education, trade unions, commerce, sport and the press. We are not here suggesting that organisation is in itself sufficient to ensure success, we are saying that it is necessary as a foundation to exploit the goodwill which exists. When properly arranged, we believe that twin towning is an exciting new way of fostering *rapprochement* at popular level. When the young people of Etrechy can make a film on their own initiative on the life of the community and send it to their 'twins' in Ostrach[19] they have made a gesture of considerable importance, and obviously one which affects the German heterostereotype of the French.

We cannot leave the matter of twin towning without reference to the German Democratic Republic. As might be expected, it has been active in this field in France. A factor here has been the express wish of many French municipalities to build a relationship with a town in each part of Germany. Many of them have, after all, left-wing councillors, which sometimes makes for additional problems in twin towning between France and West Germany, as in the case of Amiens and Dortmund. The Communist faction on Amiens Council voted in 1960 for good relations (*herzliche Beziehungen*) only, not for a formal twinning.[20] Indeed, on occasion the conclusion of an arrangement with a city in the GDR by a French town has resulted in it losing its partnership with a West German community, which promptly broke off the relationship. By 1970 there were 130 Franco-GDR twin townings, far fewer than between France and West Germany, but by no means negligible, although in the light of the recognition of the GDR perhaps less harmful to Franco-West German reconciliation than they might have been.

The intermediary in East German contacts has frequently been the *Fédération Mondiale des Villes Jumelées* (FMVJ), founded in 1957 in Aix-les-Bains and which, as its title shows, deals with extra-European ties as well as those on the continent. The federation is undenominational and non-political, in the sense that any city can join, and membership does not imply acceptance by the FMVJ of the political system of the state to which the municipality belongs. This enabled the GDR authorities to use the association as an instrument in its drive for recognition. Twenty-eight East German municipalities were members in 1970, exactly three quarters of which had a partnership with a French community. In another thirty-three cases the French twin alone is in the FMVJ, so that in one way or another the federation has served as an agent. This is certainly not in accordance with its own wishes. When in 1969 the GDR members of the FMVJ tried to get recognition of their political state written officially into partnership charters as an obligation on the twin, the FMVJ management rejected it unanimously. The GDR has tended to exploit the phrases about political nonalignment, in other words, in the FMVJ's charter. The FMVJ incidentally, unlike the other twin town federations, aims at establishing good relations between the partner communities, a rather more limited concept than that of 'partnership' envisaged by the UIM/IBU or the *Conseil*.

In France the CGT and the French Communist Party have naturally contributed to contacts. Another organ has been a private society called (in abbreviation of a longer title) *Echanges Franco-Allemands* (EFA), founded in Paris in 1958. The association gave the procurement of French recognition of the GDR as its main goal. It possessed a special committee for twinning, particularly active in those cases where a French municipality had already fixed up a partnership with a town in the Federal Republic. Ambiguity in the actual concept of 'partnership' has occasionally been exploited. The GDR press announced that an agreement had been signed between Dunkirk and Rostock. This was denied by the French authorities as it transpired that the only signatory on the French side had been the local leader of the EFA, who possessed no official authorisation from Dunkirk at all.

Sometimes a triangular accord France-West Germany-GDR has been brought about. Amiens has a link with Dortmund and Görlitz, St Etienne with Wuppertal and Zwickau, Lyon with Frankfurt (on the Main) and Leipzig. In Paris even individual *arrondissements* have links with districts in East Berlin. Most French communities with contacts, either by an actual twinning or simply municipal exchanges with no actual agreement, lie in the northern and eastern parts of the country. Although there is often some logical basis, such as Boulogne linked to another port, Stralsund, some connections seem pointless except for propaganda. An illustration is Magdeburg with 260,000 inhabitants, linked with a small town in Lorraine which has about 10,000.

The use of partnerships for political purposes is indeed unmistakable. One instance is Halle-Grenoble, where great efforts were made to sign an agreement in 1966–67, due no doubt to the coming winter Olympic sports in that city in 1968. The partnership was perhaps to prepare the way for the GDR team, entering the international sports arena for the first time as an independent team. Even more obviously political was the wording of the agreement in 1960 between Longlaville and Calbe/Saale which spoke of the common struggle against 're-emergent Fascism and militarism in West Germany'.

Included in the exchanges are the usual political conferences and information journeys. Teachers, journalists and even magistrates or lawyers are often aimed at here, in the hope of gaining political influence for the GDR in the long run. There are cultural programmes and inevitably youth activities; these include holidays in the GDR, but obviously do not take on the scale of similar exchanges between France and the Federal Republic. Nonetheless, as children can easily be impressed, there is a clear long-term potential gain for East Germany in these activities.

Whether recognition will facilitate twin towning with the GDR or not remains to be seen, as much of the activity hitherto has been directed at securing recognition in itself; now that this goal has been achieved, presumably GDR propaganda will take a fresh course. But we wish to emphasise here that the existence of so many councils in France with Communist control inevitably gives the East Germans a footing at municipal level, and this is a fact which the West Germans have to live with.

Quite apart from twin towning, the peoples of France and the Federal Republic have found a number of other points of contact since the war. One of these, the relationship between ex-servicemen in both countries, arises directly from the history of conflict between the two countries. The response in France to the treaty was encouraging from the old soldiers. Their association announced at once that it wished to aid in the task of reconciliation. Contacts with similar organisations in Germany now became the order of the day; ex-servicemen on both sides began to meet frequently. Sometimes twin towning has provided the necessary framework for the encounter; on other occasions it has been the military unit itself, as when old soldiers of the French 152nd Infantry Regiment met those from the German 21st Division. The first ever encounter between the two units had been on the battlefield in 1940.[21] This no doubt gave an extra dimension to the *rapprochement*. Verdun has figured largely in this type of meeting, because of the symbolic significance which it has now assumed in reconciliation. On the fiftieth anniversary of the battle, a joint ceremony took place in the presence of the German ex-servicemen's association. A vigil was held at night in the fort of Douamont, the scene of especially bitter fighting in 1916. This now seems to have become traditional, as in 1968 the same kind of event took place, with a pilgrimage to Douamont cemetery, with both French and German soldiers' songs being sung. Other battlefields have been the venue for similar ceremonies, as in the case of Hartmannsweilerkopf in 1969. On this occasion two World War veterans, one from each side, handed torches to a young German and Frenchman who led a joint procession to the crypt where 1,200 soldiers of both nationalities lay.

It would be too optimistic to suppose that all has been sweetness and light on the ex-servicemen's front since the war. Occasionally the celebration of wartime events has jarred on the nerves of one side or another. On the twentieth anniversary of D-Day, for example, de Gaulle offended German susceptibilities by omitting any reference to Franco-German reconciliation during the celebrations. The Ramke affair proved to be even more of a sore point in the early fifties; this former general had been held in France for six years without trial. After escaping he returned voluntarily and was given five years more, a sentence described in German ministerial circles as 'a painful disappointment'. Adenauer took the case up and Ramke was at once released in June 1951, to return to a hero's welcome.[22] The war has sometimes cast its shadow on inter-city relationships as well. In 1966 a delegation from Montbéliard was invited to its twin town Ludwigsburg, to celebrate the 262nd anniversary of the latter's foundation. The date of the event unfortunately clashed with two others, the funeral in Ludwigsburg of Sepp Dietrich, a wartime SS general, and Memorial Day in France for the victims of the wartime occupation. The mayor of Montbéliard saw himself obliged to refuse the invitation, although he did suggest another date.[23] In this case there was no permanent rupture in Franco-German relations at municipal level, but the effect of such events has to be taken into account nevertheless. The Arnoud affair in 1963–64 also provoked hostile reactions among ex-servicemen, this time in France.[24] Their national association passed a resolution deploring the 'docility' (*mansuétude*) of the Federal government in sheltering former members of the OAS and SS war criminals as well. In particular they referred to Lammerding, who was tried for the Oradour massacre but never extradited (although condemned to death at Bordeaux in his absence).

In some other respects, however, wartime events appear actually to have assisted reconciliation. In 1966 the leaders of refugee organisations in both countries met for the first time to discuss their problems with one another. There have been encounters between other war victims, such as former POWs or concentration camp internees. On one occasion, French wartime prisoners visited a refugee camp at Friedland for Germans who had fled from East Prussia in 1945, and organised a spontaneous collection among themselves for them.[25] It is hard not to feel that gestures of this nature are worth a great many long harangues on the subject of reconciliation. In France, the graves of fallen German soldiers have been so well-tended since the war that in 1972 the president of the West German war graves service laid a wreath on the tomb of the Unknown Soldier in Paris in grateful recognition. Even the medical treatment of war-wounded has been used to foster bilateralism, as when twenty Frenchmen badly injured in the war received help in Germany, against twenty similar Germans in France.

Since 1945, wartime memories have occasioned many concilia-tory gestures, but also some less pleasant acts. As psychological impressions can hardly be quantified we can only offer illustrations of both kinds of occurrence. One useful area to study here is that of *rapprochement* carried out by religious associations or indi-viduals on both sides: these have been furnished by Catholics and Protestants alike. Very often it has been a case of direct expiation, as when German youth volunteers re-built the church at Taize and handed it over to the local Protestant community. On another occasion a synagogue was constructed at Villeurbonne within the framework of a German Protestant programme of atonement (*Aktion Sühnezeichen*). This type of gesture has not been confined to Protestants: in 1962, to offer only one illustration, the Catholic bishop of Cologne presented a French commune with two bells to replace those burnt by German troops in 1944. Such actions have a precedent set in 1920, when a Frenchman, Pierre Ceresole, invited young Germans to share in the reconstruction of war-damaged France.

Relations between professing Christians in the two countries have a long and varied history, which even the Second World War did not entirely interrupt. The dialogue continued in the post-war years, to which two sources contributed. The first was the work of the French military authorities in their zone; evangelical pas-tors set up holiday camps for youth, for example.[26] Secondly, international associations provided an organisational framework. Both French and German representatives attended a world con-ference of Protestant Churches under the leadership of Bishop Bell at Stuttgart in October 1945. At the beginning of 1946 the president of the French Ecumenical Council invited German evangelical leaders to a meeting in Geneva. By 1950 articles were appearing in French periodicals on the necessity for a bilateral Protestant dialogue, said to be worthwhile just because it was so difficult.[27] The following month saw the foundation of a fraternal Franco-German council, to be concerned with political and econ-omic matters as well as the purely spiritual. The joint conferences took place biennially until 1964, when the work in general was superseded by the creation of a European organisation. Informa-tion exchanges were a regular occurrence, as were those between pastors themselves and their parishes.

Sometimes the latter type of exchange has taken place as a result of twin towning. A French vicar from Avignon spent a year in Wetzlar as a guest incumbent at a local evangelical church.[28] In another case, the war itself provided the direct link when four French Catholic ecclesiastics returned to the village where they had been prisoners and celebrated Mass in the church.[29]

The Catholic Church as such has played its part in reconciliation, quite apart from individual contacts. At Whitsun 1963, for example, a bilateral reunion took place at Strasbourg on the invitation of the local archbishop. Joint youth seminars with the participation of lay associations have been arranged from time to time. Sometimes the vocation has provided the instrument, as when French and German Catholic journalists met, which they now do regularly, to discuss political matters in a common religious framework. Town partnerships are used by Catholics as well; to choose only one example from many, a Catholic delegation from Valenciennes visited Düren in 1960, to be warmly received by their co-religionists.[30]

There can be little doubt that visits, conferences, etc. against a background of shared religious belief are a potent factor in reconciliation, to say nothing of the gestures of atonement on the German side which we have mentioned. It should be pointed out though that contacts can sometimes illuminate profound divergences of outlook as well as revealing common ground. A French priest on a visit to Westphalia in 1952 was shocked to find that the inhabitants, although regular communicants, allegedly made little connection between the tenets of their faith and daily life.[31] He felt a certain superficiality of belief in general. Equally, a joint Sorbonne conference on Catholicism and politics illustrated certain differences in contemporary outlook between the faith in the two countries. It was suggested that the persecution of the Church in Bismarck's famous *Kulturkampf* had produced a rather anticentralistic tendency in German Catholics, which lent itself naturally to European federalism. This is a rather different attitude from that of the Gallican Church in France, also conditioned by historical factors. A further divergence arises in voting practices. There is a strong conservative trend among German Catholics not visible in France, where the spectrum of political allegiance among Catholics is on the whole far wider. The laity also exercises a somewhat greater intellectual influence on French Catholicism than in the German case. We are not seeking to deny the value of contacts by these points, we merely wish to underline yet again that ostensibly corresponding associations in two countries do sometimes, indeed usually, differ in practice. This makes for difficulties in the dialogue, but it also has to be said that it makes the same dialogue even more necessary if reconciliation and mutual comprehension are to be anything but mere phrases.

Another fairly obvious way of meeting other peoples today is tourism. It would be quite impossible to measure the effects of this phenomenon qualitatively, but it has become a mass pursuit. Here again bilateral exchanges have been frankly one-sided. In 1970–71 only 836,000 French people visited the Federal Republic, whereas in the calendar year 1970, 1,745,000 had gone to Spain. In fact, for the first half of 1971 over twice as many Dutchmen as Frenchmen went to Germany. It is true that these statistics include all visitors, not necessarily tourists as such, but even when due allowance has been made for this, it is evident that the French do not regard Germany as much of an attraction for holidays. The reverse, however, is not true, in that the number of Germans travelling in France remains impressively high, nearly two million in 1970.[32] As we have pointed out in previous chapters, the Germans tend to have an image of France as a tourist country, but what complicates the matter is that whilst spending some time in France they may merely be going to Spain or Portugal anyway. The French, for geographical reasons, are rather less likely to use the Federal Republic as a route to somewhere else. But in any case it appears probable that revaluation of the mark is the primary factor in determining French tourism in Germany. Statistics seem to confirm this thesis, as the number of Frenchmen visiting across the Rhine in 1962 was actually higher than the 1970–71 figure.[33] As living standards are now rising and access to Germany for Frenchmen is so easy it is rather hard not to feel that the exchange rate plays a decisive part in the matter. We must point out, however, that another factor may well be the existence of the OFAJ itself. The mass contacts which it facilitates are not necessarily included in official tourism, as the sojourn in the other country is quite often made in a family. This applies to twin town exchanges as well, estimated in 1969 to have comprised at least 200,000 people.[34] Under these circumstances, it becomes impossible to calculate exactly the true extent of mass contacts between the peoples, let alone measure their impact. All that we can safely say is that quantitatively they are almost certainly greater than ever in peacetime, and that the Germans seem keener to effect a visit than do the French. It is said that they still feel slightly unsure of themselves in France; this is partly because of their affluence, which allegedly gives some French the impression that the Germans are now the Americans of Europe. This will not alter for the foreseeable future, and makes one rather wary of automatically evaluating all mass contacts as being necessarily good in terms of international relations.

Apart from tourism, a common vocation has often provided the criterion in forming links between the two peoples. Jurists in both countries have met quite frequently since the war. At a Bad Godesberg conference in 1956 they discussed the legislative systems of both countries, and in particular the techniques required in judgement as part of a magistrate's skill. Similarly a discussion on civil law was run at Chantilly on a bilateral basis. On another occasion there was a trilateral colloquium on liberty of information in the GDR, West Germany and France, organised by the International Jurists Commission. As far as exchange visits are concerned, the familiar obstacle of language arises; there have been far more German jurists visiting France than vice versa.

Vocational contacts have, of course, not been confined to jurists; even dentists have managed to meet in a bilateral atmosphere. Funds have been created to enable study periods to take place for members of the profession in the other country. The scale is frankly limited but this is nonetheless a gesture.

Indeed the range of possibilities which has been utilised to bring French and Germans together is impressive, if on occasion a little artificial. When a meeting between Germans of French origin and Frenchmen of German descent is arranged it is hard not to feel that almost any excuse is being employed to lend an air of *rapprochement* to Franco-German relations. However, the basis of the link is often quite solid; one particular example is the existence of flourishing Franco-German choirs at Paris and Munich. Sports encounters have become a common event in bilateral relations in recent years; one source gives a total of 80,000 since the war.[35] Links have been established between the medical and nursing professions in both countries; Stuttgart and Strasbourg have begun practical exchanges at the level of local clinics. Even more emphatic as a gesture have been the actions of Frenchmen in providing blood in Germany. Fifteen members of the national blood-donors' associations offered blood for the sick in Berlin and donated the fee to the German Red Cross. Strasbourg citizens have performed a similar action in their twin town Stuttgart. When events of this nature figure in the local press it must surely make some impact on the German consciousness. Another meeting point is furnished by the presence of French troops in Germany. It is difficult to estimate their contribution, if there is one, to Franco-German understanding, as soldier-civilian relationships are often bad, even when both share the same nationality. As far as the two armies themselves are concerned, there have been the usual exchanges between military units, and joint manoeuvres, but this is now common virtually throughout Western Europe as a result of NATO. At the level of the ordinary soldiers there have been the usual efforts at reconciliation, as when German Protestant troops took part in an evangelical pilgrimage at the invitation of the *Aumonier-Général* of the French Army.

One other flourishing Franco-German institution worthy of mention is the mixed marriage. These were said to amount to about one thousand annually in 1961, but have now trebled in number.[36] As one might expect, they provide a marvellous opportunity for prejudice to assert itself, where cultural upbringing is so different. French girls choosing a German husband have the usual mental image of a cold, wet country inhabited by blonde, disciplined barbarians. School books have often provided them with a jumble of impressions, where Bavarian castles jostle with wine feasts and Dürer engravings are mingled with memories of Siegfried or the rat catcher.[37] After the marriage they find to their amazement that the French work longer hours than their neighbours, who are not always disciplined either. The anti-militarism is surprising as well, with 14,000 objections on conscientious grounds to military service in 1969 alone. German stereotypes about the French come to the surface too; they are astounded to meet a blonde blue-eyed French girl and question her to find out if she is of Germanic descent. They are not always able to conceal their conviction that the French are dirty and lazy, and the girls frivolous. In France there is sometimes an even more extreme reaction. One family actually got letters of condolence when the forthcoming mixed marriage was announced; in another case a girl was refused permission by her parents to marry a German. Acquaintanceship with the future in-law usually smooths out these obstacles (which may in some cases arise from social distinctions anyway).

Even after the wedding, cultural differences can produce friction. German housepride occasionally seems grotesque to the newly married French girl, as her neighbours appear to be forever waxing and polishing. They are shocked by German magazines with nude women on the cover, and the mania for organisation, born apparently of a fear of improvisation, is irritating. The German husband, on the other hand, finds to his dismay that family relationships are wider-reaching across the Rhine than in his own country. At reunions he appears to have married into a sizeable part of the entire population of France. One could probably sum up by saying that Franco-German marriages are an interesting socio-psychological phenomenon but as their scale is numerically still limited they are clearly not a great factor yet in the field of relations as a whole.

Thus we are left with a whole gamut of bilateral activities, covering almost every conceivable social group and occupation. Only time can show the real value of such institutions as twin towning, tourism or vocational and religious exchanges. What is certainly new is the scale of contact which modern communication networks and living standards make possible. However, even twenty-eight years after the cessation of hostilities the war still occupies a place on the bilateral scene, and certainly influences the French stereotype of the Germans. When, in October 1968, the inhabitants of Tulle discovered that the SS chief responsible for killing ninety-nine hostages there in 1944 was living in Düsseldorf, they obtained his telephone number and rang him day and night.[38] The slightest hint of neo-Nazism, or what might be so construed, arouses hostile demonstrations in Paris, e.g. when German politicians came for talks after the 1966 NPD local successes in Hesse and Baden. The real difficulty lies in ascertaining exactly how much of this sort of reaction is general in France and how much arises from individual pressure groups. But the consequences of the war still make headlines in France occasionally.

Sometimes modern bureaucracy can produce hostile reactions on the other side of the Rhine and perhaps undo to some extent the efforts at reconciliation made in other fields. In one case, selected in order to show just how deep an impression official regulations can make, a German refugee in France wanted to visit his father who had returned to Germany after the war. The son, originally only five years old in 1933 when the family emigrated, had applied twice for French citizenship, only to have his request rejected on both occasions without any explanation. As a stateless person he was then refused a travel pass. Apparently some stateless Hungarians had gone back to Budapest in 1956 under the protection of a French permit and taken part in the uprising. To avoid a recurrence a blanket regulation was passed, applicable to all stateless persons, irrespective of the nature of the regime in their country of origin. The German newspaper featuring the story contrasted French rules with those of neighbouring Belgium, far more tolerant in its attitude to German refugees from Hitler.[39]

Equally, however, and this makes the whole question complicated to evaluate, simple personal contact can achieve wonders. In 1970 a frontier dispute over territory in Wissembourg (Alsace) was settled by the mayor of Kandel after the case had been dogging governmental circles for years. He cultivated the friendship of the mayor and other local officials in Wissembourg on the French side, got on to personal name terms and eventually the whole affair was dealt with to everyone's satisfaction.[40] There is no doubt of the value of human contacts, but the problem even today is extending them to cover a larger segment of the general public in both countries, coupled with those of differing cultural backgrounds and administrative procedures. It seems likely that these variations will continue for the foreseeable future, but at least there is now some considerable degree of personal relationships to redress the balance. There are still breakdowns in the dialogue, but surely the overriding fact is that both sides are anxious in so many cases that the links should be kept up, and indeed tied more closely. But genuine understanding on both sides as far as the bulk of the population is concerned is clearly still some way off. Nevertheless, we should not overlook the progress that has been made since the war.

Before we leave this subject, we should point out that there are still some 40,000 German workers in France today. Mostly they are former prisoners of war who remained outside Germany after the 1945 collapse. Many returned in the fifties when the economic miracle began to develop in the Federal Republic, but it is said that those who stayed on in France have gradually come to adopt French ways. As we said in Chapter 6, it was partly in order to look after their interests that the DGB set up its Paris office in 1948. Four years later a special German-language journal the *Parisier Kurier* was founded, published fortnightly, which still continues in existence with a circulation of 30,000 copies. Linked with this is a special organisation for social work among Germans domiciled in France; this is run under DGB auspices, and contains representatives of the embassy, German churches, etc. on its management committee. Appeals for charity to aid Germans in distress is one of its main functions. It is interesting that this enclave should now continue to exist, and it has even been said that its presence assists *rapprochement*, in that many Frenchmen are given a chance to work and live alongside representatives of a people whom they might otherwise not get to know.[41]

Notes

1   Unless otherwise stated this account is based on *Deutschland-Frankreich Heft*, 22 June 1969, pub. by UIM/IBU, pp 3*f.*
2   *Allemagne*, no. 2, June/Aug. 1949.
3   *Goldenes Buch der deutsch-französischen Städtepartnerschaften*, UIM/IBU, Stuttgart, 1962, p 27.
4   P. O. Lapie, 'La Coopération franco-allemande', *La Nouvelle Revue des deux mondes*, Feb. 1973, pp 289*f*; 'Note sur les jumelages européens', Conseil des Communes d'Europe, Jan. 1972, and *Goldenes Buch*, op. cit. for these statistics.
5   *Deutschland-Frankreich Heft*, 25 May 1971, p 2.
6   The information on motivation and the wartime example are from H.-J. Garstka, *Die Rolle der Gemeinde in der internationalen Verständigung nach dem zweiten Weltkrieg gezeigt am Beispiel der deutsch-französischen Verständigung*, Stuttgart, IBU, 1972.
7   Ibid., pp 64–7 and 91*f.*
8   *Correspondance*, 31 Mar. 1964, p 16; *Allemagne*, nos 55–6, Nov. 1958 and no. 34, Dec. 1954 to Jan. 1955; *Deutschland-Frankreich Heft*, 23 Feb. 1970, p 19.
9   According to Dr Kühn-Leitz of the Franco-German Society, Wetzlar, in a personal interview.
10 Garstka, op. cit., p 97.
11 *Goldenes Buch*, p 125; *Deutschland-Frankreich Heft*, 22 June 1969, p 18.
12 Garstka, op. cit., pp 98*f.*
13 Ibid., pp 80*f.*
14 *Mitteilungsblatt für die deutsch-französischen Gesellschaften*, no. 6, pp 80*f* and no. 13, pp 29*f.*
15 This account based on M. Schröder, 'Die Beziehungen von Rheinland-Pfalz zum französischen Nachbarn in der Gegenwart', *XV Jahrestagung des Arbeitskreises Deutsch-Französischer Gesellschaften*, Mainz, Oct. 1970, pp 59*f.*
16 H. Neubauer, 'Wirtschaftliche Verflechtungen zwischen Rheinland-Pfalz und Frankreich', ibid., pp 63*ff.*

17 *Mitteilsblatt*, op. cit., no. 26, pp 113*f* and no. 16, p 12.
18 Ibid., no. 16, pp 35*f* and p 51.
19 Cited by Mme Sergent, of Conseil des Communes d'Europe in a personal interview.
20 This account is based on Reime, op. cit., pp 23*f*.
21 *Correspondance*, no. 54, 15 Oct. 1964, p 13.
22 F. R. Willis, *France, Germany and the New Europe 1945–1967*, London, OUP, 1969, pp 148*f*.
23 *Frankfurter Allgemeine Zeitung*, 9 May 1966.
24 Arnoud, an OAS leader, was kidnapped by French police in Munich to be taken to stand trial in France: the result was a diplomatic row at high level in 1964.
25 *Correspondance*, no. 32, 16 Oct. 1963, p 15.
26 P. Conord, 'Protéstants allemands et français', *Documents*, Nov./Dec. 1968, pp 113*f*.
27 For example in *Allemagne*, no. 5, Feb. 1950.
28 *Deutschland-Frankreich Heft*, 25 May 1971, p 18.
29 *Correspondance*, no. 54, 15 Oct. 1964, p 14.
30 *Goldenes Buch*, p 143.
31 *Allemagne*, nos 20–1, Nov. 1952. For an analysis of the two churches and the conference, see ibid. no. 47, Feb./Mar. 1957 and no. 48, Apr./May 1957.
32 *Statistisches Jahrbuch*, 1972, p 278, and *Annuaire Statistique de la France*, 1971, pp 440*f*.
33 *Correspondance*, no. 50, 15 July 1962, p 13, for the 1962 figures.
34 *Deutschland-Frankreich Heft*, 23 Feb. 1970, p 9.
35 P. O. Lapie, op. cit.
36 Ibid., and *Documents*, no. 2, 1964, p 102.
37 See W. Haeg, 'Mariages franco-allemands', *Documents*, May/June 1970, pp 38*f*, on which this account is based.
38 Nass, op. cit., p 209.
39 *Süddeutsche Zeitung*, 2 and 12/13 Aug. 1972.
40 *New York Times*, 30 Aug. 1970.
41 Information on the newspaper and the social work from Herr Preuss in a personal interview. For a more general description see H. Kepper, 'Allemands en France', *Documents*, no. 3, 1968.

Chapter 8

The Role of
Private Initiative in
Franco-German Understanding

There is no doubt that the work of individuals, either alone or grouped together in private societies, has contributed to reconciliation since 1945. The associations active in this field tend to fall into two groups, the purely bilateral and that comprising organisations dedicated to international understanding in general, which includes Franco-German *rapprochement*. We shall devote more space here to the first grouping. It has to be said at once that there are now a very large number of associations which deal with Franco-German relations in some way or another. A conference on the theme in 1957 was attended by representatives from no fewer than fifty-six organisations, mostly unofficial ones.[1] As it is impossible here to describe the work of each in detail, we have to confine ourselves mainly to the purely bilateral societies. A further point to be made in advance is that private societies are not necessarily wholly financed by unofficial means, as subsidies from municipalities or governments are frequently available. But as they are founded on individual initiative and have no power of political decision, it seems fair to distinguish them from official cultural departments and institutes.

Much of the initial impulse towards a better understanding appears to have originated in the ranks of the French Resistance in the war years. The collapse of the Third Republic led to some serious thought about the shape of post-war France and its relations with its neighbours. By 1944 the Resistance journal *Combat* was calling for a just peace and a new, united Germany.

In other words, the concept of a neighbour divided into a number of small independent States was not held to be a solution.[2] Linked with this was the idea of a European Union, which precluded any possibility of a peace settlement based on hatred and revenge. French Socialists in their organ *Le Populaire* had already advocated similar views, going so far as to suggest a world federation of free states in 1943.[3]

Once hostilities ceased and the French occupation got under way, contacts were established, the first really being on the sports field or in youth encounters in general. The military authorities set up a special section to organise this, whose leader, Jean Moreau, played a leading part in bringing young people of both nationalities together.[4] Chronologically, the next step was that of Jean du Rivau, a priest with the occupation who in 1945 brought into being the *Bureau International de Liaison et Documentation* (BILD) with a German counterpart. The two organisations began the publication of a review, dedicated to contemporary affairs in both countries and to Franco-German understanding, under the title of *Documents* (in the German version *Dokumente*). By 1948 two more organisations had been founded, the *Deutsch-Französisches Institut* at Ludwigsburg, and in Paris, again on private initiative, the *Comité français d'Echanges avec l'Allemagne nouvelle*. As these three were the pioneers in the post-war field, we shall consider each one separately.

The *Comité* was begun by Emmanuel Mounier of the review *Esprit* in May 1948, when he invited a number of persons interested in reconciliation to his offices. These included Alfred Grosser, a political scientist who had been in the Resistance and in October 1947 had published articles in *Combat* on German youth and its problems. Another guest was Joseph Rovan who had been in Buchenwald during the war, and had already written for *Esprit* on post-war Germany. From this meeting the *Comité* emerged, which in 1949 founded its own periodical *Allemagne*. Other committee members included J.-P. Sartre, a French Germanist Robert Minder, Robert d'Harcourt of the French Academy and eventually Vercors, novelist and former Resistance member.

The committee saw its primary task as the presentation of the two peoples to one another. In addition, the need was felt to encourage democratic trends in post-war Germany. It was seen that France would get the neighbour she deserved, as a result of her post-war attitude to Germany. This feeling was exemplified in Rovan's articles *L'Allemagne de nos mérites*. It was recognised that psychological preparation was necessary if bilateral encounters were to be successful and to this end study groups were set up, especially for French students at the Institute of Germanic Studies at the Sorbonne. Guest speakers were invited from Germany, the first being Eugen Kogon, himself a former concentration camp victim. The *Comité* acted as intermediary in exchanges of various kinds, either for groups or individuals, particularly for young people from the two countries. It was felt that contacts had to be cultural in the widest possible sense, to include trade unionists as well as students. In only its second number, *Allemagne* was castigating the occupation authorities because of their more traditional approach to culture, which it was felt appealed to the '*bonne bourgeoisie*' only. Hence its presentation of regular lectures at the Sorbonne; a typical example of those early years was the discussion in 1952 by journalists from both countries of the influence of the press in France and Germany.[6] In 1947 Mounier also devoted a special issue of *Esprit* to the German problem, which evoked a considerable response in the French public.

Initial reaction to the *Comité* in France was slight. The total circulation of their review was some 5,000 (including copies sold in Germany). Attempts at arranging hospitality for Germans, especially students, in France often met with indifference. Early issues of *Allemagne* repeatedly stressed how hard it was to find accommodation, particularly in the provinces. Even when in places such as Lille, Rheims and Dijon help of this nature was forthcoming, there was no one prepared to take care locally of the necessary paperwork involved. Finance was also a problem, though less serious, as a subsidy was available from the French Foreign Office. Despite this aid, the *Comité* never allowed any French officials on its management board, in order to remain independent. In spite of difficulties the review appeared until 1967; by this time events had rather overtaken it, as the political relationship had become so close, and organisations such as the OFAJ were officially covering some of its earlier functions anyway. Before we turn to another association we should point out that the *Comité* was always ready to co-operate with other bilateral groups in conference work, exchanges, etc. *Allemagne* also provided its readers with regular book reviews of German publications available in French, and occasionally itself made concrete gestures of reconciliation, as well as encouraging it in other ways. In 1950 for example, the committee sent a football to a refugee children's village in Württemberg.[7]

Parallel with the work of the *Comité* was that of BILD, which was actually the first genuine bilateral association after the war as it had a branch in Germany itself. Originally du Rivau began his work in Offenburg in the French zone, where in September 1945 the first number of *Documents/Dokumente* saw the light.[8] By the end of 1947 the circulation of *Dokumente* attained a figure of 50,000 copies, a sure sign of the need that it was filling in a Germany hungry for news of the outside world after the intellectual claustrophobia of the Third Reich. BILD did not confine itself to the area of information alone; regular conferences between journalists and intellectuals in both countries were arranged, participants including Robert d'Harcourt, Mounier, Wilhelm Hausenstein (later German Ambassador in Paris) and Heinrich Böll.

As the frontiers began to open a little, mass contacts were sponsored. These sometimes took the form of children or youth exchanges, or those between apprentices. By 1969 the family or vocational origins of the participants in the programmes covered a wide range of categories; the exchanges are normally carried out on a reciprocal basis between families.[9] Especially worthy of mention are the three-year-long activities commencing in 1951, whereby refugee children from Schleswig-Holstein camps were given six weeks' summer holidays with French families. To organise accommodation, appeals were made in fifty-two different publications in France, which elicited replies from all over the country. An interesting by-product of the programme was the interest which it stimulated in German problems. The mere presence of the children caused numerous articles in the press and as a result young people from all parts of France then volunteered to work in refugee camps.

In addition, BILD has carried out a large-scale programme in France to acquaint the public with contemporary life in the Federal Republic. A travelling exhibition was initiated to visit the smaller communities, consisting of three glass buses full of information on Germany and its relations with France. It went to over 100 towns and was seen by some 400,000 people in the course of eight months. Welcome visitors were those classes of schoolchildren who frequently came *en bloc*. Sometimes an individual of riper years would tell the exhibition organisers of how he had been a prisoner in Germany in the war years, and even produce a letter from the farmer to whom he had been allocated, with a request for a translation.[10] A solid substratum of goodwill was discovered.

Whilst BILD and the *Comité* were working in France, similar tasks were undertaken on the other side of the Rhine by the *Deutsch-Französisches Institut*, founded in 1948 at Ludwigsburg. Among the first members was Dr Theodor Heuss, later President of the Federal Republic.[11] The aim of the society was to foster reconciliation via a continuous dialogue on current affairs, and on problems affecting both peoples. It had to find a collaborator in France to achieve this, and not unnaturally did so in the *Comité* and later in BILD also. The Institute is not attached to any political movement and lays stress on the widest possible definition of cultural exchanges. It is an independent, private institution, although subsidies have been accepted in exceptional cases from the French.[12]

One of the chief activities from the beginning has been the exchange programmes between young people in various ways. The exchange can be on a family basis, or between groups, through study courses, au pair placements or vocational visits, when young workers or professional people enjoy a stay across the Rhine in a work situation similar to that in their own country. This particular type of visit was sponsored as early as 1951 by the Institute, with French *Stagiaires* being assisted to spend one to two months in a German enterprise. This is excellent in principle but the scale was frankly limited; between 1951 and 1962 about 1,200 young Frenchmen and Germans were helped in this way, the overwhelming majority (960) being French.[13] This perhaps reflects a certain initial lack of response to German overtures in France, as experienced by the *Comité*. However, as time wore on the disproportion got less, not least because the Institute found a willing partner in a Parisian technical college.

Apart from professional/vocational exchanges other forms of bilateral encounters have included study trips for young business-men, technologists, students and school-children. Even the visit of a youth choir has been sponsored. Additionally the Institute acts as intermediary for the twinning of schools and colleges; munici-pal partnerships have been assisted. A number of language courses have been carried out. Equally there have been conferences and discussions on a joint basis at the Institute itself, for example a five-day lecture series in 1968 on Claudel, on the occasion of his centenary (with participants from Switzerland and Austria, as well as from France and Germany). A totally different event exemplifies how varied the activities are. This was an intensive course for future industrial and administrative cadres, organised in collaboration with French commercial colleges and the *Ecole Nationale d'Administration*. Apart from procuring important personal contacts, the course had an intrinsic value for all interested in Franco-German commerce, now increasingly important.

Quantitatively the Institute's work has been impressive. Between 1951 and 1967 over twenty-three thousand persons took part in its activities. Since 1964 it has worked with the OFAJ, and in many other cases with other private organisations. It has often acted as a meeting-place for all those interested in reconciliation, as in 1957 and again in 1964 when the aims and organisation of the OFAJ were discussed. The Institute has also produced four volumes dealing with Franco-German relations and is now bringing out a fifth. But despite the many fields in which it is active we feel that its greatest contribution has been the pioneer work of the fifties, just like the *Comité* and BILD. These three associations played the main part, at the level of private initiative, in securing a new constructive dialogue in the post-war years.

As well as those mentioned there are now four main bilateral societies which need to be described. On the French side there is the *Association France-Allemagne* founded in 1963 as a private society. This, a purely French organisation, contains notables from the political arena among its membership, for example, the senator Jacques Baumel. At the time of the foundation the president was Jacques Vendroux, vice-president of the European Parliamentary Assembly, and Maurice Schumann was vice-president. Another member was General Noiret, a deputy and head of the Franco-German parliamentary friendship group. Indeed the society's connections seem very high-powered. In 1964 the guest of honour at one of its dinners was Adenauer himself, then in Paris to receive an honorary distinction from another organisation. The society organises other functions, as in 1965 when the German president of his country's Huguenot association gave a lecture on how these latter fared on their arrival in Germany, a subject naturally of great interest to French Protestants. Similar historical or literary themes have been dealt with at other conferences. The *Association* awards two annual prizes to the Frenchman and the German who have contributed most to reconciliation in the year; a recent recipient was Professor Carlo Schmid.[14]

A genuinely bilateral society is the *Deutsch-Französischer Kreis*, centred on Düsseldorf. Its committee again includes many well-known people from the world of politics and finance, such as Jacques Rueff, who is a member of the sister group in Paris, the *Cercle Franco-Allemand*. In Germany, Walter Scheel is on the committee. The two sections are not numerically equivalent, as three quarters of the membership is German.[15] Most members belong either to the CDU or the FDP although the *Kreis* is in principle non party-political. The numerical difference is partly explicable by the fact that the *Cercle*, although now recognised as equivalent in status and intention, is eleven years younger. As one might expect from the composition of the membership, the societies are rather more concerned with political and economic questions than with the more traditionally cultural, and so do not belong to the ADFG (see pages 162-4). They do not undertake any programmes of youth exchanges or language courses similar to those we have already mentioned, having rather as their aim the direct promotion of European integration, initially at the economic, later at the political, level. They do, however, arrange for exchanges between young people who are members of their own societies in France and Germany. It is their belief that a private society may exercise considerable political influence if enough of its members are prominent in the world of finance and politics, as so many of theirs are. They aim also at bringing the French point of view to important Germans, and vice-versa, and strengthening the personal contacts between them. The societies also have influential support in the business world; the German Federation of Industry is a member, as are many firms themselves in both countries. These societies are the only ones which work to a long-term planned programme, drawn up by the German deputy president, Dr Forsteneichner, in 1951.

Since its foundation in 1950, the *Kreis* in Germany has held a number of discussions and lectures on topical themes, not necessarily always Franco-German pure and simple, although clearly this subject has been dominant. The speakers have usually been prominent industrialists, military leaders or politicians, including among others Adenauer, Couve de Murville, Scheel, Maurice Schumann and Marshal Juin. Among industrialists who have spoken was Paul Huvelin, head of the French employers' association. It cannot really be said that the two associations reach a wide audience, but within limits they both have an influential one in the world of business and politics.

A rather similar organisation is the *Deutsch-Französischer Arbeitskreis*, founded in September 1966; it has only about 100 members, more or less equally divided between French and German.[16] The organisation claims to be the only genuine joint society, in that the presidium consists of members of both nationalities, rather than having a separate grouping in each country. Most people in the association are journalists, officials or deputies, with a certain trend towards the Right politically. The Germans are nearly all CDU/CSU orientated, the French membership having a rather wider spectrum, although no members of the new left-wing coalition are included. It would not be unfair to say that, like the *Kreis*, this organisation also is bourgeois in character.

The birth of the society in 1966 was conditioned by current events in Europe, particularly the need to give a new impulse to European integration. At a subsequent meeting between the Düsseldorf journalist, Diethard Gottschalk, and M de Lipkowski, later Secretary of State at the French Foreign Office, it was decided that in view of increasing nationalism, as represented by the NPD, there were two current priorities. One was the British entry into the EEC, and, proceeding from it, the integration of all West European states, the other European security in general. Lipkowski's attitude was influenced no doubt by his own background; his father had died in a concentration camp and his brother had been shot by the Gestapo. He composed a brief for both governments on British entry into the EEC, and its widening in general, which was dealt with at the February 1968 consultations between de Gaulle and Kiesinger. From the subsequent Hague Conference in December 1969 came a new drive towards closer European relations.

Additionally, the society has been concerned with Franco-German relations as such; it carried out a poll among members of the *Assemblée Nationale* regarding the need for closer co-operation, which evoked a favourable response from all parties, and laid the results before the two governments. Similarly to the societies previously mentioned, this association does not seek to effect mass contacts or to further cultural relations so much as to win friends amongst influential people for European integration and security. Its chief difference from the *Kreis* lies in its greater stress on politics than on business, plus the fact that it is not concerned with lectures or conferences.

The final association which we have to consider among the bilateral is the *Arbeitskreis der deutsch-französischen Gesellschaften* (henceforth ADFG). This is a union which acts as the central organisation for affiliated friendship in various French and German cities. The ADFG was founded on private initiative, the moving spirit being Dr Elsie Kühn-Leitz from Wetzlar in Hesse. On the occasion of the seventieth birthday celebrations of the German President Theodor Heuss in 1954, Dr Kühn-Leitz met the Chancellor, Konrad Adenauer, in Bad Godesberg, who suggested that she should dedicate herself to Franco-German relations because of their importance for Europe. Dr Kühn-Leitz then founded a Franco-German Society at Wetzlar with the help of the French cultural authorities, and the French officers present at Wetzlar. A number of similar associations had sprung up all over Germany (there had already been one in Berlin in 1927, closed by the Nazis later). In 1956 the French Embassy in the West German capital invited representatives of several Franco-German societies to a study course in Paris and Lille. This enabled the leaders of the various associations to get to know one another and it was decided to hold a congress in Wetzlar in the following year. Delegates came from twenty-six different societies, and passed a resolution demanding a federation called the Working Circle of Franco-German societies, to which twenty-one delegates agreed.[18] The central committee acts as co-ordinator, arranges annual congresses and distributes an information booklet two or three times a year. Each affiliated society, of which there are now nearly 100, remains independent. Of these member societies, three quarters are in Germany. This discrepancy is partly attributable no doubt to the fact that club life in general is more developed there than in France. A further factor is the different population distribution, in that in France there are fewer cities large enough to make the foundation of a Franco-German society worthwhile. Also, one has to remember that in the Federal Republic there are a large number of French garrisons, and many members of the societies in the areas where they are stationed are simply French troops themselves. In other words, the fact that three quarters of the societies are based in Germany does not imply that a similar numerical proportion obtains in respect of individual membership. There is a French commitment to reconciliation too. The actual size of the societies is variable: in Lyon there were 476 members in 1963, exactly one per thousand of the population. This is not a large percentage, and the ADFG tends to be, like the other societies we have mentioned, bourgeois. Many of its members are Romanists or Germanists by profession; this came out strongly when in 1971 it was suggested that the annual congress should be held in September, in the holidays, as so many French members were teachers. This implies that many people in the organisation are already orientated towards the other country by their vocation.

The ADFG federation has a somewhat wider range of goals than some of the others we have mentioned, in that it concerns itself with Franco-German understanding in general. This implies not merely lectures and discussion-groups, but also the furtherance of twin towning, youth exchanges, hospitality for French groups and similar activities. It has to be made clear, however, that as the ADFG is a federation comprising nearly 100 different societies, the emphasis often varies according to local circumstances. In general the individual associations in Germany fall into one of three main types. The first group is in the south-west where French garrisons are to be found. It was often the case that the military authorities played a large part in founding these centres. Tübingen with over 1,000 members in 1963 and Baden-Baden are especially active and well-equipped. The societies in the second group work with local German officialdom, particularly the educational authorities, in regions where there are no French troops. In Dortmund, for example, the city's municipally-run Foreign Institute co-operates closely, providing a French library and a hall for joint discussions, youth meetings, etc. Finally, there are some affiliated societies which lay most stress on more traditional activities, in particular, lectures by prominent politicians, such as the late Paul-Henri Spaak or Professor Walter Hallstein.

The ADFG has both a management committee and a board of trustees (*Kuratorium*), the latter comprising members drawn from various sectors of national life in both countries. The German trustees include O. W. von Amerongen, President of the German Industry and Trade Association, Dr Holzamer of the second television channel, General von Kielmansegg, formerly of NATO, Ernst Majonica, a CDU member of Parliament and President of the German Council of the European Movement, and Albert Preuss of the DGB office in Paris. Among French representatives are Professor R. Mallet, Rector of Paris Academy, Jean Mistler of the *Académie Française*, former ambassador A. François-Poncet and François Ceyrac, president of the national council of the French employers' association. Membership is in other words both varied and influential.

Financially the ADFG is private, but nonetheless because of its links with France and local authorities in Germany it does receive some subsidies. In Weiden the local society was receiving 20,000 DM annually from the city in 1963. Other official donors include the French Embassy (2,000 DM in 1971) the city of Mainz and the *Land* of the Rhenish-Palatine, and also the Federal Ministry of Foreign Affairs. When the annual congress was held in Caen the local council gave 10,000 francs towards the expenses. All in all, the subventions are not large, but that given by the French Embassy suggests that the national government considers that the ADFG does a good job for Franco-German friendship.

This belief is intelligible in the light of the work carried out by the different societies for reconciliation. One sphere has been youth exchanges and the training of leaders by way of seminars. A typical example is that organised in Lille in 1963, lasting a week and designed to provide youth organisers with the necessary background of knowledge required for OFAJ programmes. In 1971 a part of the annual congress was devoted to youth problems. At this time there were nineteen individual societies with a special group of their own for young people. Altogether there were 1,500 young members in the German societies (about three quarters of them German, the remainder being young French soldiers). School exchanges also form part of the programmes, sometimes in the framework of twin towning, as in the case of Wetzlar and Avignon. Special sports festivals are also organised within the twin town framework. Society members are active here as well as in furthering contacts.

Closely linked with this is the language work undertaken, which often means in effect the promotion of French in Germany, to which we have already referred in Chapter 4. It is interesting to note that when French was introduced into some kindergartens in the Rhenish-Palatine in 1971 the initiative was said to have originated from the ADFG's annual congress at Mainz the previous year.[19] Sometimes individual French societies run their own language courses as well, as in the case of Caen, which began them in 1960 and by 1963 had already had 400 enrolments. The interest in the promotion of the partner's language arises partly from the fact that so many members are professional teachers themselves. Language courses can also be linked with twin towning. Members of the Bayreuth Society, who were Romanists, carried out such a programme for young people from 1964 onwards, partly as a result of the partnership with Annecy. Much of the work involved in twinning itself stems from people who are ADFG members, and who provide a great deal of the necessary enthusiasm. The case of Valenciennes and Düren provides an illustration. Many German towns have popular education colleges for adults and young people which themselves run language courses. These have been utilised by the Franco-German societies for their own members, in addition to their own private courses.

As well as its own many activities, and co-operation with the OFAJ and the French Embassy or Institutes, the ADFG is always ready to collaborate with other private societies similarly orientated. To this end it regularly publishes information on them in its own bulletins, and thus acts as a kind of clearing house in terms of information for those interested in private initiatives for reconciliation. The list of organisations with which it has co-operated is certainly impressive, but too long to give in full. It should be stressed incidentally that not all bilateral societies are necessarily affiliated to any of those associations mentioned here; there are still some at local level which prefer to remain completely unattached.

As well as the purely bilateral organisation there are a large number of international bodies now which include Franco-German activities in their programmes as part of their work for international understanding. These are indeed so numerous that only the briefest possible sketch can be given, but they clearly need to be mentioned since their programmes do have relevance for our theme. One of the most important is the *Europäische Akademie* at Otzenhausen in the Saar. This runs seminars and discussion-groups on contemporary problems, and has a strong bias towards a united Europe. Occasionally there are joint seminars for French and Germans, not necessarily on political topics. In April 1973 a week-long conference was organised on the question of after-care for ex-convicts seen in the light of prison life in the two countries, and in Eastern Europe, and in the differing judicial systems in general. The previous year saw a conference between parliamentarians from Lorraine, the Saar and Luxembourg to discuss their common regional matters. The *Akademie* is financed partly from subsidies, and each different conference usually has its own sponsor. Altogether about 10 per cent of participants are French often NCOs or officers posted to the Federal Republic. This entails a certain selection in the presentation of the subject-matter to avoid an overly obvious slant towards integration. In fact, in 1967, two years after bilateral seminars began, there was considerable trouble because of French official aversion to integration as interpreted at Otzenhausen, and in the following year no joint encounter could be held. Since then, however, the dialogue has been successfully resumed. Apart from military personnel, French students, apprentices and young teachers have participated.[20] A valuable after-service for OFAJ work was provided when young people from Alsace-Lorraine and the Saar who had met at an OFAJ-sponsored course on the neighbouring country then came together again at the *Akademie* to discuss more intensively how far the 'European idea' had become rooted in their respective regions.[21] Although primarily multilateral in its approach, the institute has rendered considerable service to mutual comprehension between Frenchmen and Germans on political and social issues.

Another German association concerned with international exchanges is the *Deutsche Auslandsgesellschaft*. Privately founded in 1949 to encourage better international relations at popular level, it tends, as its head office is at Lübeck, to concentrate on the Nordic countries. It now receives financial aid from cities, *Länder* and the Federal Republic, and in 1954 joined in a private societies' federation for those associations concerned especially with international youth exchanges. The organisation has also arranged a variety of lectures and conferences since its inception, quite a number dedicated to French themes. School exchanges have also been established with France, and from 1965 study groups have visited Germany from across the Rhine in *Gesellschaft*-sponsored trips. The scale has remained fairly limited however.[22]

Another interesting German association, multilateral in outlook, is the *Europäischer Austauschdienst* of Frankfurt. This works with a similarly-orientated French organisation CDLI in Lyon, as far as its relations with France are concerned. It sends groups of local councillors, officials and jurists on visits to France and provides hospitality for similar French visits to Frankfurt and other parts of Hesse. The scale is not large, but qualitatively the visits are well worthwhile. Typical programmes in 1970 included a group of magistrates and lawyers to study French law and judicial administration on a ten-day trip, and another of councillors and local government officials to learn about municipal administration in France, especially in Paris. If subsequent letters from participants are any guide the visits are held to be of great value. Additionally the society co-operates with the OFAJ for youth exchanges and places au pair girls in France, as well as paying guests with French families.[23]

France also has a number of organisations which include Franco-German exchanges in their general programmes. There is in the north the *Centre Départemental d'Echanges Internationaux du Nord* (CDEIN). This is concerned with twin towning among other things, and works closely with BILD, the ADFG, the *Conseil des Communes d'Europe*, the IBU, etc. It arranges study trips to the Federal Republic, especially for students and pupils. Seminars are run, much like Otzenhausen; an illustration is the 1972 joint function for young agriculturalists of both countries on the subject of agriculture in the EEC. Social workers, school teachers and officials have also taken part in bilateral discussions on themes of topical or professional interest. School exchanges are a feature of CDEIN programmes. It should be pointed out that the director, M. Martin, is himself a member of the French counterpart to the ADFG so that there is an emphasis on recon-ciliation in the CDEIN's work.[24] In 1963 a youth leaders' training seminar was run jointly by the two societies, to give only one example of work in common.[25]

These descriptions by no means exhaust the list of bilateral or multilateral associations, which today are really quite thick on the ground, as 'integration' and 'reconciliation' have become such popular catchwords. A difficulty in judging their worth lies in the fact that they tend to be quite variable in their methods, although usually inspired to working towards similar ends. It is hard to compare a relatively small organisation such as the *Deutsch-Französischer Arbeitskreis* with the ADFG, bigger in scale and more orientated towards youth activities and culture in general than directly towards trade or politics. As one French source said of German friendship societies, they differ in quality but they are always positive in their approach.[26] The question remains, is goodwill enough? What contribution has private initiative to make?

There does not seem any doubt at all that in the immediate post-war years the pioneer work of the institute at Ludwigsburg, of BILD and of the *Comité* in Paris, was of lasting value in assisting the dialogue to be taken up once more. One prominent participant has claimed that the generation of young men who made contact over the frontier at that time are today the foundation, to a certain extent at least, of cordial Franco-German relations.[27] This does not seem much exaggerated. At their best, private societies can be at least a reinforcement to official policies, or an instrument. The OFAJ decided to utilise them in youth exchanges as soon as it was founded. At their worst they often consist of old ladies listening to a lecture on Molière, finishing with coffee, simply as an evening's diversion. It seems to us that when they work for school exchanges, afford language courses, arrange seminars on current themes, further worthwhile town partnerships, they are performing positive tasks in the cadre of reconciliation. That local authorities and the two governments find them of use can perhaps be inferred from the financial aid they offer them. We suggest that those societies which offer some properly-worked-out programmes are of value in promoting understanding, that is, where the events have a definite aim, as opposed to lectures on traditional cultural themes. In particular, we feel that study groups, visits and seminars on topical questions on a bilateral basis are worthy of furtherance. Just bringing French and Germans together is not enough in itself. But when German councillors visit France to acquaint themselves with local government there this surely must have real value.

Before we leave the subject of private initiative we must make two further points. Firstly, the efforts made have been repeatedly dogged by the relative lack of response on the French side as compared to the German. Obviously there are exceptions, but as a generalisation this appears to be true. This applies especially to the promotion of individual visits, for which demand continues to be less in evidence in France. Social conditions are probably a factor here, in that housing conditions there are still relatively poor. But it is a problem to be recognised. Secondly, whilst welcoming private initiative we should not overlook that international politics take precedence in determining relations, and that this still applies even in an era of easier communications and the mass media. After all, private enterprise has worked in the field of reconciliation already, even in the nineteenth century.[28] Between the wars similar efforts proved unavailing.[29] If the prospects for the various associations are now better, it is largely because of the improvement in the political atmosphere, which will continue for the foreseeable future to be the determining factor; there is no reason, however, why private initiative cannot back up governmental policies, indeed, we have seen already that it does.

We should finally point out that there are a large number of active associations in the field of bilateral friendship and European unity which do not belong to any of the organisations we have mentioned. There are at least twenty-five Franco-German societies, each in a different city in either of the two countries, which are outside any general federation. As to the total number of associations with similar goals to the ADFG, one of its recent publications in September 1973 could list as many as fifty-one (of which the majority were in France). Our account of what is being done by private initiative cannot possibly be described as exhaustive, but should be seen rather as a series of brief case studies on its role in *rapprochement*.

Notes

1 The conference proceedings are published as 'Die Bedeutung der privaten Initiative für die deutsch-französische Verständigung', *Arbeitskreis der privaten Institutionen für Internationale Begegnung und Bildungsarbeit*, Cologne, 1957.

2 Ziebura, *Die deutsch-französischen Beziehungen*, etc., p 30.

3 C. H. Pegg, 'Die Résistance als Träger der europäischen Einigungsbestrebungen in Frankreich während des zweiten Weltkrieges', *Politisches Archiv*, 5 Oct. 1952, pp 5197f.

4 A. Grosser, 'Deutsch-französische Zusammenarbeit nach 1945', in *Deutschland-Frankreich*, vol. III, pp 17f.

5 This account of the foundation based on *Allemagne*, nos 80–2, July/Dec. 1963.

6 *Allemagne*, no. 19, Summer 1952.

7 Ibid., no. 7, June/July 1950.

8 E.-V. Couchoud, 'Die Gesellschaft für Uebernationale Zusammenarbeit', (the German title of BILD), *Deutschland-Frankreich*, vol. III, pp 28f.

9   For an analysis, 'A la rencontre de la jeunesse allemande par les échanges individuels inter-familiaux. Cinq Ans d'Echanges Franco-Allemands', *Education et Echanges*, Paris, 1969, pp 19–21.
10 *Documents*, no. 6, 1960, pp 750*f*.
11 The first president of the Institute itself was Dr Carlo Schmid, then an academic at Tübingen University, now official German Co-ordinator for Franco-German co-operation.
12 'Zwanzig Jahre' Sonderdruck der Reihe, *Deutschland-Frankreich*, Süddeutsche Verlagsanstalt, Stuttgart, 1968, p 6.
13 Ibid., p 17.
14 The Association activities are frequently listed in *Correspondance*.
15 The information here provided by the German Vice-President, Dr Forsteneichner, and *Mitgliederverzeichnis und Veranstaltungsfolge*, 1971, pub. by the Society.
16 Information from the founder, Herr D. Gottschalk, in private correspondence and an interview with the authors, and D. Gottschalk, *Zwischenbilanz*, Düsseldorf, Droste Verlag, 1970.
17 The French title is *Cercle de Travail des Associations Franco-Allemandes*.
18 Unless otherwise stated the account here is based on an interview with the ADFG Vice-President, Dr Kühn-Leitz, and the Society's own information sheet, *Mitteilungsblatt für die deutsch-französischen Gesellschaften*.
19 *Documents*, Nov./Dec. 1970, p 95.
20 For example, a joint youth seminar in 1970 on school life in the two countries sponsored by the OFAJ. *Correspondance*, no. 172, 29 July 1970, p 22.
21 Information from Herr Schlicht, Herr Hesedenz and M. Fournier of the *Akademie* in a personal interview.
22 Private reports, *Deutsche Auslandsgesellschaft*, 1949–69.
23 Private correspondence with the Society and its yearly reports, 1963–70.
24 *Rapport d'activités*, 1971–72 and private correspondence.
25 *Mitteilungsblatt*, no. 17, July 1964, p 78.
26 *Le Monde*, 11 June 1963.
27 A Grosser, 'Deutsch-französische Zusammenarbeit nach 1945', op. cit., p 19.
28 See R. Marquand, 'Un essai de création d'un institut allemand à Paris en 1826', *Etudes Germaniques*, no. 12, 1957, pp 97*f*.
29 W. D'Ormesson, 'Une tentative de rapprochement franco-allemand entre les deux guerres', *Revue de Paris*, Feb. 1962, pp 18*f*.

Chapter 9

A Brief Survey of Bilateralism and of European Cultural Work at Multilateral Level

So far in this book we have been dealing with Franco-German relations, but before we make any evaluation of them we ought to underline that their experience is far from unique. Both governments maintain a certain level of cultural activity in many other countries apart from in that of their immediate neighbour. In order to set the Franco-German relations in perspective therefore, we need to describe these undertakings. Equally, we have to pay some attention to multilateral cultural activities, which take place in the framework of the various supranational bodies, private or official, which now exist inside the European Community. A brief description of the organisational structure of these relations in Western Europe should help us to assess exactly how much of the Franco-German experience could profitably be considered as constituting a model for Europe of the future. This is a theme to which we shall return in our final chapter.

The French government devotes a considerable amount of financial resources to fostering cultural relations with other countries. In 1970 the total sum spent amounted to nearly 846 million francs, two thirds of the Foreign Ministry's entire budget.[1] This includes money used for scientific and technical collaboration, which makes it difficult to arrive at an exact comparison with the Federal Republic, which allocated 307 million DM to its cultural funds in the same year, including, as in the French case, the cost of its own schools abroad.[2] Expenditure of this magnitude clearly implies a wide range of activities.

Both governments have, in fact, signed a number of cultural agreements, apart from their bilateral one already described. In 1968 the Federal Republic had twenty-three such treaties with eleven different European countries. The usual formula is to set up a standing joint commission to supervise the execution of the accord; often there is a special sub-committee for youth exchanges under this also. West Germany has one such with six other European countries apart from France. All this is impressive, but was nonetheless surpassed by France in 1968, as the latter country then had the thickest network of cultural agreements of any West European power,[3] no doubt a reflection of its traditional drive to spread French culture and its language abroad. It must be emphasised, however, that many governments engage in the furtherance of their culture in other countries without necessarily concluding formal arrangements, one example being Switzerland.[4]

West Germany for its part maintains with many peoples the kind of links and exchanges which we have described in previous chapters. This does not mean that an equal stress is placed on each type of activity in each individual country. In the case of the Netherlands the emphasis in personal exchanges with Germany tends to fall on the future leaders of the two countries rather than upon a wider spectrum of youth. In Anglo-German contacts on the other hand, a great deal of attention is paid to musical events and to long-term projects of a social nature, or professional/vocational exchanges. Religious bodies in both Britain and Germany have also been active in promoting contacts; since 1967, Methodists in both countries have been organising joint actions, to choose only one illustration. Academic relations have also been close between the two countries; in 1966–67 there were over three hundred German language assistants in Great Britain, by far the largest number in any foreign country except France. At the same time nearly half the foreign assistants in the Federal Republic came from Great Britain. The West German Rectors' conference has links with Great Britain, Italy, Scandinavia, Yugoslavia and Turkey, as well as with France. A similar state of affairs is true of university, etc. partnerships. In 1968 fifty institutes of higher education in Munich had established contacts between them with 270 similar institutions in Europe, including seventy in East European countries.

At the level of national cultural policy the same applies; there were in 1970 as many as 116 different Goethe Institutes abroad, of which only eight were in France. To put this into further perspective, Greece had six, and Italy seven.[6] The Federal Republic had teachers or establishments of some kind in ninety different countries in all. Youth contacts are a further reflection of how widespread German cultural activities were. In recent years West Germany has been reinforcing this aspect with many countries, not necessarily all in Europe. There has been an increase in this respect with Great Britain since the cultural accord signed by the two governments in 1965. Two years later young foreigners visiting the Federal Republic spent a total of 778,114 nights in youth hostels; although the French had the greatest single figure in this respect, their proportion of the total was little over one quarter, despite the OFAJ and its works. Twin towning plays a part in Anglo-German youth exchanges; by 1968 nearly two hundred such partnerships included organised contacts for young people within the range of their functions. In 1971–72 exchanges with the Federal Republic were by far the biggest item in British bilateral youth contacts sponsored by the government.[7]

A similar picture could be painted of French activities with third countries, although it would be tedious to do so in the same detail. We shall merely point out that France maintains institutes and cultural centres all over the world, in 1969–70 nearly two hundred all told, of which only twenty-two were in Germany.[8] As a result of a meeting between Heath and Pompidou, France and Britain are now to augment their youth exchanges considerably, the British government having made a sum of £100,000 available for this purpose.[9] There are a large number of Anglo-French town partnerships with the usual programme of activities. Educationally both countries have set up the usual contacts already described here. There is, for example, a joint commission of civil servants which meets yearly to facilitate exchanges. Britain and France have, of course, signed a formal cultural agreement and there are a large number of exchanges, both in the academic field and in secondary education.

Before leaving the question of Franco-German relations with third countries we should underline that Great Britain itself is beginning to show more interest in the furtherance of European culture rather than in promoting its language and way of life in the Commonwealth as formerly. The Duncan Report of 1968 stressed the need for closer links in cultural terms with the Continent. In March 1972 Mr Rippon announced a plan to spend

£6 million over four years on relations with European countries. There was to be a strong emphasis on language-teaching, youth exchanges, educational contacts and twin towning. The British Council already has engaged in a great deal of work on the continent, running six libraries in France and four in West Germany among its other varied activities. From these latest moves it seems clear that the British government feels that the kind of contacts which we have been describing are financially worthwhile in terms of selling one's image abroad. This can in a way be seen as an endorsement of the Franco-German bilateral relationship.

Over and above all cultural activities fostered jointly by two national governments, there is another level to be considered, which may be called the multilateral, in that it is supervised by some international institution, either private or official. The number of these has proliferated in recent years especially in Western Europe. We shall begin with a purely international organisation, UNESCO. According to its charter, it has the task, among others, of furthering international understanding. To this end it organises regional conferences, including some in Europe. Exchanges have been arranged between teachers, scientists and apprentices from various countries and in addition teaching material has been produced, as well as films and exhibitions. On occasions sub-regional conferences have been arranged between Communist and non-Communist countries alike, as in the Balkans in 1963 and 1965. In November 1967 UNESCO convened a meeting of European Education Ministers in Vienna to deal with higher education; five years later it sponsored a discussion at Helsinki on cultural policies in general. UNESCO thus contributes its share to the exchange of views and information in the various fields which together form what may be called cultural relations in the broadest sense. Another Pan-European meeting of Education Ministers took place at Bucharest in late 1973, also under UNESCO auspices.

Among other official supranational bodies playing a similar role is the OECD. This was at first rather more concerned perhaps with the technological gap between Europe and the USA than with education as such. It has built up a number of study groups dealing with training and research. In 1963 the OECD arranged a meeting of scientists and educators in Paris and since 1967 has regularly published a bulletin, *Science Policy Information.*

It has now set up an experimental Centre for Educational Research and Innovation (CERI), as well as an Education Committee. From 1 January, 1972, a separate programme on educational building was initiated as well. The committee works in three areas of educational research, of which higher education is one, the others being reform and innovation, and planning and management. A considerable number of publications containing the fruits of these activities have been brought out; it should be remembered that not only West European countries, but the USA, Japan, Canada and Australia are OECD members. Attention has often been given in such reports to the special problems peculiar to individual states. Studies of Portugal, Greece and Turkey are three examples. As mentioned in Chapter 3, reports are frequently rendered on the current state of education in a particular country, for example France and West Germany.

CERI was first established in 1968 and has concentrated on four major areas, educational opportunity, including innovation in higher education, curriculum development and educational technology. For the period 1971–74, another programme has developed embracing the links between education and society, innovations in teaching and learning, and a study of how these latter may be more effectively employed.

The separate programme on educational building was established in 1972 to cover a three-year span, based on financial contributions from sixteen member states. The aim is to bring about a more effective exchange of ideas on the subject between individual countries in respect of the technology of school construction: one aspect is a study of how industrialised building methods can be adapted for schools. The OECD has thus included in its programmes a wide spectrum of activities ranging from education to science and technology, the latter dealing with environmental problems among others. Other organisations facilitating technical collaboration and advancement include the ECSC (according to its 1951 constitution), Euratom and the EEC itself. The latter is especially concerned with vocational training and the furtherance of exchanges between young workers.[10] These last three organisations have a common press and information service which among other things informs the younger generation about European integration, and perhaps in itself spreads the idea of Western Europe as one community. Additionally there are twice-yearly meetings of civil servants at Brussels to deal with the co-ordination of policy on matters affecting youth in all its aspects, the influence of which is difficult to assess.

We should point out that the European Parliament at Strasbourg also has a body, known as the Committee for Cultural Affairs and Youth. In 1963 the Parliament called for the establishment of common policies for educational organisation and for closer co-operation in those areas where the resources of a single country no longer sufficed (presumably technological collaboration was meant). The resolution also expressed the desire to see more inter-European co-operation in order to preserve that heritage which all European peoples derive from certain aspects of a common past. The Parliament has engaged in a programme of cultural education and youth affairs since then, although the results do not seem to be very impressive. The Commission at Brussels has also set up a Directorate General for research, education and science.

Curious as it may seem at first sight, one of the organisations most active in the immediate post-war years in the realm of educational collaboration was the Brussels Treaty Organisation, which had its own cultural commission. This held three different study courses between 1949 and 1951 on education, which resulted eventually in a brochure, *The Civilisation of Western Europe and the School*. By 1961 four more courses had been held, when a general European civics campaign was also launched.

Even closer co-operation between the various Ministers of Education inside the Western European Union (WEU) pact also began to develop after 1959. In that year the Dutch Minister of Education invited his counterparts to discussions at the Hague. This was followed by similar events at Hamburg in 1961, then at Rome in the following year and at London in 1964. At Hamburg, to take one example, such common problems as the teaching of modern languages were discussed. It was agreed to exchange information regularly, and in 1965 an educational documentation centre was founded, within the Council of Europe.

Parallel with these events went a close association at university level, for which a general Rectors' conference, again in the framework of the WEU, provided the organisational structure. In 1955 the first such meeting took place, and four years later at Dijon an even wider circle of countries was represented. The next discussions, at Göttingen in 1964, saw the participation even of some countries from outside Western Europe, such as the GDR, Czechoslovakia and Poland. Themes on the agenda included the relationship between the universities and the economy in general, research, student responsibility and the relationship between universities and technical colleges with the problems which it brings.

In 1959 a European Cultural Fund was established, administered by the Council of Europe, which in the following year instituted its own Committee of Higher Education and Research, composed of Rectors, Vice-Chancellors and civil servants. In 1961 came the Council for Cultural Co-operation (CCC). This is a quite distinct body from the Education Ministers' conference to which we have previously referred. Broadly, the conference consists of politicians who discuss and adopt policy resolutions, whereas the CCC is made up of senior national officials who together devise the Council of Europe's cultural and educational programmes, and their financing. Unlike the conference, it has a large permanent secretariat of European civil servants. This does not, however, imply that the two organisations never work together; as early as 1961, the conference which met at Hamburg charged the Council of Europe with such problems as adult education, *équivalences* and further education. Similarly, the conference can and does call on the CCC to carry out particular tasks on its behalf. The picture is thus one of co-operation, not competition between two overlapping organisations.

Before we examine the work of the CCC more closely we should refer briefly to the Education Ministers' conference after 1964. As recently as 1969, at the sixth conference, M. Faure advocated giving the function a permanent character, a suggestion which he linked with the concept of a European Office of Education. Two years later at Brussels his successor as national Education Minister, M. Guichard, reinforced his colleague's proposals; the Education Ministers accepted the idea of a standing conference, but a European Office is probably still some way off, except perhaps as a co-ordinating body. In fact, in December 1971 a working party was initiated by the CCC to examine more closely what the work of such a body would be likely to consist of. A further complication has been the coincidence of the new proposals with a period of financial retrenchment. All we can say is that the concept, whilst encouraging and exciting in principle, will clearly need a vast amount of careful, specific planning, as European educational systems tend to be so very varied, according to differing national experiences in the past.

Before we come to the CCC we should point out that the Council of Europe has itself produced some solid results in practice in respect of cultural collaboration. At its first-ever sitting in 1949 the Consultative Assembly set up a cultural/academic committee, which since 1967 has been divided into two bodies, dealing respectively with culture and education on the one hand, and science and technology on the other. This latter committee has developed a lively activity since then, with a series of papers and recommendations having been produced by various working groups. Additionally, it has run three conferences on parliament and science. It is currently attempting to mount a European joint expedition to the Antarctic. The Culture and Education Committee has organised a number of symposia on higher education. For example, in 1970 it worked on the question of a common mathematics syllabus. Professional training and its co-ordination has also engaged the Council's attention. Articles 118 and 128 of the Treaty of Rome are concerned with this aspect of integration, and on the proposals of the European Communities Commission in July 1971 the Council undertook an analysis of the needs of the member countries, and produced a report.

The CCC, in which twenty-one states are now represented, includes three parliamentarians to represent the Consultative Assembly, and its operational activities are financed by the European Cultural Funds instituted in 1959. These are composed of direct contributions from member states and from donations, but are rather limited. Starting from just under one and a half million French francs in 1962, expenditure rose to nearly two and a half million in 1966 and just over three million in 1971.[12] These are not large resources in view of the role which the CCC could play in facilitating the growth of integration in the fields of educational and scientific endeavour, quite apart from in activities such as youth exchanges. However, it has to be borne in mind that the CCC's staff are paid for out of the general budget of the Council of Europe. Additionally, the European Youth Centre and the European Youth Foundation (of which more later) are also separately financed. On some occasions CCC-sponsored activities which take place in member countries are often paid for by national funds. Thus the true financial backing for the CCC may well amount to as much as fifteen million French francs.

Its own goals illustrate how wide the Council casts its net; they are defined as the preservation of Europe's cultural heritage, the transmission of relevant information between member states, the improvement of educational standards, the question of *équivalances*, the furtherance of freedom of movement and transfer in the academic world, technological and scientific co-operation, extra-scholastic education and the revision of school textbooks. This is a long and imposing list, which clearly could use more money than it gets. The CCC devoted much of its efforts in fact to education, and research into this subject in particular; school education and research took nearly two thirds of the 1971 budget, with extra-scholastic education, youth and culture accounting for the remainder. These latter are now financed through the Youth Centre and Foundation referred to above.

Organisationally the CCC has built up three committees to deal respectively with the subjects of higher, secondary and extra-scholastic training. Much of their time is spent on comparative studies in these particular fields. There is now so much to undertake in relation to the funds available that in 1971 the decision was taken to concentrate on a smaller number of projects in the future. At the same time an administrative change was introduced, in that two steering groups were initiated, one for full-time education, the other for educational technology.

Despite financial limitations a certain amount of good work has been accomplished since the CCC's inception. In 1964, for example, a series, *Education in Europe*, was published giving information yielded by comparative studies. Another major project concerned research into language-teaching. Other programmes have included road safety education in schools, research into reading skills and into teacher-training. A compendium entitled *Permanent Education* was produced in 1971; later conferences have produced model programmes for an integrated educational policy. Symposia for leaders of educational policy in their own countries are a frequent occurrence in CCC-sponsored programmes, as for example in the Strasbourg colloquium in November 1971 for junior university staff.

Another task undertaken has been the inspection of various centres with a view to discovering whether or not they could undertake a European role. An *ad hoc* group was set up for this and in 1971 visited four such places, including the International Textbook Institute at Brunswick. Its opinion was that, given the fulfilment of certain conditions, each institute would be suitable for the designated function. Further recommendations were made regarding the co-ordination of member states of the Council of Europe insofar as the proposed work of the centres would be concerned, so that activities could begin as soon as possible. It was also suggested that each member state should set up a counterpart at national level to each proposed European centre. In 1972 a language centre (CILT) in London concluded an agreement with the Council of Europe to take on a 'European' role in language-teaching. If CCC proposals bear fruit elsewhere a whole network of individual research institutes for different particular educational fields could be linked to one European body in each case, which would obviously result in a much closer exchange of information and ideas. Such an arrangement would possess obvious intrinsic value, but extrinsically it would have the additional advantage of simply furthering integration as such. As against this, the accent by a European body or national government on any one place of higher learning could conceivably cause resentment in some others in the same country.

Two other extremely useful CCC undertakings have been in the domain of youth activities and in that of *équivalences*. For the first, a European youth centre has been opened in Strasbourg where the first course began in October 1963. The centre is dedicated to awakening the idea of European integration in the youth of today and providing relevant training-courses, mostly for youth leaders. The involvement of young people in the problems of today also forms part of the programmes; these take place now in a specially constructed centre in Strasbourg. The Committee of Ministers, incidentally, has now taken the decision to support a European Youth Foundation, to promote co-operation among young people. The necessary Statute has been prepared and signed by all member states of the Council of Europe. The Foundation is now in operation with an annual budget of just over four million French francs.

Work on the vexed question of *équivalences* is now proceeding at CCC level as well as elsewhere. In March 1971 a meeting of experts from fifteen member states, plus observers from UNESCO and various European Communities' organisations as well as of some outside bodies, was held in Bonn.[14] It was recommended that member states should inform the Council of Europe of their national information and documentation centres concerning *équivalences* and related matters. They should also circulate lists of recognised secondary education diplomas, and leaving certificates, etc. and of national *équivalence* regulations. The object of these suggestions is clearly the co-ordination of policies as a first step in the wider recognition of purely national qualifications. It has also been recommended that the CCC's committee on higher education and research should concentrate on standardising study records, among other tasks. Linked with work on *équivalences* is, of course, the question of academic mobility, discussed by experts from nine member states at Strasbourg in November 1971. One speaker suggested four strands which needed to be woven together in order to produce a coherent policy in this respect. Firstly, there should be more systematic exchange of information, secondly, increased rights for teachers and research workers to permanent training, thirdly, *équivalence* agreements, and, fourthly, facilities to help foreign academics to be easily accommodated into their new post. The conference as a whole seems to have felt that the whole matter would be settled only in the course of time, by a long-drawn-out system of agreements and negotiation. As we remarked earlier, the question of academic and professional stand-ardisation cannot be easily solved, but at least some start has been made multilaterally by the CCC as well as at Brussels.

Finally we should draw attention to an interesting project which the CCC has undertaken in the more purely cultural realm. A 1971 conference in Switzerland worked out the details for a wide-ranging research programme in eleven European cities, each in a different country. The idea is a recognition of the growing importance in culture and leisure activities of the municipality, although as the CCC points out, the latter does not always pursue an integrated consistent policy. It has therefore suggested to the eleven selected towns certain ways in which a better overall scheme may be produced; each town was to have its own programme over the period 1972–74, but in the framework of a common general plan. A co-ordinating body was to direct operations in each municipality; civic leaders were due to be invited to a joint discussion on the results obtained; these will be publicised among local authorities all over Europe. This appears to us to be a thoroughly worthwhile, and indeed exciting, project. When pub-lished, the results should be of immense help to councillors engaged in drawing up schemes for leisure activities, etc. in their own areas. This is particularly true at a time when the phrase 'the quality of life' is very much the order of the day. Any experiments which help us to employ our free hours in some profitable way should presumably be commended, since in the future we are likely to have so much more time at our disposal, and the local authority can obviously play a role here. Incidentally, the scheme has now been extended to fourteen different municipalities.

Of course the CCC, like UNESCO and similar bodies, has to depend very much on the willingness of national governments to collaborate with it. This may seem a rather obvious point, but in the description of multilateral schemes and projects it may easily appear that the Council is totally independent of others, especially as it has its own funds. We simply wish to underline that much of its work is achieved not merely with the active co-operation of national governments, but often on their initiative. One example here would be the French suggestions already mentioned regarding a European Office of Education. Similarly, the question of a European Youth Foundation was the result of a West German suggestion. In a sense the CCC is itself simultaneously initiator, co-ordinator and collaborator.

The work of the various bodies described in the foregoing has found concrete expression in a number of accords and conventions which the various national governments have signed in the last twenty years. Their list is impressive even if agreement in principle has sometimes been easier than realisation of the same principles in practice. In 1953 the first general accord dealt with *équivalences*, in particular in respect of leaving certificates. December of the following year saw the conclusion of a general European cultural convention open to non-member states. The signatories bound themselves to ensure the study of the language, history and civilisation of other European states in their own country, and to further exchanges and cultural co-operation. Here one may legitimately feel perhaps that the recognition of such principles was the main thing achieved in itself. Further agreements from 1956 onwards dealt with the question of common acceptance of study periods as qualifications for admission to higher education, recognition of academic titles, the exchange of TV programmes, and of production rights concerning them, and in 1965 a joint regulation against pirate radio stations. It would be wrong, however long-drawn-out the implementation of such accords may be, to underestimate the very real degree of collaboration, and indeed integration of policies that they imply.

But the Council of Europe has itself produced, in a 1970 report, a sober assessment of the worth of these conventions individually in practice. The first, on diploma *équivalence*, is regarded as useful in general, the second equally so in respect of modern languages. But the 1959 accord on academic titles has allegedly had almost no effect. The Council in its report felt that bilateral *équivalence* agreements on the whole have been successful, where based on a thorough examination of study courses; but multilateral accords not so constructed seem to have been less effective in practice than in theory. Above all, it is felt that what is always an essential prerequisite is a supply of exhaustive information on the subjects concerned in each country, perhaps based on information centres.

Textbook revision has also been carried on at international level. A recent report commissioned at Brussels and composed by M. Henri Janne, formerly Minister of Education in Belgium, has recommended new history books drawn up to expunge 'nationalistic, biased passages'. It has even been suggested that language teachers should be replaced by machines because human instructors distort a foreign culture in explaining it. Its reception has been stormy, as several countries simply do not see the EEC as having the right to intervene in national education. In any case, although removing 'biased passages' can be useful, as we saw in the Franco-German case, there is an obvious limit to this; ultimately there is a British viewpoint of Waterloo and a French one, as A. J. P. Taylor has pointed out in relation to the Janne proposals.

Official bodies have also sponsored in one way or another a good deal of additional co-operation in the wider field of cultural relations. Sometimes this takes the form of what might be termed traditional activities, such as art exhibitions. The Council of Europe, in deference to its goal of preserving the common European heritage, has held fourteen such events since it began in Brussels in 1954 with *Humanist Europe*. In September 1972 London saw the *Age of Neo-Classicism* as its contribution, the second time that it has been the venue. The exhibitions are arranged by national States with the support of experts in other countries; the CCC has already developed plans for individual events of this kind up to 1978 at least.

The mass-media have been increasingly the subject of international collaboration in recent years, for example by 1971 eight film weeks had already been sponsored by the CCC. In addition it produces its own films, mostly documentaries. The joint information services of the other European bodies contribute also by producing films, usually with some emphasis on integration as such. A studio has been built in Brussels, which is available for the production of TV and radio programmes as well. Incidentally UNESCO also has its own film and television council. There is now, of course, a considerable interchange of radio and TV programmes between all European countries as well as a number of co-productions usually undertaken on a bilateral basis. Various festivals, such as that at Montreux, have been initiated. Technically, co-operation has undoubtedly been of value to all participants, but the purely European programmes which have been brought about, such as the Eurovision Song Contest or *Jeux sans frontières*, have often been of a disappointingly low quality. In view of the exciting possibilities inherent in the capacity of TV programmes to cross national borders, it seems a pity that more use of them has not been made in this respect.

As sport is an important leisure activity today the CCC has naturally devoted some attention to this area. The Belgian government has donated a clearing-house in Brussels to be used for the planning involved in the concept of sport for all. Four principles have now been established as being of paramount importance here. There should be close co-operation between the public and private sectors at all administrative levels, the Consultative Assembly should draft a European charter to demonstrate agreement on certain principles, whilst a long-term plan is also essential in which the clearing house can play a useful part. Finally there should be a certain degree of division of labour between individual states in order to ensure the implementation of common planning.[15] In other words, a joint approach to the whole matter should be carefully prepared in order to realise a joint project; all this again quite clearly implies the advancement of integration in itself in yet another area of contemporary life. The Sport for All charter has now been drafted and waits approval from the Committee of Ministers.

Before we leave the domain of officially or semi-officially sponsored activities in a European framework we should draw attention to some other aspects of integration not so far covered in our account. For example, there is now a European Association of Teachers founded in 1956, and which in 1968 already had over 30,000 members;[16] these are organised in national sections, and each one produces its own periodical. The Association advocates the creation of a federal state in Europe, and hopes to introduce a better understanding of the problems of the area, and its common heritage, in schools. To some extent it is active in the field of educational revision, particularly for history, geography and language manuals. The existence of such an association at scholastic level must surely exercise some influence in the future insofar as winning the coming generation for the European idea is concerned.

Equally interesting in this respect is the so-called *European Schools Day*, which has taken place yearly since 1953 under the joint patronage of the Communities and the Council of Europe. This is a contest in which the pupils and students of countries in the EEC, plus those of Norway, Sweden, Austria and Switzerland participate.[17] The goal of the competition is described as awakening a feeling of 'Europeanness' in the contestants, who are divided in three ascending age groups: their interest is to further European civilisation and its contemporary problems. Every year each age group gets a different exercise, which, for the youngest, is based on drawing and painting, and for the two older an essay competition. In 1967 the task for the youngest participants was the decoration of a schoolroom to illustrate a general European theme of their choice. For group three, aged sixteen to twenty-one, an essay had to be written on a recent aspect of European integration, and their attitude towards it. All entries are judged first at national and then at supranational level. This again appears to be a constructive idea, which must assist in getting young people accustomed to think in European terms, and to see themselves as members of a larger community than the national state.

Whilst still on the subject of education we should point out that there are now a number of European schools which have been founded in various countries, partly subsidised by the Communities, although in comparison with national institutions the scale is still minute. One example is the one in Karlsruhe, opened in September 1962;[18] the first pupils to take the *Abitur* did so in 1968, the school originally having been founded at primary level, and expanding later to the secondary. In March 1967 there were 372 pupils, drawn from various countries, as were the 30 teachers. It is frankly difficult to see much future in these institutions. As in the case of the Franco-German joint *lycées* they must be usually boarding schools, which implies a financial elite, or they must have heavy state or supranational subsidies, which in either case is a certain drawback. Some of these schools now take an international *Baccalauréat*, a project originally undertaken in Switzerland. By 1969 it had so grown that 650 candidates, many from countries outside the Common Market, sat the examination. Most were from multinational schools. Finance for further development has now become available from various private funds such as the Ford and Gulbenkian Foundations.

Almost inevitably a European university is being founded. This was first foreseen in the Euratom Treaty, curiously enough. Discussions began in 1958 and it was decided three years after to establish it in Florence. Negotiations were very long-drawn-out, due to disagreement about the actual structure; then difficulty arose about naming the rector, which was eventually left to the Foreign Ministers of the European Community. After sixteen years, the university was due to be opened in August 1974. Initially there will be between forty and fifty postgraduates, which it is hoped to raise to 250 in the course of time. The affair is illustrative of the snags inherent in such joint undertakings, where nine separate countries have to be brought to accord, and also perhaps of Community bureaucracy: these two points are obviously connected with one another in practice. Clearly cultural differences will produce some delays in matters of this nature, but if the appointment of a rector has to be left to Foreign Ministers then it would seem that better administrative organisation in the Community might produce rather more rapid results. Surely this could have been decided at a lower level?

There is also a College of Europe at Bruges, opened as long ago as 1949, with a convinced advocate of European cultural unity, Henri Brugmans, as director. The College was really born of the 1948 Congress of Europe, where Denis de Rougement proposed a centre for cultural exchanges. Other delegates to the Congress, notably Salvador de Madariaga, took up the idea, with the idea of a postgraduate centre specialising in European civilisation. The suggestion of Bruges as the site came from another 1948 Congress delegate, and eventually the College opened its doors on 12 October, 1950. It now takes in about fifty students annually.

One other interesting aspect of 'Europeanisation' at university level is the sheer growth of dissertations devoted in recent years to the subject in general. In 1970–71, for example, the number of doctoral theses dealing with integration being written in France and West Germany alone amounted to 535 (compared to 266 in the year 1966). In a way it is encouraging that in European universities as a whole the greatest single aspect being considered is that of the legal questions involved in integration, with economic matters coming in second place. We choose the word 'encouraging' because Europe can only be united by overcoming specific legal and administrative hurdles, as well as cultural and economic ones. It is also interesting to notice that the German graduates tended to concentrate on questions affecting publicity and economic competition, the French and Italians on agrarian matters and the Dutch on supranationality as such.[19]

Apart from official organisations there are now a number of private or semi-official associations which also work for European unity in the cultural field, just as there are Franco-German friendship societies; equally, the contribution of these other associations has to be taken into account, however briefly. There is at Geneva a European Cultural Centre, founded in 1950, to further the consciousness of the cultural heritage and European solidarity. The Centre is a recognised meeting place, and pays special attention to education. Meetings of prominent academics, intellectuals, and of the leaders of the mass media and publishers have been convened, so that in a sense the institute is a forum for integration. Slightly different is the European Cultural Foundation, originally founded in 1954 in Switzerland but transferred two years later to the Netherlands. The Foundation organises cultural events of all kinds, including youth encounters,[20] although this aspect is now of diminishing importance. Its major activity in recent years has been concerned with the shape of things to come, under the title of 'Europe 2000'.

There is, of course, a whole network of international organisations for young people, which are literally too numerous to mention. These have sometimes a political or religious goal, but which can nonetheless consider European themes. In 1964 the first ever conference of Young People of the Left took place in Paris, to choose one illustration, which reminds us perhaps when we talk of 'Europe' or 'integration' that not everyone necessarily has the same ideas on these subjects.

Private initiative also plays an important part in complementing the work of official bodies in the realm of the education of the coming generation in European terms. Here one obvious example is the *Europäische Akademie* at Otzenhausen, which we referred to in connection with Franco-German reconciliation, and which casts its net wider than bilateral relations. As the title of one of its own publications implies, it regards integration as a challenge to political education.[21] Consequently the *Akademie* gives many seminars and courses on current European themes to groups of mixed nationality, or solely to young Germans. An example of the former was the week-long study-group in 1973 for students of technical colleges in West Germany and for those at a Dutch institution based on a comparative study of educational systems in the two countries, and of teacher-training as well. A typical seminar for Germans only was that given to young soldiers of the IIIrd Corps on the significance of the Security Conference for the East-West dialogue in general. There are a number of similar institutions in the Federal Republic, for example at Berlin and Lerbach, which today run seminars on the European idea.

Adult educational associations often supplement these courses in effect by affording study trips abroad. In 1973 the French organisation *Peuple et Culture* initiated such events for Frenchmen, visiting both Britain and the Federal Republic.[22] Thus private or semi-official enterprise complement in various countries the work of the supranational organisations insofar as adult education for Europe is concerned.

In the realm of twin towning the most important association is clearly the *Conseil des Communes d'Europe*, which, as its name implies, seeks to further integration by means of town partnerships. The association was founded at Geneva in 1951 in order to develop a municipal confederation in Europe; it is partly subsidised by the French government and cannot be held to be purely private. It is an organisation of some importance, however, in furthering unity, at local level in this case, which may be equal in significance to national or regional initiatives in the long run. We have to emphasise that the *Conseil* by no means confines its activities solely to the realm of twin towning, as it organises discussion groups, seminars and conferences for mayors and civic leaders in general. Partnerships are seen as one method among many whereby a uniform system of communal administration may be attained, as one step on the path to integration. By June 1967 the claim was made that over 50,000 European municipalities had officially adhered to the *Conseil*, with national sections in nine different countries:[23] there are, especially in France, innumerable regional and local committees to facilitate administration. Every two years there is a congress, known as the *Etats-Généraux des Communes d'Europe*. These have taken place regularly since 1953, each time in a different city. The association maintains a close co-operation with other European institutions, notably the Council of Europe.

Even if one accepts that the harmonisation of municipal administration in Western Europe is a very long-term goal indeed, it is nonetheless true that the *Conseil* is over the whole range of its activities yet another force making for unity. Especially significant is the approach, the concept of producing integration from below, as it were. There seems no reason to suppose that this is in opposition to a similar movement at governmental level; indeed, in an era of easy communications and popular international contacts on a large scale, the winning of wide sections of the electorate for any idea in itself is bound to influence national political decisions in the long run. It is presumably of some significance that leaders in various countries have acknowledged the association's work, since in so doing they commit themselves to supporting its aims, a statement of faith which could later be held against them if necessary.

In the field of municipal collaboration another body which should be mentioned is the European Local Authority conference, perhaps from the British standpoint more important than the *Conseil*. The conference meets every other year in Strasbourg and has machinery to ensure continuity. It helps local authorities especially to maintain co-operation with the Council of Europe.

On the other hand, an empirical analysis of communities in Western Flanders reveals that motives in forming these links are very mixed, and frequency of actual contact varies enormously from place to place, according to the respective geographical locations of the municipalities involved. Moreover, only four out of thirty-eight gave European integration as the motive in forming the partnership.[24] It would appear that twinning has in many cases become little more than a prevalent fashion and its influence should not be over-estimated.

The description which we have given here of the work of various organisations cannot pretend to be exhaustive. All we wish to achieve by this chapter is to demonstrate firstly that Franco-German exchanges, and the 1954 accord, are far from unique, in order to put previous sections of this book into perspective. Secondly, we wanted to show how a considerable number of supranational associations, usually official but sometimes private, have sprung up in the field of cultural relations, using 'culture' in its widest possible meaning. It now remains for us in the remaining chapter to assess the Franco-German experience as a possible European model. Further to this, we have to examine the relationship between popular contacts and foreign policy in the light of Franco-German reconciliation, and how far they can affect the stereotype of oneself and one's neighbour, which is clearly linked to foreign policy in itself. We shall also have to consider bilateralism as such in the field of cultural relations, and determine in which areas and to what extent it is either in opposition to multilateralism or rather may complement it.

Notes

1 *Correspondance*, no. 189, 15 June 1973, p A.
2 'Kulturabteilung des Auswärtigen Amtes', *Jahresbericht*, 1970, p 24.
3 G. Hindrichs, *Kulturgemeinschaft Europa*, op. cit., p 17.
4 Ibid., p 17.
5 *Das Studienseminar*, Band XII, 1967, p 34.
6 Kulturabteilung, op. cit., pp 74*f*.
7 British Council Annual Report, 1971, London, HMSO, 1972.
8 *Correspondance*, no. 189, 15 June 1973, p A.
9 British Council, op. cit.
10 Hindrichs, op. cit., p 32.
11 For a fuller account see A. Haigh, *A Ministry of Education for Europe*, London, George Harrap & Co., 1970.
12 Ibid., p 36, and Council for Cultural Cooperation Annual Report, 1971, Strasbourg, 1972, p 97.
13 Council for Cultural Cooperation, op. cit., pp 25*f*.
14 Ibid., pp 55–6.
15 Ibid., p 68.
16 Hindrichs, p 92.
17 Ibid., pp 92–4.
18 Hindrichs, Commission of the European Communities, p 96.
19 Universities Studies on European Integration, no. 7, 1972.
20 Ibid., pp 46–8.
21 For example, 'Europäische Integration—Herausforderung an die politische Bildung', 1970, *Dokumente und Schriften*, no. 7.
22 'Présentation des activités', 1973, *Peuple et Culture*.
23 *Le Conseil des Communes d'Europe. Son organisation—ses buts—ses activités*, June 1967, produced by the Conseil.
24 'Les problèmes culturels dans L'Europe du nord-ouest', produced by CDEIN, June 1973.

Chapter 10

The Franco-German Experience as a European Model

It was once pointed out by the late Theodor Heuss that whereas you cannot create culture with (governmental) policies it is possible to make culture itself an instrument of foreign policy.[1] Indeed, both France and West Germany have done so for decades. But as we have already stressed, the old concept of a national cultural policy is now fading to some extent, and more and more the emphasis falls on co-operation with other countries in Europe. Linked with this is the idea of presenting a picture of the contemporary scene in one's own society to other peoples. Of course, there is still a place in national policy for what might be described as traditional culture, Racine and Goethe, Montaigne and Lessing. We are not implying either that modern states have ceased to include such aspects of their way of life in their cultural programmes abroad, nor that they should do so. It is simply that the emphasis is changing because of the very nature of our society, where political democracy and almost unlimited chances for foreign travel now are the commonplaces of the contemporary scene. Never before in history have the people of different nations had such an opportunity for getting to know one another at the level of personal acquaintance.[2] Moreover, this phenomenon is temporarily linked with the closer political and economic links steadily being forged, in Western Europe especially, within the EEC. This is why the bilateral exchanges between France and West Germany seem so interesting from a wider standpoint. They have indeed several aspects which should engage the attention of those interested in still closer associations in Europe today.

Firstly, however, we should make it clear that in one respect the

Franco-German experience is unique. Here are two nations whose whole recent past (until 1945) has been clouded by enmity and strife, to a degree perhaps not comparable with the history of any other two countries in Western Europe in recent centuries. This has two consequences, which to a certain extent counteract one another. On the one hand there was more work to be done after 1945, but on the other there was perhaps, at least after the mid fifties, a correspondingly greater readiness to bury the hatchet, just because the past had been so frightful. This is clear from the statistics of twin towning; by 1951 eight Franco-German partnerships had been established, by 1961, ninety.[3] One can, in fact, distinguish three phases as far as twinning is concerned. Up to 1954 little occurred, then from the cultural accord of that year onwards there was a far greater degree of activity, culminating in the 1963 treaty and the subsequent unprecedented scale of popular exchanges. Thus the two official agreements neatly fulfil the role of milestones along the frequently rocky road of post-war reconciliation.

The same threefold division can be applied at the political level, as one former member of the French Cabinet has pointed out.[4] This he characterises as liquidation of the past (phase one), the recognition of new needs (phase two) and the planning and realisation of an entirely new type of policy as the last phase. We are not implying that these three periods coincide temporarily with those in respect of cultural relations mentioned above, but clearly it would be surprising if no empirical connection existed between them. Since 1956 there have been no real obstacles at political level to *rapprochement*, once the Saar question had been regulated.[5] This collaboration at governmental level is intimately tied to reconciliation between peoples, and has to take priority.

This emerges clearly from opinion polls. German economic strength can always cast a shadow on the relations between the two peoples. Whereas in 1968 the proportion of those questioned in France in one sounding who thought Germany wanted to use the European idea in order to dominate her neighbours amounted to one quarter, three years later it had risen to nearly two fifths. Similarly, those 'mistrustful' of German intentions went up from 25 per cent to 38 per cent over the same period.[6] Admittedly, in both instances there was only a minority which was suspicious, but the point we are making is that it was an *increasing* minority, due to German industrial weight inside the EEC. How this could be

linked to popular attempts at contact can be seen from the motiva-
tions behind twin towning. In several cases the need to underpin
the 1963 treaty has been given as the grounds for concluding a
partnership.[7] It is easy to imagine that a worsening of political
relationships could produce setbacks for popular exchanges. It is
very heartening to read that in 1972 the West Germans chose the
French as their favourite neighbours.[8] But German economic
predominance, and perhaps also *Ostpolitik*, could still conceivably
produce a political reaction from the French from which popular
exchanges would inevitably suffer. We do not wish to be pessimistic, or in any way undervalue what has been achieved since the
war by the efforts of so many people in the field of Franco-
German *rapprochement*, but we do feel obliged to reiterate the
precedence which political decisions take over popular sentiment.
This is tempered to some extent by the results of the most recent
opinion poll available to us on Franco-German relations. Carried
out in September 1973, this suggested that fear of a powerful
neighbour was on the decline in France, at least over the period
1971–73. Over half those questioned felt that Germany would
never again be a menace to France; the proportion among young
people incidentally was nearly three quarters. This showed a
striking difference from a similar sounding taken two years
previously. The results are all the more impressive as most
participants felt not only that West Germany was stronger, but
would remain so in the next ten years. It would appear that the
French are learning to co-exist with German economic pre-
ponderance.

All this clearly raises the further point, namely the whole effect
of mass contacts on international understanding. What is crucial
here is the distinction between liking your neighbours on the one
hand, and comprehending them, and their problems, on the other.
We shall return to this theme presently but firstly we have to
examine what evidence, if any, can be produced by opinion polls.
Soundings taken in the Federal Republic between April and
December 1965, exactly at a time when many Germans would be
travelling in France and therefore have personal experience of it,
showed an actual worsening in popular feelings about the French.[9]
But as de Gaulle was following his famous *chaise vide* policy at
Brussels at this time, political events had clearly again intervened
and made an analysis of the effects of mass contacts impossible to
achieve. Because of this, we cannot say with any assurance that

they do contribute either positively or in a negative fashion. In passing, it has even been said that the highly favourable image of Britain among German youth might conceivably be due to a lack of acquaintance with the country and its inhabitants.[10]

To this slightly pessimistic view of mankind in general we can offer two rejoinders. Firstly, those engaged in twin towning most emphatically believe it to be worthwhile, in terms of removing prejudice. Of 208 municipalities questioned, 167 were quite positive about this.[11] Secondly, we want to make a clear distinction between international understanding on the one hand and actually liking people of another country on the other. In the euphoria, especially on the German side, which followed the 1963 treaty, it was apparently assumed that one had only to bring the two peoples face to face and an era of undying friendship would be the automatic result. Among those at the centre of bilateral links, a more sober and cautious air now prevails; most appeared in our interviews to be prepared now to settle for mutual comprehension.

It seems to us that what binds people together ultimately is common interest. A nation is, in the phrase of Ernest Renan, *un plébiscite de tous les jours*. This presumably applies to any political community. There are thus four logical possibilities in the area of relations between peoples: firstly, if there is neither mutual understanding nor common interests, so that no basis for integration exists; secondly, popular comprehension without common political interests, which in the long run is unlikely to prove a secure foundation for closer association. Then one could imagine nations having political, etc. interests in common, but without at the same time any real degree of mutual understanding, or even direct acquaintance, at popular level. In other words, the actual situation as it is in the EEC today. Such a relationship can, we feel, endure, as can be seen from such links in the past as the *entente cordiale*. This understanding put an end to centuries of Anglo-French enmity and contributed to Allied victory in two world wars. In other words, it was a viable partnership which achieved its main objectives. But seventy years after its birth the average Briton knows next to nothing about France, and doubtless most Frenchmen have little understanding of Britain. The two countries thus achieved a working relationship within the framework of individual national independence, which the passage of time has done nothing to alter.

If, however, we wish for something beyond this in the Europe of the future, namely a genuine integration between peoples over and above the nation state, then common interests, whilst necessary as a basis for European feeling, are not in themselves enough. This is the fourth logical possibility, a foundation of economic and political goals to begin, and then some degree of comprehension between the different peoples, which in its turn strengthens the feeling of solidarity and permits a greater degree of political integration. It appears that the corollary for us here is that the Franco-German experiences since the war must be assessed by a definite criterion. How far have they contributed to actual mutual understanding at popular level, which would entail the possibility of them serving as a model for a wider, European context?

Before we turn from these general observations to an examination of the exchanges in more detail, we feel it is only fair to both France and West Germany to point out that the preamble of the 1963 treaty in itself spoke of bilateral collaboration as a stage towards a united Europe.[12] This implies clearly that there is no necessary antithesis between bilateralism and multilateralism, where the first may be a step towards the second. Those at the centre of Franco-German co-operation have frequently claimed this as an aspect of their own work.[13] These statements must be tempered with one qualification at once; much of the Franco-German work has been applicable to them alone, as it springs from their common experiences, and would have no significance outside this context. Ex-servicemen's meetings at Verdun are an illustration of this.

With this reservation made, we can now consider each aspect of Franco-German *rapprochement* in detail. Undoubtedly youth exchanges are the most important of these, as far as the future is concerned. Here it must be said immediately that propaganda about unity among young people today is to some extent at least merely preaching to the converted. The point has often been made to us, that for the youth of today Europe is already made, a feeling which does not necessarily imply attachment to any existing European institution. We should indeed sound a note of warning whilst on this theme. A decline in old-fashioned patriotism does not mean that any new allegiance to a supranational body has replaced it. It has been said that the events of May 1968 elicited little response from students that could fairly have been called 'Europeanism'.

However, in the context of reconciliation, 59 per cent of young people questioned in one French poll in 1963 gave it as their opinion that the past should be forgotten as far as Franco-German relations were concerned. More than a quarter expressed a willingness to accept a European nationality.[14] It was surely significant that five years later the percentage of French people suspicious of German motives was markedly lower in the fifteen to twenty-four age group than among those questioned who were fifty years of age or older.[15] A more 'European' feeling among German youth than among their elders has frequently been demonstrated by opinion polls in that country.[16] In a way the willingness among young people to forget the past and build anew is even more encouraging in France than in Germany, as, statistically speaking, youth forms such a high proportion of the total population in the former country.

The goodwill, and readiness to collaborate, are there, but before enthusiasm of readers of such polls mounts too high, it is as well to underline that popular sentiment is again necessary but not in itself sufficient to ensure any real success in youth exchanges. Moreover, more than half of those questioned in the 1963 French sounding had never even been outside France. Of young Germans, one commentator has written 'Instead of symbolically burning frontier posts, they might have done better to spend some time studying the political, economic and social problems that had to be solved before the European dream could become a reality.'[17] This exactly parallels our view of youth contacts and perhaps that of the OFAJ as well; the Office admits that the euphoria of 1963 had given place five years later to a more sober assessment of the possibilities. The road which leads to Europe can never be paved with good intentions alone. It is necessary to emphasise this at a time when the whole concept has been brought to the point where sheer vague repetition is threatening to empty it of any real meaning.

The Franco-German experience is therefore instructive as a potential multilateral model. In fact, as early as 1964 hopes began to be expressed that the OFAJ could lead to a European Youth Office. A *Bundestag* resolution to this effect was passed in December of that year.[18] Similar views were maintained at an OFAJ colloquium four years later.

Unfortunately, there has been no agreement yet as to the administrative framework. Under which European body should such an apparatus be placed? It would appear that the chief practical lesson that such an organisation could learn from bilateral exchanges is the need for careful planning, and con- centration on quality in structuring programmes rather than upon mere quantity. One thing, however, that a European Youth Office should not do is subsidise mass travel. This is partly because young people now undertake journeys abroad anyway, and there seems no need for state subvention, except perhaps for youth hostels or other means of cheap accommodation. The advent of the Advanced Passenger Train in the late seventies, and eventually perhaps the Channel tunnel, will make foreign travel even easier for private persons and, therefore, reinforce this point. Linked with this is the question of comprehension, which tourism is unlikely to foster. One can hardly expect a stay of fifteen days' duration in a strange land to produce any real understanding of its way of life.

This surely implies concentration of effort on such programmes as *Connaissance de France*. There seems no reason why a European Youth Office should not organise similar courses for the youth of all countries in the EEC. As to whether political questions should be discussed at seminars or meetings of this nature, there seems no real reason why not. Indeed, there would be little point in trying to introduce, say, Italian youth into the contemporary British scene unless themes such as Northern Ireland or wages and incomes policy were brought under review. Sweeping awkward issues under the carpet simply nullifies the whole rationale behind the encounter. Since the activities to be fostered in this way place the emphasis on comprehension of the current cultures of other peoples they should presumably, in order to maintain their quality, be confined to relatively small groups, whom we may as well call the activists. By this we mean young trades union leaders and businessmen, students, young professional people, etc., those who will play an active part in forming future public opinion in their own countries. It is surely essential that they should come to understand the contemporary social and economic scene in their neighbours' countries.

We do not wish to imply that youth exchanges should be merely elitist, despite the foregoing. There is a strong case for using public money to subsidise the contacts between young workers too. Here again, the OFAJ scheme of a six-month sojourn in the other country, with a language course as a preliminary, is excellent in principle. In practice the scale of applications for such a stay has proved disappointing. At least partially this has been due to difficulties over the differing vocational training systems. This is a hard problem, which we shall have to face again when we discuss academic contacts. Even if a young worker does learn a foreign language sufficiently to permit him to profit from the scheme, his technical qualifications, or rather lack of acceptance of them abroad, still prove an obstacle. Of course, repetitious work on a conveyor belt may still be possible, but few people doing that kind of job would wish to move to another country to do it anyway. Harmonisation of vocational training inside the EEC will have to go a long way yet before young worker or apprentice exchanges take on any real significance in terms of numbers.

Apart from these cases, public funds might perhaps be made available on a limited scale where youth encounters take place within a twin town framework. It has already been noted that young people play a disproportionately large part in such contacts; in one empirical study as many as one third of all encounters were concerned with young people only, apart from their presence at many others. There is some further evidence to suggest that in addition the average youth exchange involves more people. The net result from eighty-four communities studied was that some 60 per cent of all participants were classifiable as young.[19] These statistics suggest that the use of public money as reinforcement would be justified. Again, it should be made available only in those instances where the claimants can produce a properly structured programme as evidence that genuine attempts at international understanding will be made. Encounters on the sports field or singing around a camp fire are not enough; a discriminating use of public funds can improve understanding, without any subventions being afforded to tourism as such. Franco-German experience suggests that a European Youth Office could easily become in financial terms an almost bottomless pit unless strict discipline is maintained.

One further point to be dealt with here is the question of replacing military service by some form of social service executed by the young, in a country other than their own. This has been raised, but seems to us unrealisable in the foreseeable future, since defence planning is different in the various EEC countries (with no conscription in the UK anyway). The difficulties in co-ordination would seem too great, apart from the interruption to vocational training. However, on a voluntary basis perhaps the idea might be worth taking further.

There is one other aspect of the OFAJ which we should discuss; its aid to language learning. Again admirable in principle, it costs money which might otherwise simply be given to language teaching in schools. Obviously, the lack of a common language can be an obstacle in popular exchanges. Presumably this is why so many organisations and clubs involved in twin towning are musical or sports associations. This obviously leads us on to the whole language question in the EEC, and its role in promoting integration.

No one would decry the usefulness of sport or music in popular contacts, but obviously they cannot lead to discussions of common problems of the kind that we have been favouring. Clearly language is important in furthering understanding between peoples, but once that has been said a real practical difficulty arises. Granted that no real insight is possible into a foreign culture without a working knowledge of the language in which it is conveyed, how does one teach all the EEC languages at school? After all, there are now seven, with possible future additions to come to the list. Even if one mentally discards what, with due respect, may be called the minor ones, there are still English, German, French and Italian. There are three logical possibilities in a future EEC schools programme; either it includes all the member languages, or some, or none. Since the first choice is surely impractical and the last absurd, we are left with the second. The question then arises, should we have one official language, or choose the three most important, as being probably the greatest practical number in view of pressure on the modern school curriculum: if we choose three, they would presumably be English, French and German.

In effect, the language problem has two aspects. Firstly, there is the question of a common language insofar as ordinary social contacts are concerned, of the kind which we have been describing. Over and above this there is the need for a thorough grounding in the language in which a particular culture is expressed, as the essential prerequisite to arriving at a comprehension of it. It is not really necessary to have a complete grasp of French or German in order to participate in twin towning activities in France and Germany. But it is hard to see how one could arrive at any real understanding of their way of life without a mastery of their languages.

Since it is above all understanding that we are aiming at, it would seem that one solution to the problem would be for an

EEC educational agreement to limit foreign languages taught at secondary level to three, as the maximum obtainable in practice. As far as we can see, the only alternative really available is to go for one alone, which undoubtedly would be English. It is interesting to note in this connection that when in 1963 both French and German youth were questioned in one poll, a majority of both considered that English was more important than their neighbour's tongue. The inevitability of the use of English as what might be described without irony as the *lingua franca* of today has been recognised in other quarters in France, more recently.[20] We accept that there is some opposition elsewhere in that country to the primacy of English (*vide* Chapter 4),[21] but actual practice is likely to see English used more and more as an international medium. But satisfactory as that might be for employment in youth exchanges in general, twin towning, etc., we feel that in order to obtain a deeper insight into the culture of others there should be at least two foreign languages at secondary level. In actual practice we recognise the difficulties involved in any attempted limitations in modern language teaching, especially when the claims of Spanish and Russian are considered. Perhaps in England and Wales a possible solution would be for LEAs to arrange facilities as soon as possible for teaching French and German in all grammar and comprehensive schools. Perhaps itinerant teachers could be made available in each school area for any other languages, which parents may desire for their children.

In fact, French appears to have established a near-monopoly position in many schools, a situation unlikely to change in the near future as it is virtually the only one ever taught in primary schools. A corollary to the battle over French in the Federal Republic would appear to be one over German in Britain. We see no reason why the West German government should not demand parity for its language in our country, parallel to that demanded for French in the Federal Republic. Even if it were loath to do so, we feel that educational authorities in Britain should take a close look at the language position in our schools, in relation to the probable future situation within the EEC, where West Germany will predominate economically for the foreseeable future.

Linked with the language question is that of academic exchanges, and mobility in general. There has recently been a good deal of sometimes rather imprecise talk about an intellectual Common Market, which seems almost to imply complete academic mobility in the EEC. We are in reality a very long way indeed from reaching anything like that state. This is due partly to the whole question of communication again, and the lack of a common language, and partly to the very thorny problem of *équivalences*.

As far as the first is concerned, we have already pointed out that exchanges of teachers, students and *assistants* tends very much at the moment to be confined to linguists. We are not decrying the value of such programmes; an English schoolmaster who spends some time in a foreign country will clearly teach its language better on his return. It has been claimed during our interviews abroad that such exchanges have already assisted quite considerably in the teaching of the neighbour's language both in France and West Germany. We have to reiterate, however, that Romanists and Germanists are already orientated towards another country anyway, and that therefore most academics or students are really quite untouched by exchange programmes, even today. This emerges quite clearly from the relevant statistics: in 1968 West German universities had only 1,507 students from the other EEC countries, plus Britain (including 590 from France and 332 from Britain).[22] These are limited numbers, to put it no more strongly. Part of the reason for the smallness of the scale seems to be the sheer administrative difficulties still encountered in such programmes. One example has been given of two universities, one in Britain and the other in France, which devoted a great deal of time and care to an exchange involving three students.[23]

If an intellectual Common Market actually meant anything in concrete terms, it would presumably designate a state of affairs something like the medieval situation, where Sorbonne students could be divided into five separate nations, and when student and academic mobility was a genuine reality. We must stress that this is unlikely to be brought about in the EEC in the near future, and without careful planning may never be. We shall discuss later if it would even be desirable. What we want to say at the moment is that unless institutions of higher education in the various countries do not co-operate far more closely in drawing up facilities for more widespread exchanges, it will always be easier to opt simply for one's own country and no intellectual Common Market will ever see the light of day. What is really wanted over a long-term period is a thorough rationalisation in higher education in Europe, to avoid wasteful duplication of effort, both inside differing nation-states and in the EEC at international level. This obviously has to be a long-term objective, because of the wide variations existing at the moment, and also because of the vexed question of *équivalences*. These have to be dealt with individually and the whole problem will take at least another decade to resolve; the more pessimistic of our interviewees gave twenty years as a more likely period. The adhesion of Britain, Ireland and Denmark has certainly done nothing to help.

It seems to us that there are three quite separate areas where a good deal of hard work needs to be done to ensure greater freedom of movement both to students and academics, of which *équivalences* is only one. The other two are in intensified language teaching and in that of much closer administrative collaboration between the various institutions involved. In order to accelerate harmonisation in the whole field of higher education there seems no reason why individual national governments should not play some part. We are not advocating a kind of legally-enforced collaboration, we are merely suggesting that if a programme of action were drawn up at EEC level there seems no reason why the political channels should not encourage its implementation, per-haps by financial means rather than by administrative fiat. But above all, we must move simultaneously on three connected fronts, to produce an internally-coherent programme. Languages, *équivalences* and rationalisation of effort at European level are complementary. Progress must be planned for all three simul-taneously if an intellectual Common Market is ever to mean any-thing in concrete terms. But this merely raises the question as to what it could mean, say, in higher education. How can a particular university be open in practice to all European students? There are, for the foreseeable future, simply too many administrative obstacles, such as the lack of agreement over how courses should be run, university finance, etc. Ultimately, the real question here is do we want co-ordination or integration, a point which we shall discuss later.

There are some problems which need to be hammered out now at EEC level, where progress could perhaps be made more rapidly. For example, why should a teacher wishing to spend some time in another country have trouble over his pension and possibly even over his promotion prospects at home? Such questions could be dealt with at international level, we feel.

As we have indicated in previous chapters, some progress has been made in textbook revision and at genuine European collaboration, but far more needs to be done. Ten years of co-operation between France and Germany has produced some results, but essentially there are still two widely-diverging national systems despite this. We cannot feel too optimistic at present regarding academic mobility and rationalisation. In this field Europe is nowhere in sight. When there has been much more hard work in the areas which we have indicated, and rather less bandying of glossy sentimental phrases, then it may be. It is indeed difficult, as the Franco-German experience has shown, to harmonise in educational matters where structures and institutions differ; when this point is taken to the multilateral scene then obviously the difficulties become even greater.

Just to take some recent events will illustrate what we mean. The West German Rectors' conference has opposed the whole idea of a European University as a separate institution. In fact, the Rectors/Vice-Chancellors of European universities took a similar line in a September 1969 resolution. Similarly, in 1968 the UK delegation to the Council of Europe felt unable to accede to a new scholarships convention precisely because award-making bodies here are normally local authorities. As the delegation said, 'Without their co-operation, United Kingdom accession would be meaningless'. Thus structural diversity in administration complicates the entire problem. It is worth pointing out here that in West Germany each *Land* possesses different diplomas; the degrees granted by British universities today vary considerably in value according to which university awards them. The whole question of *équivalences* is so complicated that it will certainly require decades to achieve co-ordination, let alone integration of studies. Whatever an intellectual Common Market is, it will not be here in the foreseeable future.

There are two further matters before we move to another theme. We have already noted the interesting experiments carried out at Saarbrücken and elsewhere in joint *lycées*, and in those designated as bilingual. There is nothing further to add to our previously expressed opinion that in order to be multinational the joint *lycées* would need to be boarding-schools, and we do not consider this to be politically acceptable, since it is suggestive of elitism. In the UK the future of boarding-schools seems very much in doubt, and even granted that the European ones would not be private, it seems unlikely that the idea would catch on. Presumably a demo-cratic educational structure is the logical corollary of a democratic society.

Secondly, in case we seem to have painted our academic picture of limited harmonisation rather too darkly, we should like to point to two such cases where careful planning has produced real results. One is that of the collaboration between the *Grandes Ecoles* and the *Technische Hochschulen* which we described in Chapter 3. Another example is afforded by tri-national co-operation between polytechnics or their equivalents in Britain, France and West Germany. The institutes participating are ESCAE of Amiens, the *Fachhochschule* in Bielefeld and Leeds Polytechnic; these have drawn up a programme in common, the object of which is to produce multilingual management executives for work in the EEC. A two-year full-time course is offered, with periods both of study and business placement in each of the three places concerned. The course incidentally is open to students from other European countries. Intensive language training will be provided and successful entrants will receive a certificate accept-able in all three countries, the only difference being purely in the title. The European Commission are giving it every encourage-ment, which surely is a hopeful sign. This is an excellent case study of how to achieve concrete results, as the questions of language, *équivalences* and administrative harmonisation have all been dealt with in the framework of a joint course.[24]

Insofar as trade relations are concerned, it seems likely that it can play some part in bringing peoples together, indeed the course we have just outlined shows its significance. This should not be exaggerated, as past experience suggests that political harmonisa-tion normally precedes that made in the economic structures of differing states. Nonetheless, the *Zollverein* did help to foster German unity in the last century, and no doubt the EEC will con-tribute to political union in Europe. Apart from this there is the further matter of fusion to produce European companies of sufficient size to exploit the inventiveness of its citizens, and pre-vent a total colonisation of the EEC in technological terms by American firms. A corollary here is the vast economic power which multinationals, usually American, are beginning to wield. European governments really have two connected problems, firstly how to build their own giants, and secondly, how to control both their own and other people's once they are created. The question of control has not yet been raised in the case of what might be termed indigenous companies because as yet very few have been constructed. Legal and administrative obstacles have been too great; linked with this are the existing arrangements between individual European and American firms, which may sometimes preclude intra-European collaboration.

What is certain is that the multinationals imply trade union multilateralism in its turn. The giant companies now cross frontiers and re-allocate what amounts to a very sizeable proportion of the western world's assets at will, with all that that implies both for politicians and trade unionists. When even 3 per cent of the multinationals' liquid assets were transferred in January 1973, the move temporarily closed the world's money markets.[25] Faced with power on this scale the unions can scarcely do other than seek a multilateral solution. Under these circumstances bilateral relations are clearly not far-reaching enough: the European unions as a whole must work together. It is fortunate, therefore, that they should now have taken a big step towards unity by forming the ETUC (see page 126, note 24). Their original divergences lie outside the scope of this book and we can only regret in passing that they weakened the power of workers' associations in modern Europe as a whole.

There is one further point to be made here about bilateral economic and union relations, namely their value in Franco-German *rapprochement*. Even allowing for the fact that technical collaboration or union contacts between the two countries are insufficient in themselves to deal with the problems posed by American dominance, nonetheless it does not mean that they should necessarily be discontinued. It seems important to us that the two nations should continue their dialogue in as many areas as possible.

This applies even more forcibly to twin towning. One of the most interesting aspects is the snowball effect, for want of a better term. By this we refer to the participation in twin town activities by the citizens of neighbouring municipalities, whose town is not directly linked with the foreign one. This phenomenon was reported in one study by nearly a half of the towns replying to a questionnaire (102 out of 208).[26] The local press is said to exercise a considerable influence in publicising the events in the whole district.

As already reported, municipal partnerships include a large number of youth exchanges, which back up the OFAJ (by which they are subsidised) in bilateral relations and could be utilised in a wider context by a future European Youth Office. In winning youth for what might be called the European idea, such contacts are obviously useful, especially when run parallel with school partnerships. Here it is worth pointing out that in recent years the number of municipalities giving European unity as the chief motive in forming a partnership has sharply increased, as revealed at the bilateral level. Whereas between 1956 and 1964 well under a third of those questioned in one sample who established a link during that period have this as the main grounds, for those forming a relationship post-1964 the proportion was nearly one half.[27] Another way in which the same attitude is expressed is in the number of partnerships formed; Bad Godesberg, for example, has formal links now with five towns in different European countries.

Two questions then remain, namely how great a proportion of the actual population of any municipality is really personally involved in the average twinning, and how far are they affected by exchanges, insofar as the removal of ingrained prejudice is concerned? To take the quantitative point first, it has to be said at once that numbers involved are very variable, so that any average is purely a statistical abstraction. Moreover, figures obtained from questionnaires tend to be suspect, as it is usually the more active partnerships which reply, a point to be borne in mind when assessing any information from the study we are quoting.[28] When this is taken into consideration it appears fairly safe to say that the number of persons involved in the 313 partnership exchanges in 1967 amounted to over fifty thousand.[29] As these are the annual figures they seem reasonably impressive. What unfortunately is lacking is any real analysis either by social class or type of encounter. This is an aspect of which we clearly need to know far more.

Apart from this there is the obvious question as to whether such contacts are of lasting value in creating better, more accurate impressions of others. Opinions vary very much in respect of this point. The leading figures in partnerships are firmly of the opinion that they have done so in the Franco-German case, which would suggest a similar effect at multilateral level. The main difficulty here is one of measurement; it may well be that some participants return with glowing reports on the people visited, but it may well also be that a certain leaning towards internationalism in the participants' outlook was the cause of the visit in the first place. How far are the prejudiced being involved at all? The lack of a definite answer to that question, if one is possible, inevitably means that a definite judgement on the whole experiment cannot really be given here. Additionally, and this applies to all international exchanges, contacts of relatively short duration can actually reinforce existing misconceptions. On the other hand, empirical investigations in this field have usually been confined to individual personal encounters, rather than being based on the kind of group contacts now being fostered. One conclusion seems, however, indisputable; the better prepared the visitor, the more successful the visit is likely to be.[30] Here we return to language and its significance in international understanding yet again.

Ultimately, what lessons can be drawn from the Franco-German experience, and from the present state of cultural collaboration in Europe? Firstly, in many respects progress has been made and valuable precedents created. We consider that this applies especially to the OFAJ and the municipal partnerships; these are linked areas where the 1963 treaty seems to have been particularly efficacious. A European Youth Office can play a great part in creating Europe, with the reservation that its financial aid is confined to qualitatively worthwhile projects, such as joint seminars on the contemporary scene in the countries concerned. But, of course, any remarks which we make about youth inevitably have to be brought into the context of education as a whole. A vast amount of work remains to be done in this field, but clearly harmonisation in educational systems, or at least a far greater degree of collaboration between European governments, is a long way off, judging by the present situation. It may well be that no real progress will be made here before some form of political integration is achieved, if it ever is. Perhaps only a genuine Ministry of Education for Europe could introduce the administrative measures necessary for complete mobility in higher education within the EEC. In any case, integration in education is probably not even desirable, given that Europe's strength culturally is exactly its diversity.

One lesson at least which bilateralism can give us is that progress will be slow and painful. Individual équivalences, to take only one illustration, will have to be dealt with one at a time, and the same applies to the whole area of education. It is as well for us to realise this; there is no philosopher's stone for European unity. This last word is, after all, only a collective noun which comprehends a whole complex of particular, concrete matters, each demanding a particular, concrete solution. We have, in the whole field of cultural collaboration, to steer an even course between two rocks on which the whole ship may founder. One represents the viewpoint of facile optimism, the idea that a few phrases about unity or Europe, etc. will bring us all together. People who indulge in this form of thinking are liable to become disillusioned over the unavoidably slow and halting realisations of their dream, due to the enormous cultural differences between the various countries in the EEC. At the other extreme some may exaggerate these divergences and arrive at the conclusion that nothing can be done.

Both views seem to us to be incorrect. The readiness of governments and of official cultural agencies to co-operate with one another shows that the will to solve the problems exists. The only real danger lies in the time-span necessary to achieve genuine integration, especially in higher education: apparent lack of progress may deter us from going on. Surely the Franco-German reconciliation shows what can be brought about by a combination of goodwill and hard work. Provided that the political atmosphere between EEC countries remains good, there seems no reason to doubt that a similar model of cultural exchanges would serve an equal purpose in reinforcing political relations. The Act of Union between England and Scotland was described as the end of an old song. By old song was meant the existing enmity between the two peoples. We have a long way to go before the old one in Europe is finally silenced; if, however, we wish to bring it to an end eventually, then popular contacts will need to be planned much more carefully in the future than they have been in the past.

Notes

1 Quoted in H. Ott, *Handbuch der internationalen Jugendarbeit*, p 100.
2 By way of contrast, Diderot, a great disseminator of British ideas in eighteenth century France, did not even meet an Englishman until he was 47 years old. R. L. Graeme-Ritchie, *France: a companion to French Studies*, London, Methuen, 1963, pp 190*f.*
3 Garstka, op. cit., p 63.
4 M. Couve de Murville, 'Die Entwicklung der deutsch-französischen Beziehungen nach 1945', *Deutschland-Frankreich*, vol III, p 50*f.*
5 As Professor Grosser has pointed out 'Faut-il encore des médiateurs?', *Documents*, Nov. 1972, pp 13*f.*

6 See *Frankfurter Allgemeine Zeitung*, 15 Sept. 1971.
7 Garstka, op. cit., p 74.
8 The French got 26% of the votes, as compared to 23% for the Austrians and 16% for the Swiss. *New York Herald Tribune*, 5 May 1972.
9 Quoted in Ott, op. cit., p 100.
10 Ibid., p 100.
11 Garstka, op. cit., p 111.
12 As did Schröder, the then Foreign Minister, in the Bundestag debate on the treaty.
13 For example, R. Schlagintweit, 'Bonn-Paris: Modelle für Kultureuropa', *Aussenpolitik*, May 1972.
14 'La jeunesse française et l'Europe', *Documents*, 1963, no. 3, pp 46*f.*
15 C. Grosser and others (eds), *Das 198 Jahreszehnt. Eine Team-Prognose für 1970–1980*, Munich, DTV, 1972, p 105.
16 For a summary of such results see Ott, pp 28*f.*
17 A. Grosser, *Germany in our Time*, op. cit., p 314.
18 Text in Ott, op. cit., pp 182*f.*
19 Garstka, op. cit., pp 100*f.*
20 Grosser, 'Faut-il encore des médiateurs?', op. cit., p 16.
21 There is a movement, not confined to France, which aims at promoting French as a recognised international medium in Europe.
22 C. Campos, 'Students and Europe', *Universities Quarterly*, p 5.
23 Ibid., pp 7*f.*
24 Details from a joint brochure, *European Management Programme*.
25 *Daily Telegraph*, 22 Sept. 1973.
26 Gartska, op. cit., pp 107*f.*
27 Ibid., p 74.
28 Garstka's questionnaire was answered by 208 municipalities of the 313 inside the IBU in 1967. Ibid., p 100, where he makes the point himself about the 'activists'.
29 Ibid., p 100.
30 See W. G. Stone, *Local Authorities and Adult Education*, den Haag, 1955, p 24, quoted in ibid., p 109.

Bibliography

ALLEMAGNE, pub. by Comité français d'échanges avec l'Allemagne nouvelle, nos 1–100, 1949–67.

ALTMAYER, F., 'Das Deutsch-französische Jugendwerk', *Aussenpolitik*, no 5, 1964, pp 297–303.

ALTMAYER, F., 'La coopération culturelle franco-allemande', *L'Europe en Formation*, no. 69, 1965, pp 25–8.

ALTMAYER, F., 'Jeunesse franco-allemande d'aujourd'hui', *Documents*, no. 5, 1967, pp 41–5.

ALTMAYER, F., 'Psychologie des Jugendaustauschs', *Dokumente*, no. 23, 1967, pp 259–67.

ANDERSON, M., 'Regional identity and political change: the case of Alsace from the Third to the Fifth Republic', *Political Studies*, no. 1, March 1972.

ANGELLOZ, J., 'Pour une politique culturelle en Allemagne', *Mercure de France*, no. 302, 1948, pp 22–8.

ARBEIT UND LEBEN, 'Geschäftsbericht für die Jahre 1968 bis 1970', Arbeit und Leben, Düsseldorf.

ARBEITSKREIS DEUTSCH-FRANZÖSISCHER GESELLSCHAFTEN, *Mitteilungsblatt für die Deutsch-französischen Gesellschaften*, no. 6, Sept. 1959, no. 13, Sept. 1962, no. 16, Oct. 1963, no. 17, July 1964, no. 26, Mar. 1968, no. 34, July 1971, no. 35, Oct. 1971.

ARNDT, A. and others (eds), *Konkretionen politischer Theorie und Praxis*, Stuttgart, Ernst Klett Verlag, 1972.

ARON, R., 'Vorurteile der Schriftsteller: Vorurteile der Franzosen', *Antares*, vol 2, no. 6, 1954, pp 5–11.

BARTH, H., 'Jeunesse: Co-opération franco-allemande', *Documents*, no. 5, 1963, pp 45–9.

BAUDRILLARD, J., *Les Allemands*, Paris, 1963, Encyclopédie essentielle.

BECK, R. H., *Change and Harmonization in European Education*, Minnesota, Univ. of Minnesota Press, 1971.

BENTMANN, F., 'Frankreich im deutschen Lehrbuch der französischen Sprache', *Deutschland-Frankreich*, vol III, pp 114–15.

BERTAUX, P., 'La révolution nécessaire des études germaniques', *Documents*, Mar./Apr. 1970.

BIEBER, K., *L'Allemagne vue par les écrivains de la résistance française*, Geneva, Droz E., 1954.

'BILAN des investissements directs allemande a l'étranger et étrangers en Allemagne', *Problèmes Economiques*, no. 1,240, 7 July 1971.

BITHELL, J., *Germany: a companion to German studies*, London, Methuen, 1962.

BOEKENKAMP, W., 'Der heutige Stand des Deutschunterrichts in Frankreich', *Deutschunterricht für Ausländer*, vol 4, no. 2, 1954–55, pp 31–2.

BOEKENKAMP, W., *Umgang mit Franzosen*, Schwäbisch Hall, Eppinger Verlag, 1970.

BOENNER, K. H., *Einstellungswandel in einem deutsch-französischen Jugendlager*, Munich, Verlag Deutsches Jugendinstitut, 1970.

BONDY, F., 'Das geistige Deutschland', *Dokumente*, no. 22, 1966, pp 145–50.

BONDY, F. and ABELEIN, M., *Deutschland und Frankreich, Geschichte einer wechselvollen Beziehung*, Düsseldorf and Vienna, Econ Verlag, 1973.

BOUREL, F., 'Les échanges de jeunes dans le cadre européen à partir de l'expérience franco-allemande', *Education et Echanges*, no. 30, 1966, pp 1–10.

BOYER, B. M., 'Deux livres blancs, deux jeunesses', *Documents*, no. 6, 1967, pp 36–44.

BOYER, B. M., *L'étude scientifique des stéréotypes nationaux dans les rapports franco-allemands*, Université de Paris I—Département de science politique, Paris, 1972.

BOYER, B. M., 'Une approche scientifique des préjugés nationaux', *Education et développement*, no. 39, July/Aug. 1968.

BRUEGEMANN, R., 'Bericht über mein Jahr als deutsche Lehrassistentin am lycée d'état mixte "Jean Aicard" an meinen Nachfolger', *Das Studienseminar*, no. 12, 1967.

BRULEY, E., 'Les rencontres entre historiens français et allemands', *Les Dialogues*, no. 4, July 1952, pp 235–43.

BRUYN-OUBUTER, G. DE, 'Erfahrungsbericht über einen dreimonatigen Frankreichaufenthalt im Rahmen des deutsch-französischen Lehreraustausches', *Die neueren Sprachen*, Heft 3, March 1970.

BULLETIN, West German Government Press and Information Service.

BULLETIN *des Communautés européenes*, 'Pour une politique communautaire de l'education', Brussels, 1973, supplement.

BURGELIN, P., 'Rencontre franco-allemande de Bièvres', *Le Christianisme social*, no. 59, 1951.

CAMPOS, C., 'Students and Europe', *Universities Quarterly*, Sussex University.

CAPDEVIELLE, J. and MOURIAUX, R., *Les syndicats ouvriers en France*, Paris, Librairie Armand Colin, 1970.

'CE QUE LES Allemands pensent des Français', *Réalités*, no. 213, 1963, pp 98–107.

CHEVAL, R., 'Die deutsch-französischen Kulturbeziehungen', *Dokumente*, no. 25, 1969, pp 32–7.

CHEVAL, R. and others, *So sehen wir die Deutschen*, Mainz, Von Hase and Kohler, 1968.

'CINQ ANS d'échanges franco-allemands', *Education et Echanges*, Paris, 1969.

CINQ ANNEES DE promotion linguistique à l'Office etc., *Education et Echanges*, Paris, 1969.

COMMITTEE FOR Higher Education and Research, various reports on higher education, Council of Europe, 1968–70.

CONORD, P., 'Die deutsch-französische Aktion der protestantischen Kirche', *Dokumente*, no. 25, 1969, pp 110–13.

CONSEIL DES COMMUNES D'EUROPE, *'Note sur les jumelages européens. Un jumelage—pourquoi?, Cahiers*, nos 53, 54, 70, 72.

CORNELIS, P.-A., *Europeans about Europe*, Amsterdam, 1970, Doctoral thesis University of Nijmegen, Swets and Zeitlinger.

COUNCIL FOR CULTURAL COOPERATION, *Annual Report 1971*, Strasbourg, 1972.

COUNCIL OF EUROPE, *European conventions on the equivalence of diplomas leading to admission to universities*, Council of Europe, Feb. 1968.

COUNCIL OF EUROPE, *European convention on the equivalence of periods of university study*, Council of Europe, Oct. 1967.

COUNCIL OF EUROPE, *European convention on the academic recognition of university qualifications*, Council of Europe, 1966.

CURTIUS, E. R., 'Die französische Kulturidee', *Antares*, vol 2, 1955, pp 13–26.

DER PÄDAGOGISCHE AUSTAUSCHDIENST, Bonn, 1969–70, Sekretariat der Ständigen Konferenz der Kultusminister, etc.

D'ESTAING, G., 'Coopération et fusion des entreprises françaises et allemandes', *Politique Etrangère*, no. 2, 1966.

DEUTSCH, K., *France, Germany and the Western Alliance*, New York, Chas. Schribner's Sons, 1967.

DEUTSCH-FRANZÖSISCHE GESELLSCHAFT MÜNCHEN, pub. by the society, 3rd edn, 1969.

'DEUTSCH-FRANZÖSISCHE Vereinbarung über strittige Fragen europäischer Geschichte', *Internationales Jahrbuch für Geschichtsunterricht 1953*, Albert Limbach Verlag, Brunswick, 1958.

DEUTSCH-FRANZÖSISCHER KREIS, *Mitgliederverzeichnis und Veranstaltungsfolge*, Deutsch-Französischer Kreis, Düsseldorf, 1971.

DEUTSCHER AKADEMISCHER AUSTAUSCHDIENST, *Auslandsstipendien für deutsche Studente und jüngere Wissenschaftler 1973–74*, Deutscher Akademischer Austauschdienst, Bonn, 1972.

DEUTSCHER AKADEMISCHER AUSTAUSCHDIENST, *Etudes et bourses en République Fédérale d'Allemagne 1973–74*, Deutscher Akademischer Austauschdienst, Bonn, 1973.

DEUTSCHER AKADEMISCHER AUSTAUSCHDIENST, *Jahresbericht 1971*, Deutscher Akademischer Austauschdienst, Bonn, 1972.

DEUTSCHLAND-FRANKREICH, Heft nos 22, 23, 24, 25, Stuttgart, Internationale Bürgermeister Union, June 1969, Feb. 1970, July 1970, May 1971.

DEUTSCHLAND-FRANKREICH: *Ludwigsburger Beiträge zum Problem der Deutsch-Französischen Beziehungen*, vol II, Deutsch-französisches Institut, Ludwigsburg, 1957, vol III, Deutsch-französisches Institut, Ludwigsburg, 1963, vol IV, Deutsch-französisches Institut, Ludwigsburg, 1966.

DEUTSCHE AUSLANDSGESELLSCHAFT, *Jahresbericht*, 1963–71 inclusive.

DEUTSCHE AUSLANDSGESELLSCHAFT *Dokumentation*, 1964–69.

DIE BEDEUTUNG *der privaten Initiative für die deutsch-französische Verständigung*, Cologne, Arbeitskreis der privaten Institutionen für internationale Begegnung, 1957.

D'ORMESSON, W., 'Une Tentative de rapprochement franco-allemand entre les deux guerres', *Revue de Paris*, Feb. 1962.

DROZ, J., 'Zur Revision des deutsch-französischen Geschichtsbildes', *Deutschland-Frankreich*, vol II, pp 89–90.

DÜREN, A., 'Strukturwandel als Folge der europäischen Wirtschaftsintegration', *Europa Archiv*, no. 20, 1965.

DURRY, M. J., 'La Sorbonne à Muniche', *Revue des Hommes et des Mondes*, no. 27, 1955, pp 105–110.

ECKERT, G. and SCHUEDDEKOPF, O. E. (eds), *Deutschland-Frankreich-Europa: Die Deutsch-Französische Verständigung und der Geschicht-sunterricht*, Baden-Baden, Verlag für Kunst und Wissenschaft, 1953.

EHLERS, K. J., 'Ein französisches Gymnasium', *Die Höhere Schule*, Oct. 1968.

EMNID, *Einstellung der deutschen und französischen Jugend zum deutsch-französischen Jugendaustausch*, Bielefeld, EMNID, Sept./Oct. 1968.

EPTING, K., 'Deutschland und Frankreich', *Zeitwende*, no. 35, 1964.

'EVOLUTION des échanges franco-allemands', *Documents*, nos. 3/4, 1967, pp 222–5.

FABIAN, W., 'Verbreitung und Wirkung der zeitgenössichen französischen Literatur im deutschen Sprachgebiet', *Antares*, vol 4, no. 6, 1956, pp 6–12.

GARTSKA, H.-J., *Die Rolle der Gemeinde in der internationalen Verständigung nach dem zweiten Weltkrieg gezeigt am Beispiel der deutsch-französischen Verständigung*, Stuttgart, IBU, 1972.

GAULLE, C. DE, *Memoirs of Hope*, London, Weidenfeld & Nicholson, 1971.

GERWIN, R., 'L'exode des cerveaux', *Documents*, Mar./Apr. 1968.

GOLDENES BUCH DER DEUTSCH-FRANZÖSISCHEN STÄDTEPARTNERSCHAFTEN, Stuttgart, Internationale Bürgermeister Union, 1969.

GOTTSCHALK, D., *Zwischenbilanz*, Düsseldorf, Droste Verlag, 1970.

GRAEME-RITCHIE, R. L., *France: a companion to French studies*, London, Methuen, 1963.

GROSSER, A., 'Deutsch-französische Anfänge' in *Konkretionen politischer Theorie und Praxis*, ed A. Arndt, H. Emke, I. Fetscher and O. Massing, Stuttgart, Ernst Klett Verlag, 1972.

GROSSER, A., 'Emmanuel Mounier und das Comité français d'Echanges avec l'Allemagne nouvelle', *Deutschland-Frankreich*, Band I, Stuttgart, Deutsche Verlagsanstalt, 1954.

GROSSER, A., 'Faut-il encore des médiateurs?', *Documents*, Nov. 1972.

GROSSER, A., *Germany in our time*, London, Pall Mall Press, 1971.

GROSSNER, C. and others (eds), *Das 198 Jahreszehnt. Eine Team-Prognose für 1970–1980*, Munich, DTV, 1972.

GUICHARD, O, 'La coopération culturelle franco-allemande et les perspectives européennes', *Informations de l'Education nationale*, speech to Ständige Konf Freiburg im Breisgau, 15 Oct. 1971.

GUIDELINES FOR A FOREIGN CULTURAL POLICY, German Federal Foreign Office, Bonn, 1970.

HAEG, W., 'Mariages franco-allemands', *Documents*, May/June 1970.

HAIGH, A., *A Ministry of Education for Europe*, London, G. Harrap & Co., 1970.

HAKE, H. J. VON, 'Les relations économiques franco-allemandes', *Documents*, July/Aug. 1966.

HANDKE, W., 'Deutschland und Frankreich in der Entwicklungshilfe', *Aussenpolitik*, June 1967.

HAUSENSTEIN, W., 'Kulturelle Beziehungen zwischen Frankreich und Deutschland', *Deutschland-Frankreich*, Band I, Stuttgart, Deutsche Verlagsanstalt, 1954.

HEITMANN, K., 'L'image française de l'Allemagne dans son évolution historique', *Revue de psychologie des peuples*, no. 4, 1967.

HERTERICH, K. W., 'Les investissements allemands en France', *Documents*, Mar./Apr. 1972.

HINDRICHS, G., *Kulturgemeinschaft Europa*, Cologne, Europa Union Verlag, 1968.

HOLTHOFF, H. H., 'Der Koordinator für die deutsch-französische Zusammenarbeit', *Konkretionen politischer Theorie und Praxis*, op. cit.

'INVESTISSEMENTS allemands dans l'est français'. Dossier in *Documents*, July/Aug. 1969.

XV JAHRESTAGUNG *des Arbeitskreises Deutsch-Französischer Gesellschaften*, Mainz, Arbeitskreis der Deutsch-französischer Gesellschaften, Oct. 1970.

JUILLARD, E., 'Esquisse de régions multinationales sur le Rhin entre Mannheim et Bâle', *Cahiers de L'IBEA*, Tome V, nos 3/4, Mar./Apr. 1971.

JUILLARD, E., 'L'Alsace, va-t-elle basculer dans l'orbite allemande?', *Documents*, July/Aug. 1969.

JUILLARD, E., 'Un probleme de déséquilibre économique sur le Rhin moyen', *Studia geographica*, 20, Brno, 1971, 2nd Franco-Czech. colloque.

KEPPER, H., 'Allemands en France', *Documents*, vol 23, no. 3, 1968, pp 17–23.

KING, E. I., *Education and development in Western Europe*, Reading, Mass., Addison-Wesley, 1969.

KRAUS, W., *Gesammelte Aufsätze zur Literatur und Sprachwissenschaft*, Frankfurt-on-Main, V. Klostermann Verlag, 1949.

KRAUSE, G., *Französisches Kulturbewusstsein und deutsch-französische Begegnung*, Frankfurt-on-Main, Diesterweg, 1964.

KÜHN, H., 'Deutsch-französische Kulturpolitik im nächsten Jahreszehnt', *Dokumente*, no. 25, 1959, pp 369–72.

KULTURABTEILUNG des Auswärtigen Amtes, *Jahresbericht 1970*, Bonn, Auswärtiges Amt, 1971.

'LA BALANCE française des échanges techniques', *Problèmes Economiques*, no. 1279, 5 July 1972.

LA CFDT, Paris, Editions du Seuil, 1971.

LA COOPERATION économique franco-allemande', *Problèmes Economiques*, no. 1101, 6 Feb. 1969.

LA COOPERATION *Franco-allemande 1963–1969*, Paris, Documentation française, 1969.

'LA CRISE FRANÇAISE vue de l'Allemagne', Dossier *Documents*, May/June 1968.

LA FRANCE ET l'Allemagne face au problème de la régionalisation', *Documents*, July/Aug. 1969; speech by O. Guichard.

'LA JEUNESSE française et l'Europe', *Documents*, no. 3, 1963, pp 46–50.

LA REALITE QUOTIDIENNE *des échanges franco-allemands*, vol I (Administration —Economie), vol II (Culture), Düsseldorf, French Consulate-General, 1970.

LA RONCIERE, P. DE, 'Une année de rencontres franco-allemandes', *Documents*, vol 24, no. 3, 1969, pp 64–78.

LAPIE, P. O., 'La coopération franco-allemande', *La nouvelle revue des deux mondes*, Feb. 1973.

LAURET, R., 'Réflexions sur une image révisée du passé', *Deutschland-Frankreich*, vol. III, pp 105–6.

'LES DONNEES nouvelles du tourisme français', *Problèmes économiques*, no. 1334, 15 August 1973.

LES ECHANGES COMMERCIAUX *entre la république fédérale et la France*, Paris, Centre d'Etudes de Politique Etrangère, Apr. 1966.

LES ORGANES BILATERAUX *des relations économiques franco-allemandes*, Paris, Centre d'études de Politique Etrangère, Mar. 1966.

LES ORIENTATIONS DU VI *plan dans la région d'Alsace*, Rapport présenté par M. Jean Verdier, Préfet de la région, June 1969.

'LES PROBLEMES ECONOMIQUES des régions frontières à l'intériéur du Marché Commun', *Problèmes Economiques*, no. 1206, 11 Feb. 1971.

LES REGIONS FRONTIERES *et la polarisation urbaine dans la Communauté Economique Européene*, Geneva, Cahiers de l'ISEA, Tome V, nos 3–4, Librairie Droz, Mar./Apr. 1971.

'LES INVESTISSEMENTS directs étrangers en République Fédérale d'Allemagne', *Problèmes Economiques*, no. 1166, 7 May 1970.

'LES INVESTISSEMENTS Français a l'étranger et étrangers en France', *Problèmes Economiques*, no. 1178, 30 July 1970.

LILIENSTERN, R. VON, 'Der französische Markt und die deutsche Industrie', *Kleiner Almanach der Marktforschung*, Bielefeld, Oct. 1970, pp 51–63.

'L'INDUSTRIE Française face à l'industrie allemande', *Problèmes Economiques*, no. 934, 23 Nov. 1965.

LINNERZ, H.. 'Eine Umfrage zum Jugendaustausch', *Dokumente*, no. 20, 1964, pp 176–9.

LOISEAU, I., 'Mon éxperience de manoeuvres communes', *Documents*, no. 5, 1964, pp 92–5.

LUCAS, Y., 'Rapport concernant mon séjour a Karlsruhe dans le cadre des échanges culturels franco-allemands', *Die neueren Sprachen*, Heft 8, Aug. 1970.

MANUEL PRATIQUE *pour la coopération franco-allemande*, Paris/Bonn, Bureau franco-allemand de coopération, 1967.

MARQUAND, R., 'Un essai de création d'un institut allemand à Paris en 1826', *Etudes germaniques*, no. 12, 1957.

MAUSSER, E., 'Zweck und Durchführung des Deutsch-französischen Erziehungsaustausches', *Pädagogische Welt*, vol 23, no. 8, 1969, pp 453–4.

MINDER, R., *Bemerkungen zum deutsch-französischen Geschichtsbild*, Otzenhausen, Europa-Haus, undated.

MINDER, R., 'Deutsche Literatur in französischer Sicht', *Jahrbuch der Deutschen Akademie für Sprache und Dichtung*, 1959, pp 13–23.

MURVILLE, M. C. DE, 'Die Entwicklung der deutsch-französischen Beziehungen nach 1945', *Deutschland-Frankreich*, vol III, pp 45–6.

NASS, K. O., *Gefährdete Freundschaft*, Bonn, Europa Union Verlag, 1971.

NEUBERT, F., *Studien zur vergleichenden Literaturgeschichte, im besonderen zum Verhältnis Deutschland-Frankreich*, Berlin, Duncker & Humboldt, 1952.

NEUMANN, G., 'Deutsch-französische Austauschbeziehungen auf pädagogischem Gebiet', *Bildung und Erziehung*, Heft 5, May 1971.

NEUMANN, G., 'Internationaler Lehreraustausch', *Internationale Zeitschrift für Erziehungswissenschaft*, vol 6, no. 2, 1960.

NEUMEISTER, H., 'Der Austausch von Lehrern und Schülern mit dem Ausland', *Auswärtige Kultur Beziehungen*, no. 4, 1967, pp 285f.

L'OFFICE franco-allemand pour la jeunesse, *Connaissances et représentations*, Paris/Bonn, Office franco-allemand pour la jeunesse, July 1971.

L'OFFICE franco-allemand pour la jeunesse, *1968 Kongress DFJW—Colloque OFAJ*, Paris/Bonn, Office franco-allemand pour la jeunesse, 1968.

L'OFFICE franco-allemand pour la jeunesse, *Stages de longue durée en Allemagne fédérale*, etc.

Wer, was, wo, wie?

Richtlinien des deutsch-französischen Jugendwerks, Paris/Bonn, L'Office franco-allemand pour la jeunesse.

OFFICE NATIONAL des universités et écoles françaises, *Cours permanents pour les étudiants étrangers en France*, Paris, 1971.

OFFICE NATIONAL des universités et écoles françaises, *Equivalences universitaires franco-allemands*, Paris, 1971.

OTT, H., *Handbuch der internationalen Jugendarbeit*, Cologne, Europa Union Verlag, 1968.

PEUPLE et culture, *Présentation des activités 1973*, Paris, 1973.

PROSS, H., 'Reflections on German Nationalism 1866–1966', *Orbis*, vol X, no. 4, Winter 1967.

'QUELQUES ASPECTS de la coopération industrielle franco-allemande', *Problèmes économiques*, no. 1327, 20 June 1973.

RABIER, J. R., 'Préjugés français et préjugés allemands', *Revue de Psychologie des Peuples*, no. 2, 1968.

RAU, J., *Chancen der deutsch-französischen Kulturpolitik in den siebziger Jahren*, Bonn–Bad Godesberg, Institut für Internationale Begegnungen e.V., 1971.

REIME, S., *Die Tätigkeit der DDR in den nichtkommunistischen Ländern. IV EWG STAATEN (ohne Bundesrepublik)*, Bonn, Forschungsinstitut der Deutschen Gesellschaft für Auswärtige Politik, 1970.

RELATIONS ENTRE *syndicats allemands et syndicats français*, Paris, Centre d'études de politique étrangère, July 1965.

RENOUVIN, P., 'Les relations franco-allemandes de 1871 à 1914', *Studies in Diplomatic History and Historiography*, ed A. O. Sarkassian, London, Longmans, 1961.

RICHARD, L., 'L'image de l'Allemagne dans la " Nouvelle Revue Française " de 1919 à 1939', *Revue de psychologie des peuples*, no. 2, 1970.

RIENCOURT, A. DE, ' Nationalism in France ', *Orbis*, Vol X, no. 4, Winter 1967.

ROSS, W., 'Konzept einer auswärtigen Kulturpolitik', *Merkur*, no. 19, 1965, pp 905–22.

ROVAN, J., 'Connaissance de la France', *Dokumente*, no. 19, 1963, pp 186–7.

SALOMAN, M., *Faut-il avoir peur des allemands?* Paris, Robert Laffont, 1969.

SCHLAGINTWEIT, R., 'Bonn-Paris; Modelle für Kultureuropa', *Aussenpolitik*, May 1972.

SCHÜDDEKOPF, O. E., in collaboration, *History Teaching and History Textbook Revision*, Strasbourg, Council for Cultural Co-operation of the Council of Europe, 1967.
SEYDOUX, F., 'Le traité franco-allemand', *Politique Etrangère*, no. 6, 1963.
SICRE, J. P., 'Les Allemands à la conquête de l'Alsace', *Documents*, July/Aug. 1969.
STEINS, M., 'Images d'Allemagne en France', *Revue d'Ethnopsychologie*, Tome 26, vol 4, Dec. 1971.

TAUDIEN, K., 'Internationaler Lehrer- und Schüleraustausch des Landeshauptstadt München', *Pädagogische Welt*, vol 23, no. 8, 1969, pp 459–60.
THE EDUCATIONAL activities of the German Federation of Trade Unions (*DGB*), Düsseldorf, DGB Education Department, 1972.

'UNE COMPARAISON des potentiels socio-économiques français et allemands', *Problèmes Economiques*, no. 1323, 23 May 1973.
'UN POINT DE VUE allemand sur les possibilités de l'industrie française', *Problèmes Economiques*, no. 1262, 8 Mar. 1972.
UNE NOUVELLE POLITIQUE *d'industrialisation pour l'Alsace*, Dernières Nouvelles d'Alsace, Jan. 1972.
VERNANT, J., 'Perspectives franco-allemandes', *Politique Etrangère*, no. 1, 1967.

WALBURG, F., *Die 7 und 8 deutsch-französische Geschichtslehrertagung*, Albert Limbach Verlag, Brunswick, 1957, Internationales Jahrbuch für Geschichtsunterricht, vol VI.
'WEGE DES DEUTSCH-französischen Kulturaustausches', *Auslandskurier*, no. 6, 1962, pp 32–3.
WEINERT, H. K., 'Deutsch-französische Begegnungen in neuer deutscher Literatur', *Deutschland-Frankreich*, vol II, pp 319–20.
WILFERT, O., 'Harmonie allein genügt nicht', *Frankfurter Hefte*, July 1967.
WILLIS, F. R., *France, Germany and the New Europe 1945–1967*, OUP, 1969.
WINTZEN, R., 'Die deutsche Welle an der Seine', *Dokumente*, no. 21, 1965, pp 517–22.
WISS-VERDIER, H., 'Une rencontre d'Anciens Combattants', *Documents*, no. 4, 1966, pp 57–61.
WEIGAND-ABENDROTH, F., 'Deutschland entdecken', *Dokumente*, no. 19, 1963, pp 198*ff*.

ZIEBURA, G., *Die deutsch-französischen Beziehungen seit 1945*, Stuttgart, Neske, 1970.
ZIOCK, H., *Sind die Deutschen wirklich so?*, Stuttgart, Horst Erdmann Verlag, 1965.
ZWANZIG JAHRE, Report on twenty years' activity of Deutsch-französisches Institut Ludwigsburg, Ludwigsburg, Süddeutsche Verlagsanstalt, 1968.

Index

For Product Safety Concerns and Information please contact our EU
representative GPSR@taylorandfrancis.com
Taylor & Francis Verlag GmbH, Kaufingerstraße 24, 80331 München, Germany

www.ingramcontent.com/pod-product-compliance
Lightning Source LLC
Chambersburg PA
CBHW062021270326
41929CB00014B/2274

* 9 7 8 1 1 3 8 8 4 7 5 3 8 *